Conversations with Percival Everett

Literary Conversations Series
Peggy Whitman Prenshaw
General Editor

Conversations
with Percival Everett

Edited by Joe Weixlmann

University Press of Mississippi   *Jackson*

www.upress.state.ms.us

The University Press of Mississippi is a member of the Association of American University Presses.

First printing 2013

∞

Library of Congress Cataloging-in-Publication Data

Everett, Percival L.
  Conversations with Percival Everett / edited by Joe Weixlmann.
    pages cm. — (Literary Conversations Series)
  Includes index.
  ISBN 978-1-61703-759-7 (cloth : alk. paper) — ISBN 978-1-61703-760-3 (ebook) 1. Everett, Percival L.—Interviews. 2. Novelists, American—20th century—Interviews. 3. Novelists, American—21st century—Interviews. 4. Fiction—Authorship. I. Weixlmann, Joseph, editor of compilation. II. Title.
  PS3555.V34Z46 2013
  813'.54—dc23
  [B]   2012045170

British Library Cataloging-in-Publication Data available

Contents

Introduction

In jeans, a soft-blue short-sleeved shirt, and scuffed riding boots, Everett, forty-four, sits ramrod straight, in a straight-back chair against a wall. He is prepared, it seems at first, not for an interview but an inquisition.

"I don't usually say yes to these things," he tosses out . . . as a point of clarification. "But I've promised I would be better."

> —Lynell George, describing Everett's demeanor at the outset of their 2001 interview

Only six of the approximately seventy interviews with Percival Everett that I have identified were published prior to the release of *erasure* (2001), his fifteenth book, which appeared nearly two decades after his first novel, *Suder* (1983). As the quote above suggests, a major reason for what might otherwise be attributable solely to early-career neglect is that Everett has been much more inclined to eschew the literary limelight than to bask in it. Asked by William Starr in 1994 if it were true that he "hates talking publicly about . . . his work," Everett provided a terse response, "Yes," and he confided to Robert Birnbaum in 2003 that "for a long time I was a problem for publishers because I just . . . wouldn't go places and do stuff." Given his aversion to self-promotion, it should not be surprising that, although a few of his books have been released through major publishing houses, Everett's decided preference has been for independent publishers—most notably, Graywolf Press[1]—because "they keep you in print longer, they treat you better, and they talk about literature instead of money." How ironic, then, that the media attention which greeted *erasure*, a novel that satirizes what Everett views as the undue cultural influence of media icon Oprah Winfrey, along with racialized aspects of the book publishing and distribution industries, was to make less defensible the relative anonymity he had to that point maintained.[2] Remaining true to form, Everett would, following the success *erasure* enjoyed in hardcover, reject an extremely lucrative contract from Doubleday to distribute the paperback edition of the book as the first offering of its African American imprint, Harlem Moon, because he felt that the company would not have made the offer had it truly understood the novel, but he apparently found it less easy to dismiss the increasing demands for interviews and public appearances triggered by the novel's popularity.[3] Thus, although Everett would much rather write than discuss his writing or his writing processes, or give public readings, he has, over the past decade, become considerably more willing to carve out public time as his literary reputation has continued to grow. Novels as diverse as *Wounded* (2005), a highly dramatic book which earned major awards both domestically and in Europe, and *I Am Not Sidney Poitier* (2009), another award-winning, albeit broadly comic, work, have continued both to broaden Everett's readership and to attract more attention from members of the print and electronic media.

Everett's increased openness to giving interviews and making public appearances does not, however, mean that he has become more commercial, either in his writing or his attitudes. In fact, he remains as much the maverick as ever, producing risk-taking work that is so wide-ranging in tone, form, and subject matter that it is often described with such terms as "characteristically uncharacteristic,"[4] "uncategorizable," and "all over the map." As critic Tracie Church Guzzio observes,

> Where does one place a writer whose canon includes revisions of Dionysus, Medea, Tiresias, Icarus, *and* the John Wayne film *The Searchers* and at the same time attempts to write a "history" of African Americans penned by the most notorious political foe of integration in post–World War II America, South Carolina senator Strom Thurmond? Whose work reflects the influences of French poststructuralist theory (especially semiotics), the philosopher Ludwig Wittgenstein, Ralph Ellison, and Laurence Sterne? Who has written a children's book as well as a new introduction to *The Jefferson Bible*?[5]

While the interviews collected in this volume may not provide a fully satisfying answer to Guzzio's rhetorical questions (to which a glib response might be, *in a class by himself!*), the interviews do offer signal insights into the attitudes and practices that underlie Everett's large and eclectic body of writing.[6]

Born in 1956 in Fort Gordon, Georgia, and raised in Columbia, South Carolina, Everett currently serves as Distinguished Professor of English at the University of Southern California, where he teaches creative writing and literary theory. Interviewers have explored the author's life, his writing, and his teaching, but their success in laying bare information about his life has been far more limited than when inquiring into his writing and teaching practices. Everett does, however, speak openly about such topics as growing up in South Carolina (see Starr, "'Bored'"); his transition from pursuing a doctorate in ordinary language philosophy at the University of Oregon to his enrollment in the creative writing program at Brown University, where he earned his M.A. in 1982; the abundance of doctors and dentists in his family; his fondness for fly fishing and woodworking; his long-time devotion to training horses and mules, and operating a working ranch; presidential and "Red-state"/"Blue-state" politics (especially when responding to European interviewers); and, most notably, his views on "race" in American culture, literature, and publishing—all subjects that have, in varying ways, provided grist for his fictional mill. It is also noteworthy that Everett's positions on most subjects—at least those expressed in both his interviews and his nonfiction—appear not to have altered much over time, suggesting that his views are deeply considered. Everett's wit shines through in the interviews, but so do his thoughtfulness and his penchant for making principled, nuanced distinctions.

Perhaps it is Everett's handling of "race" and racialism, complicated subjects in their own right, that most clearly illustrates his capacity to offer carefully considered observations designed to expose, then question readers' assumptions. For many, Everett's views about "race," which he has described as "a bogus yet *real* category that's perpetuated by the culture," may seem unconventional. For example, he asserts to Garry Mulholland that "I don't see color when I'm meeting people, and I don't see myself or others in terms of their race," yet explains that "I'm not naïve. I know that there are places where the color of my skin will place me under threat." Unlike the writer Jean Toomer, who in his 1931 book *Essentials* famously declared that "I am of no particular race, I am of the human race, a man at large in the human world, preparing a new race," and unlike those currently promoting American "post-racialism," the notion that the country is now substantially devoid of racial preference, discrimination, and prejudice, Everett harbors no illusions about America's being a "race"-blind society—or, for that matter, about its *becoming* one any time soon. He wryly observes to Rone Shavers that "social injustice is not going to go away, so if you hate social injustice and love complaining about it, then this is the world for you." But the fact that what passes for social progress is often glacially paced doesn't mean that one has to accept the status quo, or that one cannot help effect small change in some people. "When I started writing," Everett tells Robert Birnbaum, "I did it because I wanted to make art and now I understand that art and politics are inextricably bound and that you can affect the world in really small ways and hope that something good happens." One way he attempts to influence readers' attitudes about "race" is to ignore racial designations in certain of his novels and stories. Another, albeit less common means is to plant a psychic landmine designed to play off the traditional reader expectation that "most characters are white unless you tell them they aren't," which he points out is "an assumption no one can [logically] make." Not until page 54 of *Glyph*, for instance, does the reader discover that the hyper-intelligent child narrator of that novel is black—a trap that has caught readers of all backgrounds off guard. When interviewer Anthony Stewart admits to "feeling kind of caught" when he first read this section of the book, Everett initially takes some delight in the success of his ploy—". . . it made you feel like shit"—then sagely counsels, "This is the culture in which we live. This is the way we're trained to read. . . . But [tha]t doesn't mean it has to remain that way."

Everett builds upon his concerns with American racialism when talking with fellow novelist Jeffrey Renard Allen: ". . . anthropologists gave up race as a category in the beginning of the twentieth century, but our culture hasn't, so race exists. Speaking logically, I am an African American novelist." But, he adds, "I'm also a 5'11" novelist. I'm, at this point, a California novelist." The designation *African American*, in short, is not an especially apt one—and it is inappropriately limiting. Everett notes that he goes to many bookstores where he sees "this section 'African American,' usually it's 'Studies' or 'Literature,' and, you know, I don't see 'White Literature.' And I . . . know what it means. It means the same thing it means when I pick up an art book that wants to call a certain art 'folk art' or 'naïve art.' It wants to put art in a separate category to make it seem as if somehow it is not quite art. And that's the problem I have." He dubs this practice "culturally offensive" when talking with his French translator Anne-Laure Tissut in 2005, and he comments to Shashank Bengali that another venue in which the "insidious" and all-too-pervasive racialism of American society shows up are reviews of his books, in which reviewers often feel compelled to identify Everett as an African American even though his text may make no mention of race.[7] And "even if the novel had African American characters," he adds, "I don't know why it makes a difference that I'm an African American writer. Reviewers feel they need to say, 'By the way, the writer is black.' I've never seen, 'By the way, the writer is white.'" At issue is unequal treatment. Everett points out another example which he finds culturally offensive—black writers' fairs—to Tine Winther: "If I were a white writer, I would not enjoy being invited to a white writers' fair."

A more substantive aspect of inappropriate "race"-based cultural delimi-
tation that concerns Everett is American readers' tendency to "want their
black experience to be inner-city and rural south." He tells Rone Shavers,
". . . I spend a lot of my time with ranchers, hydrologists, and veterinarians.
Occasionally someone [who has read my work] will say, 'That's not the Black
Experience.' And I laugh and say, 'I'm black, and that's my experience.' I know
a lot of black people whose experience is that, but it's not what people want
to think is the black experience . . . ." Unless these perceptions are challenged,
the broad range of occupational, geographical, avocational, and other forms
of diversity that characterize any group in America becomes lost. "Where
you live," Everett opines to Lynell George, "affects the way you think, no
matter what color you are." In this regard, one of the things Everett finds
important about his novel *erasure* is "that it rebels against the established
practice of pigeonholing the black experience. Black people in America are
as diverse as white people." What many readers of *erasure* may find more
worth pondering, however, are Everett's remarks to Sean O'Hagan about
what, for him, is the core meaning of the book, especially since the author
usually guards against disclosing his sense of a book's meaning, leaving that
to the reader: "I see it [*erasure*] essentially as a book about the creation of
art and all the impediments placed in front of some of us as we set out to
do that within this culture . . . . What is most interesting to me about Monk
is not his color, but his selfless examination of himself. He does not want to
be constrained or reduced by society's demands or expectations." A possible
explanation for Everett's here breaking form and speaking about his assessment of the book's meaning may lie in the fact that his statement, especially
in its last sentence, goes so deeply to the heart of his own literary sojourn.

Earlier, I remarked that Everett's views about most subjects appear not
to have changed much over time, but one thing that apparently has altered
is his *affect* with respect to "race"-related issues. He informs a number of
interviewers that when he was younger he used to become angry when exposed to racial slights, and he recounts for Tine Winther two DWB (Driving
While Black) incidents from his early adulthood in which he was pulled
over by a police officer for no good reason, questioned, and asked to show
his ID. In one of these instances, he "wasted a day sitting in prison because
I was stubborn and wouldn't give my name." The mature Everett, on the
other hand, takes exception to the fact that *erasure* would be considered "an
attack" on American culture's obsession with the limited depiction of black
experience dramatized in the *My Pafology* section of the novel. "I don't see
it that way at all," he tells Lynell George. "I see it as fairly calculated. I'm

amused more than anything. I find all of this rather silly. It's not important enough to have me disgusted with the world or life." Or, as Everett laughingly remarks to William Starr, "I guess by now I'm pretty much past getting offended. After all, you don't get mad at a snake when it bites you"—a sentiment that recalls "Monk" Ellison's rather sanguine reaction to American racism on the second page of *erasure*: ". . . that's just the way it is."

Another dimension of Percival Everett, both as a literary figure and as a person, that we learn about in the interviews is his profound devotion to his craft. There can be no doubt that his self-definition is deeply bound up in being a literary artist.[8] Relatedly, he views himself as somewhat of a loner, despite having been married for much of his adult life and despite acknowledging that he has benefited both personally and professionally from his marital relationships.[9] Writing, he remarks to Anthony Stewart, "is solitary work. Regardless of what completes the circuit, it's done alone. There are lots of gregarious and social writers who spend a lot of time with people. I don't. My experience with the world is pretty much solitary. I'd much prefer to be with a horse than a pack of people. And so that's part of my experience coming into the work. It's how I understand the world." One reason for his feeling so at home in the West, where he has spent the bulk of his adult life, and for living on and operating a working ranch approximately sixty miles east of Los Angeles for many years, is "the privacy it gives me." Jim Kincaid, a close USC friend with whom Everett co-authored *A History of the African-American People [Proposed] by Strom Thurmond*, reinforces this image of Everett when speaking with Shashank Bengali: ". . . he's very much a loner, despite being such a warm person. He has adjusted to a kind of geography in his mind of being alone a lot." These comments suggest that we should take literally his words to Fred Kirsch in 1994: "Writing is more than putting words on paper. It's a way of life." But while this "solitary work" brings him satisfaction, it is far from unbroken delight. "I almost never have fun writing," he explains to Arash Markazi. "I love my work. I love the art, but I'm never sitting there enjoying it. . . . It's that masochistic thing that a lot of people who love their work go through."

What Everett does find enjoyable is "studying," the background reading and other research required to effectively achieve his fictive ends. He tells Claude Julien that "I love to study. There's so much I don't know anything about that any time I get an opportunity to study and learn something, I will. . . . I get to study something with every novel and that's what I like." His comments to Andrew Medlin and Trevor Gore reinforce this position: "Ninety percent of my work is research. I only write books because it allows me to study. I can go out and learn about something I didn't know, and then promptly forget it, but still I love finding out about the world." There are, of course, limits to the pleasure that study typically brings. Everett explains to Forrest Anderson that doing the background research for *erasure* meant that he "had to watch a lot of Jerry Springer and Rickie Lake to get some of those voices." And in order to write the *My Pafology* section of the novel, he had to "read books I hate, and listen to these voices, which I think are fabricated. . . . I did not love learning that."

It will also come as no surprise to readers of Everett's fiction that, along with *study*, the words *ideas, questions*, and *thinking* hold a privileged place in his lexicon. As an undergraduate student at the University of Miami, he majored in philosophy, concentrating on mathematical logic, and as a graduate student at Oregon he studied ordinary language philosophy, with Wittgenstein providing the bridge across those two domains within the discipline. Everett summarized his subsequent transition, from the study of philosophy to creative writing, for William Starr in 2001: ". . . I became disenchanted with philosophy. Wittgenstein said, 'Philosophy is a sick endeavor,' and I realized that the patient, at least for me, was terminal. . . . So I started writing fiction as a better way to approach philosophical ideas." By "approach . . . ideas," Everett does not mean "propose answers"; to the contrary, his goal is to create stories in which meaningful questions are presented for the reader to respond to, perhaps finding some "truth" in the process. They are also questions for the author to consider somewhat exhaustively while writing—thus Everett's oft-repeated, Zen-like quip that "the beautiful thing about novels is I think I know something when I start one, and by the time I'm done with it I realize I didn't know anything at all."[10]

Everett most definitely does not set out to proselytize in his writing. Rather, he seeks to engage readers sufficiently in his stories that they will spend time thinking about what they've read when they finish one of his texts. In contrast to Ishmael Reed's formulation "writin' is fightin,'"[11] Everett's very different literary formulation—at least with respect to those he terms "serious" readers—might be expressed in this way: writing + reading = thinking. And he sees this thinking, in turn, serving as a prelude to readers' producing "meaning" and "truth"—or what more conventionally is termed insight. Many of Everett's comments point in the direction of his writing as a questioning process, including: "You don't have to have answers to be a writer. I don't have any. But you have to love entertaining the questions" (Kirsch 1994); "I . . . know I don't have many answers to questions. So I guess what I like to do now is raise questions so that somebody discussing my work will give me an answer" (Starr 2001); "as a fiction writer, I just want to illuminate the fact that there is something to discuss. I'm not a superhero. I'm just the writer" (Shavers 2004); and ". . . I don't approach fiction—or, more generally, writing—with the notion that I know what's true and right. I raise questions" (Mills, Julien, and Tissut 2007). He offers a similar response to the value of literary theory in the Shavers interview: ". . . it's important to watch how ideas work and how they can be manipulated. That's probably the most important question to me in the world: What can you do with thinking?" Thus, although Everett is open to readers' generating a very wide range of responses to his questions, including—or, perhaps, *especially* including—responses he had not anticipated, he is extremely canny when crafting the vehicles through which he launches these questions. While he may read theory or do mathematical logic "for fun" or "to sort of relax," he firmly believes that writing is, at base, "about loving life and attacking it and trying to make sense of it," and so, as he reminds Lynell George, he must always remain, after some fashion, "connected to" and "engaged with . . . the real world" when writing. And he certainly recognizes that, given this commitment to connection and engagement, the reader's active participation is required if his written words are to engender meaning.

Everett's construction of his relationship with readers is an interesting one, since it starts by substantively ignoring them and ends by ceding them full authority to ignore what might pass for authorial intent and create their own meaning. As he tells Jeff Allen, "I never think about audience, which, if I look at my bank account, is pretty apparent. But it's true. I just don't think about whom I'm writing for. I just think about making the book." Yet he of course recognizes that, although he must please himself while writing, "I'm not writing for myself." "The work isn't complete," he insists to Anthony Stewart, "until somebody reads it. The circuit of art isn't complete until it is received. And meaning's not made until that happens." Moreover—and this explains Everett's loathness to comment publicly about his personal understanding of his books' meaning—". . . all meaning in any work is something I stay out of completely" (or at least make a determined effort to avoid discussing) because generating meaning, as he tells Barbara DeMarco-Barrett, is "the reader's job." Strengthening this position, Everett informs Edward Champion that "once I let a book go, I have to let it go. I can't control what it does. I can't control what it means. I might have some intentions. But really, who gives a damn about what I meant? And again I can't affect it in any way. That's the beauty of doing this. . . . That's the exciting part of making a novel. It's that I have no idea what it's going to mean." Going one step further when speaking with Champion, he conceptually turns the traditional notion of authorial intent on its head when he states that "most of my creative process is a literal misunderstanding. I just love the fact that not only can we mean stuff but that we can mean something that we don't intend."

Another way in which Everett parts ways with many writers is that he approaches each novel as a wholly new project. He regards repeating oneself as boring, and he hates to be bored. Taking risks he finds both exciting and rewarding, and failures have their value if you learn from your mistakes. "Write what you want to write," he tells Ben Ehrenreich. "You gotta have faith in what you see. It might not be a recipe for success, but it is a recipe for artistic happiness." He claims that the term *experimental* is meaningless, because every novel "has its own life" and is an experiment. "The only reason I would want a particular style is so that people could identify every work of mine as mine," he tells Rone Shavers. "There's nothing at stake for me in having people recognize the work because of stylistic consistency. . . . I think that anybody who thinks they have a style—it's like watching punk rockers get ready to go out. It must take you two hours to get that look. How many safety pins do you need? . . . Send the work out there naked."

If one were to succeed in compelling dedicated readers of Everett's novels to state common features of his books, they would probably name two somewhat interrelated things: The novels are relatively short, and they end abruptly—attributes that reviewers, both favorable and unfavorable, mention with some regularity. Those who like the books often bemoan the fact that Everett leaves them wanting more, whereas more negatively inclined reviewers are wont to complain that the author has appeared to run out of steam at book's end. The interviews provide a rationale for Everett's keeping the books short and, as Rone Shavers puts it, "pull[ing] the emergency brake when you end a book." Everett, we learn, often writes in blocks of time as short as ten or fifteen minutes, "when [he] think[s he] might understand something," and he is an inveterate rewriter who "like[s] short novels" and "take[s] a certain amount of pride in having the work lean," often generating "a lot more [text] than [he] need[s] and then . . . chop[ping] aggressively." With respect to Shavers's comment about pulling the emergency brake, Everett responds, "I hope it feels that way, because if you're really into a world then you don't want it to stop and anyplace it ends, it has to . . . ," preferably "in an open-ended way." If we interpret this comment in the context of Everett's acute awareness that it is the reader who will have to arrive at a book's meaning, a logical way to initiate that thinking process is to craft an abrupt, open-ended conclusion that implicitly calls upon the reader to stop and take stock of what he or she has just read. Were all of a plot's loose ends knit together by book's end and the narrative slowly wound down, readers might feel that there is little for them to examine, and might therefore be disinclined to undertake such an examination. With respect to readers' wanting more, there is probably no easy answer . . . other than the knowledge that Everett will likely have a new book, with a new look and new issues, in print within a year or so.

Do not play to readers' interests; make them think; eschew having a discernible message; when you enjoy success with a certain type of book, change it up for the next one—Everett is certainly aware that this is not a recipe for commercial success. But being "successful" in the way society typically defines the word has never been Everett's goal. "I just want to write books," he told Lynell George in 2001. "And apparently for the most part, I don't want to write books that are terribly commercially successful. But I want to write what I want to write." For Everett, "a breakthrough book is . . . a novel better than I've written before—not that it sells more copies. If I look at what's popular, that's not exactly great company. For good or bad, I want to make better art every time I go to work." And speaking with Garry Mulholland in 2003, Everett went so far as to claim being "tickled by the fact that my work is not popular." Small wonder, then, that he counsels fledgling writers not to ask "whether something is publishable" but to "think about . . . the work and the life that the work has." In his discussion with student interviewers Andrew Medlin and Trevor Gore, Everett explains that "it's very easy for me to sit here having been published and talk about how unimportant that is but—it *is* unimportant. There are so many beautiful works of fiction that have not been published and so many truly shitty works of fiction that have been. And that's good to remember away from work. When you go to your art, it's just the art." This is the credo Percival Everett has lived and worked by over the past three decades, and is likely to continue working by, no matter what direction his new writing projects take.

This introduction differs from some others in the *Conversations* series in that it places little emphasis on the chronology of the interviews. By now, I hope the reason for this is clear. In his interviews, Everett pays much more attention to his fictional practices and the conceptual underpinnings of his approach than he does to the meaning of his works or to his development as a writer. Perhaps these "uncharacteristic" tendencies are what one might reasonably expect from this author. But this is not to say that Everett's interviews are devoid of typical elements, such as ticking off some of the books that are especially important to him—most notably, Sterne's *Tristram Shandy*, Samuel Butler's *The Way of All Flesh*, Ellison's *Invisible Man*, Himes's *If He Hollers Let Him Go*, Melville's *Moby-Dick*, and Twain's *The Adventures of Huckleberry Finn*, as well as the work of Zora Neale Hurston, Samuel Beckett, and Flannery O'Connor. More interesting, perhaps, is Everett's list of his own works to which he feels closest—*Glyph*, *Frenzy*, and *Cutting Lisa*, but not *erasure*, which he does not regard as his best book and which, as I have noted above, he found painful to write. *Glyph*, he tells Claude Julien, "was the easiest for me to write as it is closest to my own voice." Along the way, we also pick up working-titles for four of his books published under different names: *How Much Is That Negro in the Window?* (*erasure*),[12] *Making Jesus* (*American Desert*), *The Wall* (his poetry collection *re:f (gesture)*), and *Other Languages Are All We Have . . .* (*The Water Cure*).

There are also, spread across the interviews, comments about individual works that should help stir insights leading to reader-generated meaning. And while many of the interviews are wide-ranging, certain ones focus on individual works: George, Mulholland, O'Hagan, and Winther on *erasure*; DeMarco-Barrett and Stone, as well as the piece from *l'Humanité*, on *The Water Cure*; Toal and Reynolds on *I Am Not Sidney Poitier*; the inReads interview on *Assumption*; and Thea Brown on *Abstraktion und Einfühlung*, the only interview, and one of the few works of any kind, devoted to Everett's poetry.

I will briefly address one final topic—Everett's painting—before moving to a close. As people know if they have seen the 2010 volume *There Are No Names for Red: Poems* [by Chris Abani] *& Paintings* [by Everett], or have had the rare pleasure of viewing the dust jacket for his hard-to-locate small-press novel *The Body of Martin Aguilera*, Everett is an excellent abstract painter. Several of the interviews—especially those by Allen and by Mills, Julien, and Tissut—allow us to see that the painting, which has value in its own right, can also help us understand an important aspect of Everett's writing. I quote at length from the piece by Mills et al.:

> I paint because I love spreading color and not because I'm attempting to construct an identifiable scene. And that brings me to why I do paint. The relationship with visual art is a more immediate visceral, emotional one. When I look at a canvas and start spreading paint on it, it's physical. There it is in front of me and it's exciting in a very different way than writing. Starting a novel is like entering a bad marriage. No matter what I do, it's going to end badly, to be full of emotional

ups and downs. It's going to alienate me and I'm going to be alienated from anyone I know—family, friends—and it's going to last a lot longer than I want it to.
The relationship is shorter with a painting.

The inherent difficulties of engaging in a year- or years-long project such as
writing a novel, a project which the prolific Mr. Everett has undertaken on
roughly an annual basis for the past three decades, hit home dramatically
when he speaks of the comparative ease of producing a painting, itself no
mean feat. And this, in turn, should remind us of the incredible personal
and artistic commitment, as well as the uncanny ability, required to generate an opus that possesses the scope, diversity, and importance of the one to
which Percival Everett has given birth.

My most profound hope for this collection of Everett's interviews is that it
stimulates increased scholarly and general interest in one of the finest writers now working in America, and helps to provide a lens through which
to better understand and appreciate his literary achievements. Editing of
the texts has been minimal. Each interview appears uncut, and textual
changes have generally been limited to correcting the few factual errors I
encountered in the interviews' first printings and to ensuring consistency
of spelling, capitalization (most notably utilizing Everett's preferred form of
the book titles *erasure* and *damned if I do*), the format of "African American" (which is only hyphenated when it is part of a title), and the format of
the speech tags when an interview utilizes traditional question-response
format.

I am especially grateful to my research assistant for this project, Heather
Bozant, a graduate student at Saint Louis University who had the unenvi-
able task of obtaining permissions to reprint the interviews which appear
here; to Kate Tschida, another of our graduate students, who assisted me
with several aspects of my Everett research, including creating transcrip-
tions of some of his audio interviews; to the Interlibrary Loan librarians at
the University's Pius XII Memorial Library, who have provided a great deal
of printed material in support of my ongoing research into Everett's writing;
to Jeffrey Renard Allen, Ed Champion, and Barbara DeMarco-Barrett and
Marrie Stone, whose interviews appear in print here for the first time; and
to the other interviewers and publishers' representatives whose cooperation
was essential to this project's successful completion. I am also most grateful to Mr. Everett, who has at various points taken time away from what I'm
sure were to him more important tasks in order to assist me in my research,

including providing me with much of the material I used to construct the Chronology that appears here. A special debt is owing to four people who were extremely generous and caring in translating interviews originally published in Danish, French, and Italian: Evelyn Meyer of the Department of Modern and Classical Languages at Saint Louis University; independent scholar Marte Hult; and Saint Louis University students Jennifer Kinney and Roma Rae Ryan. Thanks as well to David Cowart of the University of South Carolina and Reginald Martin of the University of Memphis, without whose efforts I might not have been able to secure permission to reprint two interviews that appear here. Finally, and in many ways, I am also indebted to my wife of thirty-plus years, Sharron Pollack, who has tolerated many periods of my own single-mindedness as I have worked to see this and other scholarly projects through to conclusion over the past several decades.

JW

Notes

1. ". . . I like being at Graywolf," Everett remarked to Anthony Stewart in 2007. "It's an independent publisher, a non-profit publisher. Ironically, they're under more pressure to turn a profit than for-profit publishers, but I've never had a talk with them about marketing. I don't want to talk about marketing. I don't know anything about marketing. Nothing could bore me more than marketing. I want to talk about books. And that's what we talk about."

2. Everett has quipped to several interviewers, beginning with Ben Ehrenreich, that he did "a publicity tour" for *erasure* because he "need[ed] a new roof on [a summer] house in Canada," but I am not alone in understanding this remark as one primarily designed to elicit a laugh.

3. As Lynell George states, following years of modest book sales, " . . . interpretations, expectations, and reporters' questions [would] now encroach" and produce the need for some "adjustment" by a writer who had "always lived and reveled in remote places."

4. Joseph Bates, "The Writing Life: Percival Everett, Characteristically Uncharacteristic," *2008 Novel & Short Story Writer's Market*, eds. Lauren Mosko and Michael Schweer (Cincinnati: Writer's Digest Books, 2007), 5–9.

5. "Percival Everett (1956–)," *American Writers: A Collection of Literary Biographies—Supplement XVIII (Charles Frederick Briggs to Robert Wrigley)*, ed. Jay Parini (Farmington Hills, MI: Gale, 2008), 53.

6. As of June 2012, the month of this introduction's composition, Everett had published seventeen novels, a novella, three collections of short fiction, three books of poetry, and a chil-

dren's book. By the time this collection of his interviews appears in print, an eighteenth novel, intriguingly titled *Percival Everett by Virgil Russell*, will also have appeared, and one could add to his book tally the volume *There Are No Names for Red* (2010), a text which conjoins fourteen of Everett's paintings with poems by one of his former students, Chris Abani.

7. Regarding his novel *Frenzy*, which focuses on the Greek god Dionysus, Everett tells Ben Ehrenreich, "The only thing ostensibly African American about the book is my photograph."

8. Everett's devotion to his craft comes across directly in many ways and in many places, but perhaps nowhere more clearly than when speaking to Anthony Stewart: "When I say I make books, I have an old-fashioned and maybe arcane sense of myself as an artist. And that's all I really want to do. I don't care about fame. I don't want to be famous."

9. Many of Everett's books are dedicated to his former wife Francesca "Chessie" Rochberg, who is referenced in several interviews, and he is currently married to writer Danzy Senna.

10. This is a boiled-down variation of a stock response which Everett provides in at least six interviews. A more hyperbolic version appears in the Medlin and Gore piece, and was likely punctuated by a laugh: "Writing fiction is a beautiful, cleansing thing. I think I know something about the world when I start a book. I'm pretty quickly disabused of that notion in the middle of it, and by the time I finish a book, I realize that a lot of what I thought I knew was wrong—and that I know very little. After twenty books, I know a lot less than most people. I'm well on my way to knowing nothing at all, which is my goal."

11. See Reed's 1988 book *Writin' Is Fightin': Thirty-Seven Years of Boxing on Paper.*

12. In Everett's interview with Begoña Piña ("Percival Everett," *Qué Leer* 26 February 2012), we learn that another of the working-titles for *erasure* was *Modern Art*.

Chronology

1956	Born on December 22 in Fort Gordon, GA, to Percival L. and Dorothy (Stinson) Everett.
1957	Moves with his family to Columbia, SC, where he grew up.
1974	Graduates from A. C. Flora High School in Columbia and leaves in the fall to attend the University of Miami.
1977	Receives his baccalaureate degree from Miami, with a major in philosophy and a minor in biochemistry.
1978–80	Does graduate study in the philosophy of language at the University of Oregon.
1980-82	Does graduate study in creative writing at Brown University, earning his A.M. degree with the submission of *Suter*, his master's thesis, which served as the basis for his first published novel.
1983	Publishes *Suter*.
1984	Receives the D. H. Lawrence Fellowship at the University of New Mexico.
1985	Publishes *Walk Me to the Distance*.
1985–86	Serves as visiting assistant professor of English, University of Kentucky.
1986	Publishes *Cutting Lisa*.
1987	Publishes *The Weather and Women Treat Me Fair*.
1987–89	Serves as associate professor of English and director, Graduate Writing Program, University of Kentucky.
1989	In a speech at the Verner Awards ceremony at the South Carolina State House, criticizes the presence of the Confederate flag flying on the Capitol dome.
1989–91	Serves as professor of English, University of Notre Dame.
1990	Publishes *For Her Dark Skin* and *Zulus*, winner of the New American Writing Award.
1991	Serves as fiction judge for the PEN/Faulkner Award.
1991–92	Serves as William Robertson Coe Chair in American Studies, University of Wyoming.

1992	Publishes *The One That Got Away*.
1992–98	Serves as professor of creative writing, University of California, Riverside.
1993	Serves as visiting professor of English and honors, University of Kentucky (fall semester).
1994	Publishes *God's Country* and receives a Lila Wallace-*Reader's Digest* Fellowship; begins serving as fiction editor for the journal *Callaloo*.
1994–98	Serves as department chairperson, University of California, Riverside.
1996	Publishes *Watershed* and *Big Picture*, which was a finalist for the Paterson Fiction Prize.
1997	Publishes *The Body of Martin Aguilera* and *Frenzy*, serves as a fiction judge for the National Book Award, and receives the PEN/Oakland-Josephine Miles Award for Excellence in Literature (for *Big Picture*); "The Appropriation of Cultures" included in *The Pushcart Prize XXII: Best of the Small Presses*.
1998–2007	Serves as professor of English, University of Southern California.
1999	Publishes *Glyph*.
1999–2002	Serves as department chairperson, University of Southern California.
2000	"The Fix" included in *The Best American Short Stories 2000*.
2001	Publishes *Grand Canyon, Inc.* and *erasure*, wins the Hillsdale Award for Fiction, and serves as a Hurst Visiting Professor at Washington University in St. Louis.
2002	Receives his first Hurston/Wright Legacy Award (for *erasure*) and learns that *erasure* is named one of the year's ten best novels by the American Library Association as well as a finalist for the International IMPAC Dublin Literary Award.
2003	Receives the American Academy of Arts and Letters' Award for Fiction and serves as a judge for three prestigious awards—the PEN/Hemingway Award for First Fiction, the Hurston/Wright Legacy Award, and the Rea Award for the Short Story.
2004	Publishes *A History of the African-American People [Proposed] by Strom Thurmond, as told to Percival Everett & James Kincaid*; *damned if i do*; *American Desert*, which was named one of twenty-five Books to Remember from 2004 by the New York City Public Library as well as a Best Book of 2004 by the *San*

Francisco Chronicle; and a substantial introduction to *The Jefferson Bible*, which includes an imagined conversation with Thomas Jefferson.

2005   Publishes *Wounded.*

2006   Publishes *re:f (gesture)* and receives the PEN Center USA Literary Award for Fiction (for *Wounded*).

2007   Publishes *The Water Cure*; begins serving as Distinguished Professor of English, University of Southern California.

2008   Publishes *Abstraktion und Einfühlung* and receives the Prix Lucioles des Libraires (for the French translation of *Wounded*) as well as an honorary Ph.D. from the College of Santa Fe.

2009   Publishes *I Am Not Sidney Poitier*; begins serving as director, Ph.D. Program in Literature and Creative Writing, University of Southern California.

2010   Receives five literary awards—the Premio Vallombrosa Gregor von Rezzori Prize for Foreign Fiction (for the Italian translation of *Wounded*), his second Hurston/Wright Legacy Award and the Believer Book Award (both for *I Am Not Sidney Poitier*), the Charles Angoff Award (for his story "Confluence"), and the Dos Passos Prize in Literature—and provides the paintings for Chris Abani's *There Are No Names for Red: Poems & Paintings.*

2011   Publishes *Swimming Swimmers Swimming* and *Assumption*; inducted into the South Carolina Literary Hall of Fame.

2012   Serves as a judge for the FC2's Catherine Doctorow Innovative Fiction Prize.

2013   Publishes *Percival Everett by Virgil Russell.*

Conversations with Percival Everett

On Writing: Visiting Author Brings a Love of Craft to Classroom

Fred Kirsch / 1994

From *The Virginian-Pilot* (Norfolk, VA), 26 February 1994, B1. Copyright © 2012. *The Virginian-Pilot*. Reprinted with permission.

They'd been reading his short stories and novels for weeks, but they didn't quite know what to expect when Percival Everett came to Virginia Wesleyan College.

They thought he'd be, well, older. And serious. His writing was so spare and lean and to the point.

And probably a white guy. They were white, those doctors and hunters and guys hanging around Carlton's garage and that huge three-hundred-pound woman he wrote about, weren't they?

But when Everett arrived on campus to spend two weeks as a Lila Wallace–*Reader's Digest* writing fellow, students discovered you can't judge a book by its cover. Or a writer by his subjects.

Everett turned out to be a thirty-seven-year-old black man who not only, according to one student, is "an awesome writer" but also a guy who talked their language. A guy who knew all about staring at blank computer screens.

"To be able to actually sit down and talk to an author you've been reading is just an incredible opportunity," said Melody Budzina, a sophomore who sat in on one of the many classes Everett spoke to.

"You get so much more out of something like this. Even though we're students, he said a lot of things we could identify with."

He should have.

Everett wasn't much older than the two dozen students sitting in front of him on a recent morning in an English 112 class when he wrote his first novel, *Suder*, about a baseball player who falls into a horrendous slump that brings on a constellation of off-field problems.

It was published when he was twenty-four. Now he's at work on his sixth and seventh novels, writing short stories in between.

"Writing is more than putting words on paper. It's a way of life," Everett says.

Everett will return to Virginia Wesleyan in the fall as part of the national Writing Fellows Program, whose purpose is to stimulate greater appreciation for the written word on campuses.

Virginia Wesleyan is one of eighteen colleges selected this year (there will be sixty over the next four years) for the program, which is administered by the Woodrow Wilson National Fellowship Foundation and is the largest of its kind in the country.

"If you have to write and you don't, you're going to be miserable," he tells the students. "You've got to write. That's the way it was for me. If it's in you, let it out. But keep the day job."

By day, Everett, a lean, immaculate man, is a professor of creative writing at the University of California–Riverside. But by night and at heart, he's a writer. A writer's writer.

"You have to love the craft first" is one of the messages he brought to a class of students the other day. "The work is more important than you. And if it's good it will last a lot longer. It has the potential to endure. You don't.

"And you have to love life even more. Writing is about loving life and attacking it and trying to make sense of it. You don't have to have answers to be a writer. I don't have any. But you have to love entertaining the questions."

Like most of the students he met during the past two weeks, he didn't have "a clue" what he wanted to do when he was at the University of Miami studying science and philosophy.

But he knew what he didn't want to be.

"Some kind of physician," says Everett, who grew up in Columbia, S.C. "Everyone in my family—grandfather, father, uncles, my sister—are physicians or dentists. I thought a plumber was a doctor who had a part-time job."

The idea of being a writer didn't surface until he was in graduate school at Brown University. It was when he started "studying behavior and writing these scenes of how people behaved that I discovered I had a need to express myself. And that's how I started writing *Suder*. It was the first thing I really ever wrote."

It started out as a short story, but Everett discovered he had more to say than he thought. *Suder* turned into a 264-page novel acclaimed as a "work of comic genius . . . juxtaposing heartbreak with farce to make up a narrative that has never been told before."

Since then he's been writing "whatever is in me. The one thing I don't want to do is write the same novel or story over and over. If you're growing you don't stand still. You should be changing all the time. I couldn't write the same thing, or what would be the point?"

He hasn't.

Cutting Lisa is about a retired surgeon and an unfaithful daughter-in-law. *Zulus* features a three-hundred-pound woman who may be the last fertile woman on earth after a thermonuclear war, and *Walk Me to the Distance*, which was made into the TV movie *Follow Your Heart*, deals with a Vietnam vet.

His short stories are filled with characters ranging from a guy named Chacón Chacón to old country boy Darnell Aimes who wants to "knife wrassle" a bear, and a "born-again endrocrinologist" whose wife ends every argument by telling him "at least, I'm still a Jew."

What doesn't change is Everett's concise, almost exacting, command of the language and his understated sense of irony and humor.

"The characters are the important element," he tells students. "The plot is just something to hang them on. If you don't have people that come alive, your story won't come alive."

For the most part, Everett's characters have no color.

"I don't have people combing their Afros or turning down 125th Street in New York. Most white readers assume that most characters are white unless you tell them they aren't. Like in *Cutting Lisa*, the doctor to me is black. Others see him as white. It really doesn't matter."

Everett's new novels *God's Country* and *The Body of Martin Aguilera* will be published by Owl Creek Press, a small publishing company in Seattle.

"I don't like being published by oil companies," he says. "I'm not in it for money, anyway. Which is good. Because I haven't made that much. I'm not what you'd call a commercial success."

Everett, who is also an accomplished jazz guitarist and painter, hasn't made that much speaking, either.

Once, when asked how much it would take to get him to Brown University to speak, he told them, "I really like to play touch football with my friends. Just give me enough to buy a football. That would be great."

Praise motivates him even less than money. While his works have been highly acclaimed, Everett casts a dim eye toward reviews.

"I'm always suspicious if people give me too much praise. I always think, 'Yeah, but it wasn't that good.' You always see how much better it could be."

The only two critics that count for Everett are his wife Francesca, who teaches history at UC-Riverside, and his agent. They are the only two people who ever see his work before he sends it to a prospective publisher.

"If it passes them, then it's probably OK. Those two are absolute brutes. But if you want your writing to ring true, you have to be willing to hear the truth yourself."

In the end, Percival Everett tells the students at Virginia Wesleyan, there's only one person you write for.

"You. And you are the only person who can make you write. All the encouragement in the world can't make you write. And all the discouragement can't make you stop."

Invariably, though, wherever he goes, students who show him their work have the same question.

"They always ask me, 'Is this good enough to be published?' The question should be, 'Is this good?'"

And sometimes, says Everett, that takes a lot of work. Often he writes "twenty to twenty-five drafts" of a novel before it reaches its final form.

Makes a term paper seem like a breeze.

Author Everett Prizes Privacy

William W. Starr / 1994

From *The State* (Columbia, SC), 29 May 1994, F1. © THE STATE. 2012. Reprinted with permission.

The pain in Percival Everett's voice is palpable on the telephone from his home in California.

A question about his new novel draws a sharp intake of breath and a quiet pause before he haltingly begins his answer.

Another query about whether the Columbia native hates talking publicly about his new book—or any of his work—draws a quick response: "Yes."

It's not that Everett is impolite. Hardly. But he places a premium on privacy, and intrusions of any sort are not encouraged.

"I like living in the West. I like the privacy it gives me. I'd just as soon have even fewer people around me," Everett says.

"I was twenty when I first went to the West. The space and the harshness of the countryside appealed to me. The character of the people, I found, was a lot like Southerners, in their enjoyment in storytelling and their use of the language."

That might seem evident from Everett's just-published novel, *God's Country*, which draws its geographic landscape from the Old West in 1871 and offers up a seriocomic tale that would seem familiar to Southern yarnspinners.

God's Country is Everett's eighth book, the latest in a diverse canon that includes literary novels and short stories, a dark cautionary sci-fi tale, and a book for young readers. Like *God's Country*, that book for youngsters—*The One That Got Away* (1992)—is a story set in the Old West, which is now Everett's home.

He's the chairman of the creative writing department at the University of California at Riverside, some fifty miles east of Los Angeles. That represents another in a series of moves that have taken him farther and farther away from the Columbia home where he grew up and went to A. C. Flora High School and where his parents still live.

He was graduated from the University of Miami, studied writing at Brown University and at one time lived on Cape Cod. He was later a teacher at the University of Kentucky, then at Notre Dame, Wyoming, and now in California.

"I keep sliding to the West. Maybe next it's into the ocean," he says with a laugh.

On the other hand, he's not exactly a newcomer to that region, either. A few years before the publication of his first novel, *Suder*, in 1983, he lived for a time in Portland, Oregon, and did some work as a sheep-ranch hand.

Nowadays, when he's not writing or teaching, he's back outdoors in the West: hiking, camping, bird-watching with his wife Francesca, fly fishing, or pursuing his latest interest: painting.

He started painting seriously about a year and a half ago, and has taken to it with enthusiasm and commitment, saying it "taps a different part of me from the writing."

Asked whether painting could replace writing as his chief form of artistic expression, Everett hesitates.

"I'm halfway serious about it at this point. . . . I love writing, but it is emotionally draining. With art, there is a shorter relationship to the work. Writing is more labor intensive. It can be a destructive art form. If I work on something for several years and it doesn't work, that's a big problem. If I mess up a painting, I start over."

His first show of what he calls "abstract expressionist works" in oil will be held at the Bristol Gallery in Denver opening August 5. He and his wife will fly there for a reception, though Everett admits he's as uncomfortable talking about his painting as he is his writing.

He has agreed to do a few readings to promote *God's Country*, though the closest one to Columbia will be in Atlanta in July. He says, however, that he probably will come to Columbia later and sign some books.

The new novel, while bearing some kinship to his book for young readers in its setting and humor, is quite unlike Everett's earlier books, which include *Walk Me to the Distance*, *Cutting Lisa*, and *Zulus*. The narrative is straightforward and the humor is more in evidence, making *God's Country* a likely candidate for a wider readership.

The novel is about a black cowboy named Bubba, the best tracker in the West, who somewhat reluctantly agrees to help a gambling, drinking, cowardly womanizer named Curt Marder find his wife. She has been abducted, ostensibly by some bad Indians after they killed Marder's child and dog.

Charleston author Bret Lott calls the story "a darkly hilarious brew of Kafka and García Márquez, of *Twilight Zone* and *F Troop*." Another reviewer suggests it's a satirical Western "co-authored by Jonathan Swift and the ghost of Chester Himes."

Everett, pushed by his interviewer, concedes that he "was going for something different, playing off the genre. . . . I hope that Bubba represents something more than just the African American experience. His color is what spurs his neglect in the story, but it's as if he was offered something that doesn't exist.

"And that's the American dream, the vague idea that in America you can do anything, be anything. We're all taught that, and it doesn't exist. It isn't there. It's just a dream for whites and for blacks. That's what gives the story some layers, I hope."

Parody That's Personal

Lynell George / 2001

From *Los Angeles Times*, 16 October 2001, E1, E3. Copyright © 2006, 2012. Los Angeles Times. Reprinted with permission.

At the moment, there is something very, well, Percival L. Everett–like transpiring within author Percival L. Everett's life. He couldn't have written it better. The teasing, compact irony he now inhabits is much like the mazes and mirrors he animates on his pages. It might be premature to guess whether this predicament brings him chagrin or amusement. After all, it is still very early in the yarn.

During a break squeezed into a day of classes and meetings in his office at USC, Everett sits in a beam of last-blast summer sun, considering plots and parallels.

In his witty and withering new novel *erasure* (University Press of New England), Percival L. Everett drops readers into the suddenly upended life of Thelonious "Monk" Ellison—a black college professor edging into his middle years. A man of idiosyncratic pursuits and tastes, Monk, as he's known by close friends and family, has made a relatively quiet life for himself in reflective pursuits: fly fishing, woodworking, teaching, and writing obtuse books for university and/or boutique presses.

Ellison, like Everett, is a man who does not define himself by his race but sees it as just one of the shadings that inform his outlook.

Ellison, like Everett, writes multi-layered, "dense" books that find a devoted but slim audience.

And Ellison, somewhat like Everett, ultimately writes a book, a parody of "wannabe ghetto fiction," that receives through-the-roof attention for reasons that make him increasingly uncomfortable.

But that is where the paths diverge—slightly. Whereas Ellison suddenly finds himself in an undertow that pulls him into raucous daytime talk shows

and smarmy motion picture deals, ultimately leading him to lofty book prizes, Everett has, thus far, been simply observing an uncharacteristic blast of
attention that's kicked up around this, his thirteenth book. Better late than
never, to be sure. But, not to be a spoiler, he has his concerns.

For one thing, it's the parody that his character Ellison creates—*My Pafology*, an "authentic" take on ghetto life by Everett's invented gangsta alter
ego Stagg R. Leigh—that has prompted much of the commentary about *erasure*.

"There's a terrible irony that this book is getting a lot of attention for the
very reason that I wrote the book," Everett says, his brow furrowing just for
a moment to add gravity to an already serious face. "Everybody is interested
in the race question . . . instead of the book itself. The parody within the
parody. But . . . ," he stops himself, his expression relaxing into a smile, "I'm
just a writer. And I don't want to shade the way someone might come to the
work."

For a man who admits he has always lived and reveled in remote places, this sudden shake-up is an adjustment. After a career of modest book
sales, interpretations, expectations, and reporters' questions now encroach.
In jeans, a soft-blue short-sleeved shirt, and scuffed riding boots, Everett,
forty-four, sits ramrod straight, in a straight-back chair against a wall. He is
prepared, it seems at first, not for an interview but an inquisition.

"I don't usually say yes to these things," he tosses out, not threateningly,
but as a point of clarification. "But I've promised I would be better."

His office reflects the ease of familiarly negotiated worlds. It's crowded
with the typical trappings of an English professor—multiple volumes of *Norton Anthologies* line orderly shelves; papers and files compete for attention
with a nonstop ringing telephone and student footfalls. Photos of his wife,
Francesca, and pastoral scenes taken on their farm near the Banning Pass
dot the walls. And in a frame next to his computer, a formal, regal portrait
of his mule, named, like the main character of *erasure*, after the humorously
oblique bebop musician Thelonious Monk.

In its few weeks on the shelves, *erasure* has been called Everett's "breakthrough book." *Publishers Weekly* has, in a starred review, hailed it "an over-
the-top masterpiece"; the *New York Times Book Review* has called it "cun-
ning" and "well-calibrated." Everett weighs the "breakthrough" brand—and
the rest of the adulation, for that matter—somewhat dubiously.

"Well, one hopes that it will have financially positive effects on me," he
says, carefully stringing together words and creating chasms of pauses. "But

I don't think about it too much. I just want to write books. And apparently for the most part, I don't want to write books that are terribly commercially successful. But I want to write what I want to write.

"To me, a breakthrough book is when I write a novel better than I've written before—not that it sells more copies. If I look at what's popular, that's not exactly great company. For good or bad, I want to make better art every time I go to work."

With *erasure*, he has produced a multi-layered, tightly written novel that refuses to equivocate. It's a funhouse of manipulated reflections, lives viewed through screens and lenses. The story winds through cutaways and short stories, pieces of Greek chorus conversations among philosophers and artists, world leaders—all alternate prisms glimpsing family, academia, identity, and pop culture.

Monk Ellison is forced to confront the chaos erupting within his once orderly, even sealed-off, life—his mother's advancing age and fading memory; his withering publishing career. The devastation is made more bracing when it coincides with the rising star of an Oberlin-educated young black woman's runaway bestseller *We's Lives in Da Ghetto*.

Based on the author's two-day visit to Harlem to visit relatives, *Ghetto* is a "typical" story of a fifteen-year-old black girl named Sharonda F'rinda Johnson, pregnant with her first child, who lives with her drug addict mother and mentally deficient brother. ("A masterpiece of African American literature. One can actually hear the voices of her people as they make their way through the experience which is and can only be Black America," Monk reads on a plane trip from DC to LA in a highly respected culture magazine.)

His familial loose ends and that last straw become kindling—the impetus leading Monk to divine the persona Stagg R. Leigh—who pens the rebuttal—*My Pafology*—as told by Van Go Jenkins. But both the parody and persona ultimately threaten to erase not just Monk's ambitions but Monk himself.

While much is played for laughs, *erasure* is a trenchant examination of the labels and assumptions that the outside affixes on others, and that many, in turn, unquestioningly affix on themselves. There is a lot here, but that is typical of an Everett story.

His books defy easy category. *Suder* (Viking, 1983), his first novel, published when he was twenty-six and in graduate school, focuses on a black baseball player marooned in a professional and personal slump who takes to the road; *Frenzy* (Graywolf, 1996) is set in the world of Greek mythology;

Glyph (Graywolf, 1999) tracks a baby post-structuralist genius who cuts his teeth, as it were, on philosopher Ludwig Wittgenstein's *Tractatus Logico-Philosophicus.*

But Monk's story is far less fanciful, something Everett puzzled out as a daily exercise: "It wasn't hard. I just looked in the mirror for that. I've heard what he hears in the novel enough. I wouldn't say that the novel is strictly autobiographical, but our experiences are pretty close."

For instance, the experience of browsing the bookstores, reading dust jackets and scanning reviews that at once trumpet and definitively outline "the authentic black story." "It's funny," he says. "We don't have any *white* stories." *My Pafology* was Everett's response to his frustration, and it pushed the larger book into being.

Black fiction, black imprints, black themes—such labels disconcert Everett. "It's irritating when we have this weird 'life imitating art imitating life' thing going on. And it takes the wind right out of your sails if you want to write seriously."

Expectations dog writers, particularly in the realm of race: "It's frustrating," he says, even with this new work. "Everyone calls *erasure* a 'ferocious attack'" on a culture that celebrates prose that sounds like *My Pafology*. But he takes issue with the "attack" assessment of his book. "I don't see it that way at all. I see it as fairly calculated. I'm amused more than anything. I find all of this rather silly. It's not important enough to have me disgusted with the world or life."

Narrow constructs and thinly sketched caricatures persist in popular culture, says Everett, because "audiences aren't discriminating. On the one hand, I think the so-called black audience is so happy to see black people in books or on screen in any way that they'll go to see something, and the black and white audiences have been brainwashed to think that 'this is The Black Experience.' And the fact that I ride horses and fly fish doesn't make me any less black. We get cheated out of geographic differences. Where you live affects the way you think, no matter what color you are."

Born in Fort Gordon, Georgia, Everett spent time in Tennessee and Columbia, South Carolina. He studied philosophy and biochemistry at the University of Miami and creative writing at Brown. "I liked science, and I like mathematical logic." So the puzzles of science and words and people and their language "are not as different as they sound."

He's knocked about variously as a ranch worker, jazz musician, high-school teacher. Those different incarnations have enhanced his writer's ear and broadened his vision. "I write about people. Finally, my characters are people, and they talk to people in the world. I think that it is interesting that people *do* things. I like being engaged with the world in which I live. I don't create work in a vacuum. A lot of my work might be considered esoteric or, for lack of a better word, dense—I believe that it's connected to the real world."

It's a fluid, unwieldy world Everett chooses to embrace and ultimately reconstruct on a page, one dominated, finally by complex themes. "I don't feel that I'm a natural storyteller," he says. "I don't spin yarns. I don't collect family history. I'm motivated by ideas."

USC Department of English Chair Finds Writing a Chore and a Pleasure

Arash Markazi / 2002

U-WIRE from *Daily Trojan* (University of Southern California), 12 February 2002. Reprinted with permission of the USC Office of Student Publications.

Percival Everett is standing in front of a crowded audience at the Alfred Newman Recital Hall at the University of Southern California. He is reading from his latest and most critically acclaimed book, *erasure*.

The soft-spoken Everett has captured the audience's attention. They laugh at every joke and listen tentatively through every tense moment.

Following his book reading, Everett smiles as he greets students, readers, and colleagues, signing his book and shaking their hands.

He appears to be in his element.

Nothing could be further from the truth.

"Once I'm done with the book I really don't care that much about it," Everett said. "I don't look back at them once they're published. I look back at them when I have to do readings, but I don't think about them.

"If there's something bad in it, there's something bad in it. If there's something good in it, then that's not going to help me either."

While Everett, a Department of English chair at USC, doesn't mind talking about his prior accomplishments, he is more concerned about the future and how he will come up with his next novel.

"I am more interested in the process because it differs so greatly from book to book," Everett said. "I'm always curious how the next one will come. That's the exciting thing for me."

Everett's latest novel, *erasure*, has been hailed as "an over-the-top masterpiece" by *Publishers Weekly* and "a remarkable work of fiction that transcends labels" by *Bookreporter.com*.

After publishing twelve novels, one children's book, and two collections of stories, Everett is finally achieving mainstream success, but that has never been the driving force behind his work.

"I've never had a bestseller, and I'm not going to have one," Everett said. "I watch our culture and I see what sells. That's not what I write. I do make demands on the reader."

Everett, forty-five, also makes demands on himself. So much so that he actually has a hard time enjoying writing even though there's nothing that he would rather do.

"I almost never have fun writing," Everett said. "I love my work. I love the art, but I'm never sitting there enjoying it. When I'm not working on something, I feel bad even though I don't really have fun. It's that masochistic thing that a lot of people who love their work go through."

Coming from a family of doctors in South Carolina, Everett is glad that his parents didn't make the same type of demands on him, allowing him to find his own passion in life.

"My grandfather was a physician, my father is a doctor, my brothers and sisters are all doctors, so I had to break the chain," Everett said. "My parents were supportive of my pursing the arts. When I was younger they told me, 'We don't worry about you' and I took that as a statement of confidence."

With the ability to pursue his own ambitions, Everett has led a somewhat rambling early adulthood as both a student and a teacher.

He received a bachelor's degree in philosophy from the University of Miami in 1977, pursued graduate study at the University of Oregon and earned an A.M. in writing from Brown University in 1982. For the last fifteen years, he has held a number of consecutive faculty positions at the Universities of Kentucky, Notre Dame, and Wyoming, and as the head of the creative writing program at California-Riverside before coming to USC in the fall of 1999.

"I've always enjoyed the students where I've taught, but I must say that my experience with students [at USC] has been the most positive that I've had," Everett said. "I've always wanted to be in the west and now I am."

Despite being an award-winning author, Everett gets more pleasure from teaching and learning from his students than he does actually writing his next story.

"I think I'm a good teacher because I appreciate how much I don't know about writing," Everett said. "It helps because the students here are highly motivated, eager, and above all else bright, and that makes teaching a lot of fun."

But even teaching doesn't always satisfy Everett.

"I get tired of it," he said. "I have to admit, sometimes I get very exhausted. Some classes are more exciting than others."

It seems one of the few things that truly pleases Everett is tending to his horses and mules at his home near Palm Springs.

"I train horses and mules. I've been around horses for twenty years," said Everett, who keeps a framed picture of his mule next to his office computer.

"I worked ranches when I was in graduate school. I've always felt comfortable around them."

While he admits he has a strong passion for writing and teaching, Everett gets more joy from the simpler pleasures in life. "Do I write every day? No. I read every day," Everett said. "I think every day. I tend to my horses every day. I talk to my wife all day long every day. I write when I think I might understand something. Ironically, I spend less time writing now, but get more done."

"I Get Bored Easily"

William W. Starr / 2002

From *The State* (Columbia, SC), 31 March 2002, E1. © THE STATE. 2012. Reprinted with permission.

Born and reared in Columbia, Percival Everett has become one of America's most acclaimed African American writers.

The author of fourteen books, he has created novels, short story collections, and even a children's book, each one distinctly different from the others and covering a wide range of genres, from science fiction to fabulism and realism.

His characters cover a similarly wide range, from the last woman capable of bearing a child in a post-apocalyptic age to a nineteenth-century frontier cowboy to a modern black writer issuing an embittered blast against racial/political correctness.

Everett, forty-five, has written his fourteen books during the past nineteen years, beginning in 1983 with *Suder*, a funny, bittersweet novel about a black third baseman for the Seattle Mariners. His 1985 novel *Walk Me to the Distance* was made into a well-received television movie, *Follow Your Heart*.

His latest novel, *erasure*, a satiric indictment of race and publishing in the new millennium, was released to widespread praise late last year.

Acclaim has not led to bestsellerdom, however, and Everett concedes his books are not always easily absorbed by casual readers.

"I'm not ever going to be a bestselling writer," he said.

A graduate of the University of Miami with a master's degree from Brown University, he has taught at a number of institutions including Notre Dame, the University of Kentucky, and the University of California–Riverdale. In 1999, he joined the English faculty at the University of Southern California in Los Angeles.

We caught up with him at the recent South Carolina Book Festival in

Columbia, where he sat down to talk about his experiences in Columbia and his writing.

WS: What do you remember about growing up in Columbia?
PE: I have very pleasant memories of growing up in Columbia. I grew up in a hilly part of the city. My parents lived on a hill off Harden Street near the university. It was steep there, and I had fun riding my bicycle over to the river. It was a pretty healthy ride because of the hills, but it wasn't too far.

WS: When you were growing up, were you exposed to books in your home?
PE: I don't remember my family so much talking about books as I recall books being around the house and accessible. I found *Of Human Bondage* on the shelf when I was very young and thought I was doing something naughty by reading it. So I hid it and would pull it out and read it. It was wonderfully scandalous, a great book. I didn't read children's books, though. I didn't care for them very much. Any book with pictures sort of irritated me. Now, of course, I have a lot of respect for children's books, but then I didn't. (Laughter.)

WS: You didn't read children's books, but you wound up writing one yourself. How did that happen?
PE: I was babysitting my friend's five children while they were away. The kids were asleep, and I knew when they woke up I'd have to have something for them. So I wrote a story with stick figures, and they loved it. Later, I published it (*The One That Got Away*, 1992). But I haven't written any children's books since then because I don't think that way. That was an act of desperation. (Laughter.) I just got lucky with that one book; there won't be another.

WS: Did you spend much time in libraries growing up?
PE: I did. I used to sneak over to McKissick on the university campus and into the stacks. I loved that. And that was before they built the new library. The stacks were so musty and the books so strange and wonderful I could read forever. I spent a lot of hours there reading everything. But it's the smell I remember most.

WS: When did you leave Columbia?
PE: I went to A.C. Flora High School, and I left Columbia at about seventeen, I think, and went off to college.

WS: Some people might be surprised to know that philosophy was one of your majors in college. You once said one of your major influences for a time was (Austrian-born twentieth-century philosopher) Ludwig Wittgenstein.

PE: Yes, that's right. I was interested in logic as an undergraduate. I seem to have a talent for mathematical logic. I started reading Wittgenstein and became interested in language. I continued to study ordinary language philosophy, and it turns out that a lot of ordinary language philosophy was the construction of scenes in which people talked about or around philosophical questions. That was good, but I became disenchanted with philosophy. Wittgenstein said, "Philosophy is a sick endeavor," and I realized that the patient, at least for me, was terminal. . . . So I started writing fiction as a better way to approach philosophical ideas.

WS: And did you do that in conscious anticipation of becoming a writer? A literary writer?

PE: I guess I did when I finally made up my mind to write. I did write a play in high school, at least all evidence points to this since it was apparently produced. My mother claims I used to keep several notebooks full of stuff I was writing, but I don't remember that. It seems to me I had a lot of friends who read books, and that makes me sad for our culture now. Kurt Vonnegut had an army of fourteen-year-olds like me waiting for his next book because fourteen-year-olds read something then, and not just *Harry Potter* or whatever. I don't have that army, no matter how strange my work might be.

WS: You sound pessimistic. Are you gloomy about the future of writing, the future of the novel?

PE: A lot of things are conspiring against it. This bizarre talk of a visual culture, the competition of television and music videos, and the fact that no one wants to read anything "beyond their means." No one wants to be challenged by any work, and that's sad. I remember as a kid that many of my friends had no idea what Herman Hesse was talking about, but that thrilled them. That was a wonderful way to be. Now the response is, "I don't understand that—why should I read it?"

WS: If there is a common thread to your work, it may be that it is all challenging. Does that perhaps explain why you haven't yet written a book that's made it to bestseller lists?

PE: I get bored easily, so I want to write something that's difficult for me.

And interesting to me. I've never done this for money. I've done it to make art, and I have to look at myself every morning in the mirror and be happy with what I've made. That doesn't mean I've made everything perfectly because I look back now and see I would write things differently.

WS: Does that mean the person you're writing books for is you?
PE: I have to please myself, but I'm not writing for myself. I know what I think, so I don't have to go over it again. (Laughter.) I also know I don't have many answers to questions. So I guess what I like to do now is raise questions so that somebody discussing my work will give me an answer.

WS: Are you happiest when you feel your books challenge readers?
PE: Well, I'm not saddened by that. But I don't think about it. I don't think about the reader when I'm working. I think about what it is I'm producing.

WS: Your output is so diverse, so eclectic, with so many different kinds of characters and situations, so many genres. You know it's very hard to categorize you in any way?
PE: I've been lucky to have lived with a lot of different experiences. I've worked at ranches, I've been in academe, I love the outdoors, I love going to New York and Washington and Los Angeles to hear music. I think that my work is a reflection that I live in so many different places.

WS: You're at the University of Southern California now. What are you teaching there?
PE: I teach fiction writing and literature and fiction theory.

WS: Are you a demanding teacher?
PE: Well, that's what my students tell me. I just think I'm being honest with them. If I have a talent as a teacher, it's that I can completely rip a story apart and have my students laughing about it. I think they're comfortable with that because I've experienced what they're experiencing. I do the same thing to myself. That's funny because I come to fiction workshops without ever having been a student in one myself.

WS: Did you come to teaching voluntarily or because you needed something to do to support yourself while you were writing?
PE: It might have come to that. I was offered a visiting position early on,

and at the time I hadn't really thought of teaching as something I would do as a profession. But the opportunity presented itself, and it turned out to be good for me. I've been teaching since the mid-1980s.

WS: And you've always remained away from the South. Does that make you an expatriate Southern writer? Or do you see labels like *Southern writer* as having any significance?

PE: If you consider Kentucky the South, I did teach there for a while. But really I am a Westerner, and that's where I've wanted to be for a long time. I don't know what being a Southern writer or a Western writer means, though. Those are just geographic labels. I've been flattered when people have pointed out similarities between my work and Flannery O'Connor's. I'd love to be able to see the connections, but I don't. One is hard-pressed not to note the preponderance of Southern writers on the country's literary landscape. In that way, I guess, I'm in a long line of writers from the South. But is there some kind of Southern aesthetic at work in the fact that I even choose fiction as my art? There might be, but if so, I don't understand it.

WS: Many writers say their first books were something special. I wonder whether *Suder* occupies a special place in your heart?

PE: Not really. (Laughter.) I like the book. I read it now, and I realize I would write it differently because I'm a better writer now. But I don't know that I could make it a better work of art. That was a long time ago.

WS: Is your best book, then, your last book?

PE: I love all my children, geniuses and idiots alike. (Laughter.) There are three books I feel close to: *Cutting Lisa* (1986), *Glyph* (1999), and *Frenzy* (1997). *Frenzy* is special because it became sort of a love letter to my wife; *Lisa* because I see it as successfully experimental and most people read it as a realistic or romantic novel; and *Glyph* because I had so much fun writing it. It had a voice that was really natural for me. It's my humor.

WS: Your most recent book, *erasure*, was a pretty savage satire. What kind of response have you gotten to it?

PE: *erasure* was a funny, sad book, and I'm sorry I live in a world where I had to write it. I thought it would upset a lot of people, but the response has been mostly positive. A lot of publishing houses stayed away from it. I heard that one large commercial publisher worried that because there's an Oprah

Winfrey–like character in it, if they published it they would never get a book on Oprah again. So I ended up at a university press.

But I love small presses. After the success of *erasure,* many large publishing houses lined up for the rights to publish the paperback. One press that shall go unnamed (Doubleday) showed up to make a paperback offer. They wanted to do this book as the inaugural book for an imprint for African American authors. I was wondering if they had bothered to read it. My agent said the title of the imprint would be Harlem Moon. Why not call it Steppin' Fetchit, and get it over with?

The irony of it struck me. It would be really wonderful to have an imprint inaugurate and invalidate itself with the same book. But then I couldn't see doing that to my work.

I guess by now I'm pretty much past getting offended. After all, you don't get mad at a snake when it bites you. (Laughter.)

Invisible Man

Ben Ehrenreich / 2002

From *LA Weekly*, 29 November–5 December 2002, Features section, 33. Reprinted with permission of *LA Weekly*.

Perched atop a wooden stool on a temporary stage erected for the UCLA Hammer Museum's New American Writing series, Percival Everett smiles uncomfortably and tells his audience that he's tired of reading from *erasure*, his latest novel. "I'm sick of it," he says in his soft, steady voice, then reads a short story instead. He gives another reading a week later, in Brentwood this time, crowded among the stacks at Dutton's. He's wearing jeans and looks a lot more at home surrounded by books than he did under the museum lights. Everett takes a seat at the table, holds up a newly released paperback copy of *erasure*, laughs a little and begins, "First I have to tell you that I'm really sick of this book."

It's an odd way to sell books. But though he's written a lot of them (fifteen since 1983: twelve novels, two story collections, and a children's book), selling has never been Everett's priority. His novels are—to borrow a phrase he uses to describe the work of Robert Coover, whom he cites as an influence— "unapologetically intelligent," too brave and quirky to rise very high on the bestseller lists. They are almost always challenging, but rarely abstruse. Each is different from the last and deals with its own discrete formal and thematic concerns; one is set in a cataclysmic future, another in ancient Greece, another in the suburbs. They're inventive, arch, and often obscure, with bits of Latin, German, French and lots of high-cultural allusions thrown in, all somehow without pretension.

In a contemporary literary landscape that, when it doesn't just look like a mall, looks a lot like Park LaBrea—well-guarded and overflowing with joyless, comfortable, cookie-cutter structures—Everett's work is tucked way off in its own well-hidden corner, lush but skillfully landscaped, filled with strange and surprising beasts. His reviews are almost always good, but his name goes largely unrecognized, and his sales remain modest. Everett hasn't exactly helped them. Though the literary market is demonstrably more interested in celebrity than in language, he stubbornly keeps his head down, and does so without any of the paranoid staginess of better-known reclusive writers. He rarely agrees to be interviewed. He has always refused to do publicity tours for his books, though he made an exception for *erasure*, only because, he says, "I need a new roof on my house in Canada."

erasure is a biting novel about a Percival Everett–like author named Thelonius Ellison, who is frequently told, as Everett has been, that his books are too experimental and not "black" enough. In a fit of rage, he pseudonymously pens a howlingly bad ghetto screed called *My Pafology*, only to find, to his horror, that it is embraced by the literary establishment as he never has been. *erasure*'s real-world reception has been accompanied by similar ironies. The novel has received a fair amount of attention, and Everett is clearly ambivalent about its success. At Dutton's, he talks about Doubleday's offer for the paperback rights to *erasure*. "They wanted it to inaugurate a new imprint of African American authors called something like Harlem Moon," he says. "I asked, 'Did they *read* it?'" He turned the offer down.

He talks about a scene in the novel, based on an experience he had, in which his protagonist walks into a Borders bookstore and can't find his books in the fiction section, eventually discovering them on the African American studies shelves. (Of his novel *Frenzy*, which is about Dionysus, he says, "The only thing ostensibly African American about the book is my photograph.") Everett was puzzled recently after being given a book award sponsored in part by Borders. Sitting at the ceremony, observing the Borders executives all around him, he says, "I turned to one of the judges and said, 'Have they *read* this book?' I seem to be asking that question a lot."

Except in the summer, when he lives even farther away—in a remote spot on Vancouver Island—Everett lives in Moreno Valley, about ten minutes east of Riverside. A few exits to the west it's all red-tile-roofed subdivisions and endless chain stores—McDonald's, Target, Walgreen's, Kragen, anti-abortion protesters picketing outside a strip-mall medical clinic, smog hanging low like a curse. Everett's home is past all that, down a skinny road lined with pepper trees, somewhat less than green. He is miles even from a gas station, among rock-strewn hills of scrubby black-brown chaparral, for sale signs next to fields of dirt and dusty nopales. His place, though, is a little Eden, planted with wildflowers, huge beds of rosemary and purple sage, 150 varieties of roses (his wife's passion). There's a house and a separate two-story painting studio, a big old barn he hasn't figured out what to do with yet, corrals and another active barn for the horse, the two mules, and four donkeys. There's also a cat, a goat, and two dogs, a black shepherd named Zoe and a slightly crooked Rottweiler called Bosch. There was once a crow too, a jealous bird named Jim, but he disappeared one day. "He would sit on my shoulder when I wrote," Everett says. "He wrote *erasure*."

Seated in the shade on a blue Adirondack chair, Everett looks a lot less forbidding than in his book-jacket photos, in which he is invariably scowling. His eyes are lighter and softer than they look in black-and-white. He laughs freely and warmly. His speech is slow and relaxed, and he pauses occasionally to toss a battered Frisbee for the dog. I ask him why he's so sick of *erasure*. "I don't think it's my best book," he says. (That privilege he extends to 1999's *Glyph*, a hilarious academic satire and meditation on language narrated by a more than slightly precocious four-year-old.) He's happy that it's been so well received, and that it's resonated with so many people, but *erasure*, he complains, "is getting attention for all the wrong reasons." I ask him what those are, and he answers, "The race stuff"—which seems an odd complaint for a book that is largely *about* race. It's not just the ironies of his life unpleasantly mirroring his art that irk him. And it's not that the book has caused unwanted controversy, though he had anticipated that it might. Instead, "There's been a lot of people getting onboard and agreeing with me, and there's nothing more boring than that."

Pressed as to what he would have liked readers to concentrate on, Everett shakes his head. He doesn't know, he says, then adds, "I don't really want to be present. That's the only problem I have with the book—the character resembles me so much that it's harder for readers to divorce me from the work, and my mission has always been to disappear."

In the interest of forestalling his complete disappearance, here are a few facts about Percival Everett. He would likely wish to remind us that facts are different from truths, the latter being the domain of literature. With that caveat in mind, Everett is forty-five years old. The son of a dentist, he grew up in Columbia, South Carolina. He put himself through college playing guitar in Miami jazz clubs, then worked as a schoolteacher for a while. At some point he fell in love with the West ("I liked the openness," he says, "the idea of the openness"), went to grad school in Oregon to study philosophy, working on sheep and cattle ranches all the while. He left the University of Oregon to enroll in Brown University's writing program, and wrote and sold his first novel, *Suder*, while at Brown. Soon thereafter he began teaching, first in Kentucky, then at Notre Dame (where he met his wife), then in Wyoming, then at UC-Riverside (where his wife now teaches Assyriology) and now at USC.

Everett keeps busy. He sleeps about four hours a night, but only, he says, because his wife has been encouraging him to sleep more. Left to himself it would just be two or three. He spends a lot of time painting, colorful abstract work reminiscent of Kandinsky or Klee. He reads a lot, "not so much fiction as everything," he says. He rereads Samuel Butler's famed Victorian novel *The Way of All Flesh* every year ("It makes me mad as hell that he wrote it and I didn't"), and returns frequently to Ralph Ellison's *Invisible Man*, Chester Himes's *If He Hollers Let Him Go*, Zora Neale Hurston, and Flannery O'Connor, but he can get just as lost, he says, in service manuals for machinery. He writes a lot too, but says he's trying to figure out a way to write less. He does woodworking and did a lot of the construction on the ranch himself. In Canada, during the summer months, he fly fishes. He's learning to slice wine bottles in half. He maintains an insect collection. Of course, he teaches, both writing and literature, last year chairing USC's English department. And then there are the animals.

It's not just that he owns a lot of them—Everett clearly loves animals. When a golden retriever walks into Dutton's, his eyes light up and he stops talking in midsentence. Back at the ranch, his own small-scale Noah's Ark, he cooks chicken and rice every day for creaky old Bosch, who stopped eating dog food when he got a stomach infection. After a walk in the hills, he notices that Bosch is limping and gives him a cortisone shot in each haunch, murmuring tenderly to him all the while. At least four times over the course of the afternoon, Everett mentions, unbidden, that he really does like people, until it seems he's trying to convince himself. At one point, though, talking about gun control, he qualifies: "I don't have a lot of faith in *all* people." And walking through the hills in the public land behind his house, he points to the trash spilling down a neighboring hillside. "People are worse than anybody," he shakes his head. "You just can't do anything about it."

Everett's work consistently betrays a deep mistrust of any and all human collectivities—his apocalyptic novel *Zulus* ends with its protagonist unleashing a lethal gas that will wipe out all human life and, in context at least, it seems like the right thing to do. When I ask him about this, he agrees that the mistrust is there. "And if you want to play my therapist for a bit, I've always felt alienation," he says. "That's one of the things that's culturally

African American in my work; it's the experience of people who've always been outside the center." He pauses for a second and adds, "I take that back, that's just American."

It's likely this sense of alienation that keeps Everett's work so blessedly independent, that not only gives him his skills as an observer and his uniquely skewed outsider perspective but shields him from the lures of commerce and celebrity. There is little celebration of the onward march of American culture in his work, and none of pop culture. When I ask him if he has ever been interviewed on television, his eyes widen in visceral horror. Everett wants no part of the whole spectacle. "I really hate being the center of attention," he says. "I'm not a show." He would rather be left alone to write and at times seems almost resentful that the process requires an audience. "The mere fact that I want to write fiction for a living is evidence that I'm mentally deficient," he laughs, "but I do want to participate in making truth, and I can't make it without a reader. And though I don't think about the reader, the work isn't complete until somebody reads the damn thing."

For someone who writes as much as he does, though, Everett is oddly uncompulsive about the process. He doesn't write every day or on any disciplined schedule at all. He harbors no romantic notions about inspiration and creativity. "Maybe that's why I've produced a lot," he offers, "because I am maybe abnormally relaxed about it. It just kind of happens." It's just another thing he does, like caring for the animals, woodworking, painting, or sawing wine bottles in half. And though he works hard at it, he says, "At the same time I'll leave in a second to go and play with my wife. Work always comes second to anything like that." The demands of the market—mollifying editors who demand a commercial product, showing up for readings and book signings, smiling and nodding and shaking hands—for many as much a part of writing as the act itself, don't seem to rank at all.

Later, over lunch at a Thai restaurant in Moreno Valley's "downtown"— one of many strip malls—I ask him what advice he gives his students about writing. He thinks for a moment, and I wonder if he'll warn them about the cruelties of the market, the laziness and fickleness of editors and readers alike, the hardships of creating art in a world with little use for it. He doesn't. "Write what you want to write," he begins. "You gotta have faith in what you see. It might not be a recipe for success, but it is a recipe for artistic happiness. Also," Everett laughs, "it's only books."

Color Me Blind

Garry Mulholland / 2003

From *Time Out*, 5 March 2003. Reprinted with permission of *Time Out New York*.

"I'm not naïve. I know that there are places where the color of my skin will place me under threat. But nevertheless, I don't see color when I'm meeting people, and I don't see myself or others in terms of their race." Percival Everett's deep, measured speaking voice neither preaches nor pleads. But then, neither does his literary voice, at least not in his most successful book to date. *erasure*, his thirteenth novel (he has also written two short story collections and a book for kids), is about race.

But it's also about literature, money, family, Alzheimer's, grief, the loneliness of the long-distance intellectual, and the dangers of becoming someone you're not.

Despite all this, it's very funny, too. A black comedy, of course.

erasure's protagonist is Thelonious "Monk" Ellison, an Afro-American author of academic novels that no one buys, who, in need of cash and under pressure from agent and editors, writes a parody of commercially successful "ghetto prose" called *My Pafology*, later retitled *Fuck*, under the pseudonym Stagg R. Leigh.

Percival Everett is an Afro-American professor of English at the University of Southern California who writes academic novels that no one buys ("*Frenzy* is about Dionysus. *Glyph* is a parody of critical theory") who has now written a book that has won the first Hurston/Wright Award and been named among the ten best novels of 2002 by the American Library Association, which contains said ghetto prose parody.

Are we twigging something here?

"The book isn't autobiographical but the main character is alarmingly like myself," Everett admits without reluctance. "I'm not, at least I don't think I am, but maybe deep down I'm somewhat embittered by my situation. But

I'm more tickled by the fact that my work is not popular. And I have encountered the complaint from completely white editors that my work is not black enough."

Has *erasure* been perceived in the States as an attack on Afro-American literature?

"I wish someone would! There's nothing more boring than when everyone agrees with you. The indictment really is of publishing, not individual writers." The indictment is also of dominant images of blackness: the Afro-American as either tastelessly flash, bling-bling minstrel or violent victim from The Projects, speaking in sweary slang, drowning in nihilism. Hip hop videos and Hollywood movies don't feature too many forty-six-year-old, Balzac-quoting black professors who live on a Californian ranch and keep chickens. According to Everett, the arguments over authentic blackness are even spilling into American debate about imminent war.

"Harry Belafonte recently made a comment that Colin Powell and Condolezza Rice were Uncle Toms. This is the sort of thing that depresses me, that because he doesn't share their politics they must be less black than him. I've never heard someone call Suge Knight, CEO of gangsta rap label Death Row, who recently served time for his, er, assertive way of doing business, an Uncle Tom, but does he really care about black people? What many of the pro-black movement don't seem to understand is that that sort of insult is exactly what the white establishment would want us to do."

Everett's innovatively structured satire doesn't just take a pop at gangstas and blaxploitation. The early chapters savage the academic culture that he's part of, particularly in a baffling paper Monk reads to a literary society. "It's a parody of Barthes and it's supposed to be incredibly obtuse. It is nonsense." But there are plenty of references the less well-read among us will struggle to understand.

Do you mind that I enjoyed the book while often not having a clue what you're on about?

"Of course not," Everett insists. "I want my work to be accessible. How I make the distinction between literary art and popular fiction is that I return to the literary novels that I love over and over. I will never do that with a John Grisham book and that's not to take anything from it. It's just meant to do something different." The thing that makes *erasure* stick is the finely woven detail of Monk's life; his inability to connect, to love, literally to get out of his mind and find intimacy and a true self.

Isn't *erasure* really about a lonely man who doesn't know how to grieve?

"Well, I never thought of it that way, but I think anything that anyone reads into a book is reasonable," says Everett, politely. "For me, the book is about how our culture seeks to interfere in the production of art. But then, that might be what Monk's grieving about. I can't tell you. I'm just the writer."

The Books Interview: Percival Everett

Sean O'Hagan / 2003

From *The Observer* (London) *Review Pages*, 16 March 2003, 17. Copyright © Guardian News & Media Ltd 2003. Reprinted with permission.

Percival Everett's latest novel tells us on the very first page, "I did not grow up in any inner city or the rural South." Like his creator, Monk is an academic engaged in a one-man war against the reduction of black experience to a set of stereotypical fictional tropes: the ghetto, the deep South, the angry pimp, the street hustler, the triumphant victim. It would be tempting to describe Everett's funny and provocative satire on American mores as a novel about race—and, indeed, it is his challenging treatment of that subtext that has of course garnered most critical attention—but *erasure* is a much bigger book than that and, as such, is as much about blackness as *Lolita* is about prepubescent female sexuality.

"I see it essentially as a book about the creation of art and all the impediments placed in front of some of us as we set out to do that within this culture," the soft-spoken author says, his voice still bearing distinct traces of a Southern upbringing despite a long sojourn in Californian academe. "What is most interesting to me about Monk is not his color, but his selfless examination of himself. He does not want to be constrained or reduced by society's demands or expectations. He's alert to that all the time." Monk Ellison is indeed a fascinating and not altogether sympathetic character, as indicative of his time and place as Ralph Ellison's Rinehart was to fifties America.

If Ellison's *Invisible Man* is an obvious influence, formally and politically, so too is Mark Twain, who provides the book's cryptic epigraph: "I could never tell a lie that anyone would doubt, nor a truth that anyone would believe." It is a line worth keeping in mind as you read this multi-layered and elusive text. *erasure*'s central narrative traces Monk's increasingly problematic family life: his mother's senility, his brother's struggle to come to terms with his sexuality, his sister's work in an abortion clinic under siege from

Christian fundamentalists, and his own sense of anger that his willfully difficult, postmodern novels are overlooked while inferior fictions like *We's
Lives in Da Ghetto* by Juanita Mae Jenkins sit atop the bestsellers list. In
despair, he churns out a rushed parody of the black ghetto novel, entitled
My Pafology, under the pseudonym Stagg R. Leigh. "I tighten up my belt
and then yank my pants down on my ass. The T-shirt I'm wearin' be funky
as shit. But I don't give a fuck. The world be stinkin' so why not me? That's
what I says. So, why not me? That's my motto. So, why not me? It be eleben
thirty in the mornin' . . . ."

When his agent sells *My Pafology* to Random House for a huge advance,
Monk's problems really begin. He needs the money badly, but every bone
in his postmodern body recoils against the notion of perpetuating black
stereotypes, particularly black stereotypes written as parody that white
publishing houses then find "magnificently raw and honest." As his family
problems reach a nadir with the murder of his sister by an anti-abortionist
nut, Monk simultaneously finds himself embroiled in a literary nightmare
of his own making. *My Pafology*, now retitled *Fuck* in a vain attempt at self-
sabotage by an increasingly desperate Monk, is shortlisted for a prestigious
national book award that he is helping to judge. These intertwining narratives are constantly fractured by a series of odd, and seemingly random,
imagined conversations—with Rothko and Resnais, Rauschenberg and de
Kooning, Wittgenstein and Derrida—which parody the kind of post-structuralist novels that Monk himself writes. Fortunately, Everett is one of those
rare writers who can indulge in all manner of formal boldness while still
seducing the reader with his storytelling.

"I play with form and structure a lot because my impulse as writer tends
towards the modernist," says Everett, who also teaches fiction writing and
critical theory at the University of Southern California. "Ultimately, though,
I feel that if someone was to comment on that while they were actually reading the story, I'd have failed. In spite of my concerns fictively, I really hope I
create a world that sucks the reader in."

That is certainly the case with *erasure*. Even the novel within the novel,
which consists of the entire manuscript of *My Pafology*, has a strange cumu-
lative power. This, it turns out, is something that disturbs not only Monk
but Percival Everett. "I can't even bear to read from that section because, despite all my efforts to the contrary, it works in some weird way. I guess that,
no matter how a story is told, if there is some kernel of truth, we care as
readers."

More surreally disturbing still was the initial response to the book from certain American publishing houses. "Doubleday came in with an eleventh-hour offer for the paperback rights," Everett says, grinning mischievously. "My agent rang me and said, 'You're not going to believe this, but they want to publish *erasure* as the inaugural book of an Afro-American imprint called, wait for it, Harlem Moon.' I mean, did they read the book?" Did he not, even for a moment, I ask, consider taking up their offer and running with the prank as far as he could. "I actually thought of it. It was tempting to have them invalidate themselves with their first publication but, you know, I really couldn't do that to my work."

As befits an academic with thirteen novels to his name, Everett is a scholarly writer and talker, and places himself firmly in the modernist tradition. His favorite authors are Laurence Sterne, Samuel Beckett, and Zora Neale Hurston, and he "reread[s] Samuel Butler's *The Way of All Flesh* every year just to remind myself how funny fiction can be." His previous novel, *Glyph*, was a parody of critical-theory studies, narrated by a baby who "acquires language completely and immediately, and who writes but refuses to speak." The late Roland Barthes had a walk-on role. It wasn't a bestseller. With *erasure*, he may have hit pay-dirt, not least because race—the issue he hoped to parody but not perpetuate—has gotten the book noticed. The irony is not lost on him.

"I think I represent an impulse that is essentially modernist and is certainly not unique to African Americans—a desire for a certain standard of creative excellence. I think that has all but disappeared—in music, in fiction, in culture generally. Once, to be a writer or a musician, you needed to learn your craft and have a certain talent, and then you needed to prove yourself and improve your craft each time you created something. That's gone now. It's been replaced by other impulses like this bogus notion of authenticity that bedevils music and fiction made by black people. I have nothing against ghetto novels or rural Southern novels," he continues, warming to his subject, "except that they are the only representations out there. When I see my books in the Black Fiction or Black Studies section, I feel baffled. I really don't know what those terms mean. Especially, when I look around the store and there is no corresponding White Fiction section." (Everett's original title for *erasure* was *How Much Is That Negro in the Window?*; he's not saying whether he, or the publishers, balked at it.) He pauses for a moment. "But, here we are again," he says, "talking about race. I don't want to talk about race, I just want to make art." He has succeeded in the latter, if not the former, which, ultimately, is all that really matters.

Percival Everett

Robert Birnbaum / 2003

From *identitytheory.com*, 6 May 2003. Copyright © 2003 Robert Birnbaum. Reproduced with permission of Robert Birnbaum.

Author Percival Everett grew up in South Carolina and attended the University of Miami as well as the University of Oregon, where he did graduate work in philosophy. He has an A.M. in writing from Brown University. He has published fifteen books, including *For Her Dark Skin, Zulus, The Weather and Women Treat Me Fair, Cutting Lisa, Walk Me to the Distance, Suder, The One That Got Away, Watershed, God's Country, erasure,* and a story collection, *Big Picture.* He has taught at Bennington College, the University of Wyoming, and the University of California at Riverside and is currently at the University of Southern California. Everett and his wife Francesca live in LA as well as on a ranch in California and in a house on Vancouver Island. He has a novel and a story collection coming out in 2004.

Beacon Press recently published the soft-cover (or trade paperback) editions of *God's Country* and *Watershed.* The former is something of a parable set in 1871 that features Curt Marder—an all-around loser—who as the story begins has lost his farm, wife, and dog. Marder teams up with legendary tracker Bubba, a black man, and also Jake, a recently orphaned child set upon vengeance. Everett's take on the Great American Western includes a highly amusing cast of characters, including one George Armstrong Custer.

In *Watershed,* Robert Hawks, son and grandson of two iconoclastic physicians, is a hydrologist who finds himself entangled in a Native American treaty rights imbroglio as he retreats to the Colorado wilds to fish and escape his relationship with an extremely neurotic woman. Along the way he encounters a midget Native American woman, Louise Yellow Calf, two murdered FBI agents, a toxic waste dump, a peyote-ingesting religious ceremony, the neurotic woman's ineptly suicidal father, and an inebriated female FBI agent. Need I say more?

RB: Do you care to comment on what kind of crapshoot the publishing business is?

PE: I have always ignored the business of publishing. A lot of people think I am joking when I say I am process-oriented. All I care about is while I am working on something. I really do. I like being paid like anybody else but I have ignored . . . I don't read reviews. The statements from publishers— when they come, I look at them, but I still don't see them. I just throw them away. (Laughs.)

RB: Well, strange and fascinating oddities occur at the intersection of art and commerce, I guess. Why is Beacon Press publishing the soft-cover edition of two books that you wrote seven or eight years ago?

PE: I can't really say how it happened. I am really happy that it has because it extends the lives of those books. And they weren't picked up for paper after their hardback publication by Graywolf. Part of it is that Graywolf, as great a press as it is—I love being over there—doesn't have the distribution muscle of a lot of publishers, and probably if it did it wouldn't be as great as it is. I don't know.

RB: You think there is an inverse relationship there?

PE: (Both laugh.) There seems to be, but I haven't looked at it enough to say. Helen Atwan at Beacon read the books, and because of their political stance, she thought they would be good books for Beacon. It's probably better for the books. I didn't get a lot of money from Beacon, as I would have if I was published by Bantam, but logically it makes more sense for the books. And for me, morally, it feels better.

RB: I read something about you in the *Guardian* in the UK recently. Has *erasure* been published in this country?

PE: Yes. In 2001 it was published by the University Press of New England. It was kind of an experiment for them because they do have a fiction imprint called Hardscrabble.

RB: Oh yes, they published W. D. Wetherell?

PE: Yes, it's always been New England–based writing. But *erasure* wasn't published by Hardscrabble and it was a departure for them. They treated the book well and it did well and Hyperion published the paperback. In a way the layers of irony with this book are just kind of disgusting. (Both laugh.)

RB: Do I have this right? Doubleday was launching an Afro-American imprint, Harlem Moon . . .

PE: It was a nice offer, but I really don't think if they did read it that they understood it all. I was tempted briefly to let them do it so that an imprint could be invalidated by its first publication.

RB: *God's Country* might have been funnier if some of it didn't ring so true.

PE: But then it might not be funny at all. (Both laugh.) *Huck Finn* is really funny because it is so sad.

RB: 2 *Blowhards*, a culturally astute weblog, recently tried to assemble a list of great Western novels. It was interesting to see how many books people were unaware of, including, of course, *God's Country*. Were you intending to write a Western novel?

PE: I was consciously writing a parody of that form. And in that way, no, it's not a Western because I wasn't trying to write an adventure set in the mythic West. I was looking to exploit the fact that there is a mythic West.

RB: It's all myth.

PE: Yeah, it has nothing to do with any reality. And how that mythology was invented for the West is really the American story. Not the story itself but the fact that it was needed.

RB: It falls in with a number of books that have attempted the same demythification, Berger's *Little Big Man* . . .

PE: E. L. Doctorow's *Hard Times* . . .

RB: Pete Dexter's *Deadwood*.

PE: Oh yeah and didn't Vonnegut have something . . . he floats around in times so much it's hard to know.

RB: It brings to mind Robert Altman's great film *McCabe and Mrs. Miller*, one of the first and one of the few films that is an anti-Western besides the film version of *Little Big Man* . . .

PE: Those are the only two that try to do it seriously, but of course you have . . . we don't think of it in this way, *Blazing Saddles*, may be the best example. Also we have *Silverado*, which is a fun, silly movie that exploits the genre but really doesn't have the depth.

RB: In your fifteen books, you have hopped around in terms of subject matter.

PE: And style too. I don't care much to write the same thing again.

RB: So at what point in your life did you decide that you wanted to do something as honorable as writing fiction?

PE: Well, I realized that I wanted to be really rich. (Both laugh.) That's when I decided. I was actually studying philosophy. I did the kind of philosophy known as ordinary language philosophy.

RB: Me too.

PE: Oh yeah. I just became so disenchanted with scholastic philosophy that . . . I was writing scenes anyway, to have people talk to each other about philosophical concepts.

RB: You were studying philosophy and you became disenchanted and so began dabbling in fiction—would you call it dabbling?

PE: It was dabbling—I have always loved fiction and always read it. I applied to a couple of writing programs and they asked for writing samples, and so I wrote a story and that's how it started. I have just been lucky, basically. I always feel kind of guilty about the paying the dues thing that people always talk about, and I suppose I am paying my dues now by having to still do it. But it wasn't so hard to start, for me.

RB: Honestly I could just as easily see you as being embittered. You've published fifteen books and the way I came across your work was a reference to you in one of my favorite websites, *The Minor Fall, The Major Lift*, mentioning you as an underappreciated writer. Which is why I asked you about the crapshoot nature of publishing.

PE: I just want to make my art. So far I have been able to do that and live comfortably enough. I don't care about being rich, and I really don't care about the adulation. I just want to be able to buy hay for my horses (chuckles) and now, gasoline. (Both laugh.)

RB: Have you always been teaching along with writing?

PE: Most of my career I have been teaching, and it is necessary now to live the way I have grown accustomed to living. I like teaching. I get paid fairly well to hang out with smart young people. That's hard to complain about.

RB: Not that I am trying to convince you otherwise, but I can easily see someone pissing and moaning about the half-empty-glass part of your life. Don't you think?

PE: It's just books. (Both laugh.) Who would I rather be? Would I rather be Wittgenstein or . . .

RB: No, no . . . would anybody rather be him?

PE: I think the people who like my work like my work for all the reasons that I would want them to like it. And the people who don't like it dislike it for all the reasons I would want them to dislike it.

RB: What's to dislike? There are people like that?

PE: I'm sure there are. I don't know if they dislike the way I write or the way I make my art as much as they dislike my political stance.

RB: Of course they would have to read you carefully, wouldn't they?

PE: I can pretty much relax that the people who disagree with me are not reading books.

RB: What do you make of a vein of resentment in the culture—who is to say how large it is—toward someone like Toni Morrison? I have read commentary suggesting that publishers promulgating her books privately don't like them . . .

PE: I don't get it either. Very odd. I'm sure that she could write anything down and get it published because she is going to make somebody some money. It's also obvious that she doesn't do that. There is a lot of room in the world for all sorts of books. I don't know why anybody gets really worked up.

RB: And then there are the attacks on writers like Morrison and Salman Rushdie and DeLillo and now young guys like Franzen and Foer, and it strikes me that they are being attacked by people who haven't read them . . .

PE: It's always easier to condemn something when you haven't read it.

RB: But why get so worked up? On the other hand, maybe it's a good thing that people are passionate about these things.

PE: If that's really what they are passionate about. If somebody is really offended by the artistic sensibility of some writer that would be a great discussion. But if they are simply jealous of that person's success or something personal, I don't get it.

RB: What's your life like? You teach a couple classes a semester?
PE: Yeah.

RB: You write every day?
PE: I don't write every day. I have what I call work amnesia. I don't know when I am really writing. I trust myself to be doing it.

RB: You mean that at the end of some period of time you have a book written?
PE: Yeah, that's basically how it happens.

RB: So if I asked what you are working on now you would say?
PE: I'm working on something. (Both laugh.) At some point it makes itself clear what it is, and then I will be really sad for a long time while I finish it.

RB: Why the sadness?
PE: Because that means I have to finish it.

RB: You could write really, really long books and then never get published.
PE: Yeah and that might even be more fun. If my wife says she wants to go out and play and have fun, I'll just leave work immediately.

RB: Chessie?
PE: Yeah, Francesca.

RB: You dedicate all your books to her?
PE: Damn near.

RB: I guess it keeps the peace.
PE: No, she's always surprised that I am doing it. It's because I have been so productive since I have been with her that it really is a sincere thank you.

RB: Very sweet. I noticed a couple of writers dedicate their books to their wives, Richard Ford and Julian Barnes.
PE: They're the ones who have to put up with us.

RB: Are you a different person when you are in the middle of writing something?
PE: I don't think so, but I am the wrong person to ask. (Both laugh.) I try to

talk to myself as little as possible. I have periods . . . I don't get cranky but I suppose I become a little withdrawn or a little distracted.

RB: Is writing hard for you?
PE: I say to Chessie frequently, "Okay, this is the last one. I don't want to write anything for a while." And because she knows me, obviously a lot better than I know myself, she can turn to me at any point while we are driving in the car and say, "You're working on something, aren't you?" And I won't even know it, and when she says it, I will realize it is true.

RB: That's a rare thing isn't it? To have a relationship where you accept that someone knows you better than yourself. We aren't exactly trained for that . . .
PE: Well, I wasn't trained for it. When someone says enough true things to you, you start to listen.

RB: Maybe.
PE: Yeah, it's always maybe. Other than that—the way I live, I'm spoiled in a way. I teach, but I teach two days a week and the rest of the time I am at home with my wife. She teaches too. We are always home. And we work at the same desk. It's a big desk, we're there at the same time.

RB: One of those partner's desks that were used at old law firms.
PE: I'd like to find one, but we made a semicircular glass table that sits in front of a window and we sit at either end, angling toward the same spot in the window.

RB: And you have a place in Mississippi?
PE: No, in California.

RB: Why did I think it was in Mississippi?
PE: I was just at a book conference there. Though Morgan Freeman seems to be comfortable on his farm in Mississippi, I don't think that I would be.

RB: It hasn't changed that much . . .
PE: I guess it has. I don't know if it's a function of his being a millionaire that makes him happy there. I really enjoyed the visit I just paid to Oxford at Square Books. It's a terrific town full of people who love books.

RB: It's also highly gentrified at this point. It's another piece of information that filters into the book press, when book or publishing magazines attend to real estate in Oxford, Mississippi. Apparently people who were raised there can't afford to live there anymore. It's gotten quite expensive. But that bookstore is one of the legendary independents, especially now that those kinds of stores assume the mantle of a crusade.

PE: I wish them luck. I have trouble with the chains. I don't mind the business people like Square Books or Lemuria and Powell's Books where I know that the people who own the bookstores and are trying to make money came to it because they loved books, not like the Walmart model of the bookstore.

RB: So you are not under any contractual obligation to write a book. An idea comes to you, you write the book, teach, you have a ranch.

PE: I work a lot. I must because I . . . I'm always a little ahead of myself. I have a novel that's done and waiting to come out and a book of stories. They are both coming out in 2004. So I don't really feel pressure and neither do my publishers, to want me to write something else.

RB: Having written fifteen books you apparently have the confidence and the work ethic.

PE: However misguided that thinking is . . .

RB: Who is publishing the novel and the stories?

PE: The novel is being published by Hyperion.

RB: The Disney people.

PE: Yeah, I am trying to come to terms with that . . . and the stories again from Graywolf. Fiona McCrae, the director of the press, is my editor there and she is the person I think of as my editor. I hope I can always keep a book with them.

RB: Is that the longest-standing editorial relationship you've had?

PE: Yeah, we've done six books. And we talk about literature and books. That's real different in this industry. (Both laugh.)

RB: They published a wonderful anthology of essays this spring called *The Next American Essay* by John D'Agata. I was talking about Graywolf Press with Fred Busch and he was telling me that they are financially strapped . . .

PE: It's funny how nonprofits are under this pressure to break even whereas regular presses finish in the red all the time. (Chuckles.)

RB: Accounting sorcery. Can you talk about the yet-to-be-published novel?
PE: I have never been terribly good at talking about books.

RB: Okay.
PE: It is a novel and it is kind of . . . maybe it is unnecessary for me to say it but for me it is kind of strange. (Both laugh.)

RB: When you begin a new work how much of your past books do you carry with you? I was struck by your mention of "work amnesia." Do you remember or think about your previous writing?
PE: No, I don't think about it too much. I recognize it when I see it and to some extent I'll read at readings from things I've written. I have—I don't know if it's a reading disorder—but I can't read line by line. I see the whole page, which is why I read rather rapidly. When I am giving readings I am pretty much reciting what I have just memorized while I have looked at the page. But I don't know it when I am away from the book. My wife seems to remember every word I have ever written because she tells me what I have changed at my readings because I am constantly editing myself. What I actually read is not always on the page. Given any particular day, I like the sound of some words better than others. And, of course, I am a different writer now than when I had written the thing.

RB: One can say that, and it seems that it should be true, but why do you say that?
PE: Hopefully I am smarter. Hopefully I have gotten better. And in between the time I am seeing it and the time I have written it I have probably read about two or three hundred books that make me feel differently about language. Who knows?

RB: Do you read fiction or nonfiction?
PE: I just finished judging an award, the PEN/Hemingway, so I just read a couple hundred books.

RB: Did you read all of them? I'm thinking back on the National Book Award brouhaha . . .
PE: You will have to read my treatment of that in my novel *erasure*, I have a

little fun. I judged that award a few years ago. It was a good experience, but I do make some fun of it.

RB: Sorry, I sidetracked you.

PE: Yeah, I like reading essays but I have to admit I have never warmed up to what is called creative nonfiction, things that people write a lot. I'm sure it's fine but I can't . . . I can't read science fiction and I am sure a lot of it is well-written and wonderful. It just doesn't turn me on. But I read a lot of science and philosophy and history, still.

RB: Did you read *Wittgenstein's Poker*?

PE: No, I don't know that one.

RB: It's a book about a legendary confrontation at Cambridge University between Ludwig Wittgenstein and Karl Popper. I have this sense of your life as idyllic. What is it that, excuse this word, informs what you write about? Movies, do you fish . . . whittle on your front porch?

PE: I do fish. I have horses so I don't have time to whittle. I like my life and I think I like it because I don't like so much about the world. And I can't divorce myself from it. And writing is my way of dealing with the stuff that gets me so . . . there is no profit in being mad anymore. I used to be angry all the time.

RB: So that's how we get smarter.

PE: And now I am kind of sad. It's all predictable and maybe I sound cynical saying this, but the outrage gives way to a sort of amused concern. And it's shocking and I am curious and interested in the fact that it's not shocking—what's shocking is that is not shocking. And what does it mean about people that they have always behaved in a way that doesn't let their behavior surprise us.

RB: When the hostilities began in Iraq many friends and acquaintances, my mother, they were upset. I thought most of my life the world has been in a state of more or less armed conflict. I can't remember a time of peace. I asked, "Why this and not that?" I kept telling people to stop watching television.

PE: Yeah, there's that and there is also this question when I see the Saud family having given $500 million to Al-Qaeda in the past ten years. I don't know how we choose allies and enemies. I don't know how we stood by and watched and said that apartheid in South Africa would change naturally as a matter of course and so there should be no violence there and now we are liberating people who never asked for it.

RB: The stench of untruth is oppressive here. I guess that's why you have a ranch and why I have withdrawn from my formerly urban lifestyle . . . terrible. This is a lot of weight to carry, such anger. What do you see in your students?

PE: I've been impressed with my students at USC. They run counter to every stereotype that's been created for the private university and especially the USC student. At least mine have been engaged with the world and interested and, to a one, they participate in some kind program in the community in LA.

RB: Why do you think that is? What's the stereotype—that they are disengaged and only care about careers?

PE: The stereotype for USC at one point might have been deserved—a very expensive private university . . .

RB: A football school . . .

PE: I guess it was at one point. And fortunately the football team became really bad and that always helps a university. Then the university, a number of years before I arrived, made a concerted effort to change its student body, to find better students. And what I can see is they have succeeded. I never thought I would like an institution where I taught, but the university embraces that it is set in downtown LA, surrounded by what is considered a bad neighborhood. It doesn't run from that. In fact it had a chance to move a number of years ago to some beautiful suburban setting and it didn't. It's a Los Angeles university. We have this program for kids in the neighborhood; they are spotted in middle school and if they stay with this program and are admitted to USC, they go for free. We just graduated our first student in English three years ago. It's fantastic—a $30,000 a year education that these kids get.

RB: Times four.

PE: I'm proud of the institution.

RB: Where is your ranch in California?

PE: We are about sixty miles east of Los Angeles in between Palm Springs and LA. But we live part of the time on Vancouver Island. Though we have this little farm, we still have neighbors. I like people just fine, but in Canada we are stuck in the woods and it's nice. Do you fly fish?

RB: No.

PE: We have a mile of the Salmon River on our property. So if you want to fly fish you are welcome to join us.

RB: Thanks. My dog has made me more of a nature person. Anyway, how do you plug into the informational shit stream? TV?

PE: No, but I read the papers. I never thought I would say that the Internet is good, but because of the Internet . . . I used to go to the library every week and read all the papers, and now I read all the papers online.

RB: Where did the resistance to the Internet come from?

PE: Out of habit. And also it's really bad for my students. There is so much bad information, and unless you come to it—this might sound elitist—with an education you don't know enough to edit and judge what you are getting. Even though there are a lot of bad publications, what you are getting has at least been vetted by someone.

RB: Maybe.

PE: That's true. It's been the case that you can find anything to support what you believe in the world. You have to read between the lines with every-thing, and that's what a college education is for.

RB: I thought a college education was supposed to get you a job?

PE: Luckily, I don't think that's why my students are there. I never went to college for that reason.

RB: This is a vital issue for me because my young son will be of college age in 2016 and I have my doubts about what the real value of a college education will be. As opposed to some training in how to view the world intelligently and critically and, dare I say, skeptically.

PE: I think it still will be the case that real advances in our culture will come from people with education. A lot of people will make a lot of money find-ing out a way to sell us a different kind of deodorant, and that's always been the case. But how our art changes and how medicine changes will still be by people who have some investment in the world beyond themselves.

RB: Maybe I am double-talking here because I don't want to denigrate the idea of the university.
PE: I understood what you were saying.

RB: I'm wrestling with the notion of what a degree conveys, and that the process is anything other than some rote, automatic thing.
PE: That's the bad part—the equating of the degree with the meal ticket that universities have to resist. The universities are feeling a pressure to sell themselves as places that will get their students the best jobs.

RB: What are you teaching?
PE: I teach some lit courses and mostly fiction writing. And I teach theory for writers.

RB: And why are people taking writing courses.
PE: That's a good question. I am always baffled by that. I don't know why people want to be writers. For some people it's because they love books. For quite a few it's because they have this romantic notion of . . . and I have no idea where it comes from.

RB: If I walked into a class and you were my teacher, I'd say, "Great." I'd like to have your sense of ease and your accomplishments. You are a wonderful paradigm for being a writer.
PE: Well, because of that I have been contemplating becoming an alcoholic (both laugh) so I can do my students a favor and steer them away.

RB: Do your students want to change the world?
PE: I wish they did. But honestly I can't say to them that I want to change the world anymore. When I started writing I did it because I wanted to make art, and now I understand that art and politics are inextricably bound and that you can affect the world in really small ways and hope that something good happens. I never have a message and I try to teach them to not have a message, but it's hard to do that while at the same time trying to teach them that part of the reason they are writing is to participate in the world.

RB: That would be a subtle thing. Preachy books don't deliver.
PE: Yeah, and they can't.

RB: I asked before about the body of your work, and somewhere here in our talk I got a sense of the mystery of your creative process.

PE: To some extent. I like the magic of it. I don't know where the stories come from. People will say, "Why did that occur to you?" And I have no good answer, for them or myself. And in that way it is mysterious. That's why I really love it. There is a magic associated with it. And by now . . . my students ask, "Can you teach me to write a novel?" I say, "No, because I don't know how to write a novel." And I don't. I know that I have written them. And from all appearances, I will do it again. But I have no idea.

RB: Do you outline?

PE: Everything comes differently. Every book has its own life. That's what I mean when I say I have no idea when I start. Interestingly the first thing that occurs, though I can't explain it all, is I see the shape of the book.

RB: As a geometric form or as a shadow?

PE: In a way, that's really easy—it's going to be rectangular (laughs)—but I see what the words will look like on the page and kind of the negative space they will be in. That sort of thing.

RB: How do you know when you are done?

PE: You can work it forever. I think it's done when the changes you are making don't make it ostensibly better. When you can step back and say I've changed that but nothing really has changed.

RB: How many drafts?

PE: Typically a lot of drafts. But most of the work is the research and my thinking. For *God's Country* I must have watched and read 150 Westerns so I could soak up the genre. It was not something I was into.

RB: Most Westerns were pretty hokey.

PE: I taught a film course in the Western not too long ago. A movie like *The Searchers* with John Wayne—growing up I hated John Wayne. John Wayne is great and *The Searchers* is an incredibly sick movie, from the opening scene in Monument Valley. And the beautiful part is what's being sold. Anyone who knows that region knows you can't live there. (Both laugh.) And there's this house . . .

RB: Jonathan Raban wrote a whole book (*Badlands*) about the people who were euchred by the railroads to come out to the Upper Plains. I don't know how many times you used this joke, but it cracked me up every time people would commiserate about Curt Marder's dead dog [in *God's Country*].

PE: Part of that is about how much I love dogs, but the other part is you can kill the entire Confederate army in a movie and nobody blinks, but *Old Yeller*, everybody cries.

RB: You don't tour much do you?

PE: For a long time I was a problem for publishers because I just wouldn't do stuff. I wouldn't go places and do stuff. And then with *erasure*, I needed a new roof on my house in Canada (both laugh), so I thought I am going to try.

RB: The practical side.

PE: *erasure* has done fairly well. I got the roof; there was nothing left after that, but it's better to be dry and poor than rich and wet.

RB: Do you take a longer view of your life?

PE: I have a few ideas. I paint as well. I'd really rather be painting.

RB: Were you born in this century? Oil paints, fly fishing—do you write with a computer?

PE: I write longhand actually. I used a typewriter for my first five books—a manual typewriter.

RB: Do you still have it?

PE: I gave it to a student. It was collecting dust in my studio and there was this student who I liked very much, he was admiring it. So I said, "Would you like that?" And he got all excited and so I gave it to him.

RB: I love typewriters and I think they are beautiful.

PE: And they have that—computers have too, on the hard drive—but I always loved the idea that all my words were on the ribbon.

RB: Let's see, you'd rather paint but you are going to continue to write because when it comes down to it, it's in your blood?

PE: I guess. I always avoided that kind of talk. But unfortunately it's probably true.

RB: If you had only written three or four books, I wouldn't have said that.

PE: I'm going to do it until I get it right, basically. (Laughs.) I learn a lot writing. And with every book I learn more about how little I know. So by now at the end of fifteen books I know a lot less than almost anybody. (Laughs.)

RB: Think about what you won't know when you have written thirty.
PE: My goal is to know nothing.

RB: A Zen approach to fiction. Do you associate with writers?
PE: I think it's always healthy to avoid a room full of writers. A lot of my friends are writers and we don't talk about writing. I like the way writers see the world. That doesn't mean I always agree.

RB: I agree with you. That's why I like to talk to writers. Mostly because there is an effort to individuate, to think originally. It's not like trying to say what everyone else is saying.
PE: That's right. Writers like disagreeing with each other.

RB: Unless you are in a religious cult or a right-wing name caller, why surround yourself with people who think the same way?
PE: Unfortunately people who might be considered progressive and lefty usually have a somewhat artistic sensibility and don't like to repeat themselves.

RB: Yeah, so they are not able to become practitioners of the Big Lie technique. That's pretty savvy. In order to brainwash people you have to keep repeating the same message over and over. I'd like to think that progressives also have more respect for other humans. Getting back to this idea of how to mitigate the anger we feel, we have to find something that . . .
PE: It's like what you said earlier. There were no good old days.

Teaching Voice and Creating Meaning: An Interview with Percival Everett

Forrest Anderson / 2003

From *Yemassee Literary Journal*, 11.2 (Spring 2004), 1–7. Interview conducted in October 2003. Copyright © 2004 Forrest Anderson. Reproduced with permission of Forrest Anderson.

Percival Everett, a native of Columbia, South Carolina, attended the University of Miami as well as the University of Oregon, where he did graduate work in philosophy. He received an A.M. in writing from Brown University. Everett has published fifteen books, including *For Her Dark Skin, Zulus, The Weather and Women Treat Me Fair, Cutting Lisa, Walk Me to the Distance, Suder, The One That Got Away, Watershed, God's Country, erasure,* a story collection, *Big Picture,* and most recently *The History of the African-American People [Proposed] by Strom Thurmond, as Told to Percival Everett & James Kincaid.*

A recipient of the Academy Award for Literature and the Hurston/Wright Legacy Award, he also won the New American Writing Award. He has also won the Hillsdale Award, PEN/Oakland–Josephine Miles Award, Lila Wallace Fellowship, and the D. H. Lawrence Fellowship. He currently is a professor at the University of Southern California, where he teaches American studies, creative writing, and critical theory. Everett lives with his wife in Los Angeles as well as at a ranch in California and a house on Vancouver Island.

While Everett was a guest reader at the University of South Carolina's Fall Festival of Authors in 2003, I had the opportunity to interview him at the Adam's Mark Hotel. We discussed books, painting, and horseback riding.

FA: Your writing seems to speak to basic human yearnings and the search for the self. Do the individual voices you create try to respond to these yearnings?

PE: The only reason I'm ever interested in characters in fiction is because they're searching for something, and in some way anything we're searching for has to do with self. We're always trying to figure out who we are and what we're doing.

FA: How do you go about creating each individual voice?

PE: Writers have to be the best actors and become the people we're writing about. Not just the protagonist but also the peripheral characters as well because they have to speak. You just have to take the time to become those people.

FA: Why are you interested in such diverse voices?

PE: I'm pretty bored with myself (laughs), but that's what makes the world interesting, the fact that people are different and that they see different things. That's the only way we learn anything.

FA: Some writers say their characters do not surprise them. Their work is completely mapped out from beginning to end and they work like reporters relating the events. Do your characters ever inspire or shock you?

PE: Surprise me? Well, stories surprise me. I really don't believe in this thing that characters take on this life and do what they want to do. I go to work. I am God. They do what I want, and it's my world. Is it mere recording? No, because I'm trying to shape a world and give it to you, and I don't really care what they say and do. What I care is what it means about what they say.

FA: Your settings seem to vary from book to book. Is this because you view setting as an important character in the story?

PE: Setting is character. Place is as much a character as any person. Geography might be one of the most defining features of a person's personality. The challenge is getting it right, and knowing the place, but that doesn't mean I can write about them. Sometimes the better you know something, the harder it is to present it in a way that is believable.

FA: Several of your books seem like they required a lot of research. I imagine you had to learn a lot about hydrology for *Watershed*, read a lot of Westerns to parody them in *God's Country*, and become a pop culture consumer for certain aspects of *erasure*. What sort of research do you undertake for your books?

PE: For *God's Country*, I must have read a hundred Western novels and watched as many films. I wanted to own the clichés. In *Watershed*, I learned a lot about hydrology so I could become that character. In *erasure*, I had to watch a lot of Jerry Springer and Rickie Lake to get some of those voices. I read books I hate, and listened to these voices, which I think are fabricated. Anyone who wants to be on Jerry Springer is already such a small slice. . . . That was the first book. I did not love learning that.

FA: Was it difficult to write about something you didn't enjoy learning about?

PE: It was pretty difficult. The difficult part was going to work every morning having to write that voice—the novel within the novel—hating that voice, but yet having to write in it. And then, at the end, acknowledging that the power of story—regardless of this voice that I hated—had some kind of currency in and of itself.

FA: When you begin a new work how much of your past books do you carry with you? Do you remember or think about your previous writing?

PE: There's no baggage from the previous work. I don't even care about it once I deliver it. I don't mean when it's published, but when it gets to the publisher and I'm done with the final edits and the copyediting. I never think about that work again. Except when people ask me to read from these things and I hate that so much.

FA: You don't enjoy fiction readings?

PE: Interestingly, I like meeting people and I like the fact that people read the work. But I'm always amazed and sort of curious about fiction readings. I suppose one day—I'd hate to disappoint anyone so I don't know if I would do it—but I'd love to walk in with photocopied stories and pass them out and say, "Well, let's read." There's a little bit that's . . . I wouldn't say dishonest . . . about reading, but I can do things as I read. I try to read flatly, but one can do things reading that don't occur on the page. And the real adventure in stories is what a reader does privately taking this stuff in because it can mean something so different from what I imagined. And it's not wrong, and it might even be more interesting, but that's what draws me to fiction. Meaning doesn't get made until the reader participates.

FA: Listening to you talk about the origin of meaning and the role of the author reminds me that you've flirted with postmodernism in a couple of your books, notably *Glyph*. But I've read that your impulse as a writer tends toward the modernist. What pulls you in the modernist direction?

PE: This postmodern label is one that is stylistically artificial. I'm concerned with form, and insofar as form makes meaning. I'm not only interested in what stories mean, but how they mean. I don't find that to be terribly ironic, so I find it to be amusing that we really believe we're making meaning when we create literary art.

My novel *Glyph* is presented as an experimental novel, but the fact of the matter is every novel is experimental. There's no such thing as an experimental novel. I have no idea what I'm doing at any point. My students ask me, "Can you teach me to write a novel?" and I say no. I don't know how to write a novel. I know I've done it, and I'll probably do it again, but every time I do it, it's brand-new.

FA: So, is writing hard for you?

PE: Not particularly. It's not my favorite thing in the world to do. I don't know what "hard" means. It's not like trying to put horseshoes on a wild animal, but it sure beats showing up at an insurance office.

FA: When you write a book like *erasure*, for example, or a short story like "The Last Heat of Summer," do you know at the time how good it is? What I mean is, when you're writing a book do you know while you're creating it that you've got something special?

PE: I never think whether the work is good. I think whether it's honest, whether it's true, whether I'm doing what I set out to do. It's not up to me to decide. I'm going to love all my kids whether they're geniuses or idiots and I'm not going to compare them. I don't think of that. Monticelli was considered a hack painter for a long time and now he's a master. All that stuff is politics. If the book affects somebody, then it's great. I take the advice of Samuel Johnson: When you're writing and you like it, tear it up.

FA: How do you know when you're finished?

PE: You're never done with a book. You just decide you're done. There's a difference between writers and people who are not writers. Writers can't just decide we're finished. We can rewrite something until we never write anything. And this is the guts part. You've got to let it go into the world.

That's why we name our children after all, so we don't get blamed for what they do.

Whenever you look back at a story or a novel, you're always seeing that you could have done something differently. And you'll be a better writer when you look back at it, and hopefully we all are when we look back at stories. We always see that we could have drafted something better, but that doesn't mean we could have made it a better story.

FA: You also work as a creative writing teacher. How do the roles of writer and teacher intersect?

PE: I love literature, and this is a way to help nurture literary art. I have some fine students and they're serious and they want to put work into the world. If I can help them with that, then that's something else I've done that's good and makes up for all the bad things I've done.

FA: Do you feel creative writing can be taught?

PE: I didn't say that. If you asked me that about fifteen years ago, I probably would have said, "No, I don't believe it." What I believe is that I can help somebody be a better writer. Whether I'm teaching them to be a creative writer? I don't know.

But I've watched colleagues and I've watched myself work with people and I've watched them come out of the other side better than when they came in. But they have something to start with. I can't take someone who cannot write and make that person a writer. In that way, one cannot teach creative writing. I can teach somebody how to play basketball. They might not be good at it, but I can teach them to play basketball. I can teach them to build a house. They might not build a great house, but they can build a house. I cannot teach somebody how to write a novel.

FA: Because there's no out of bounds and no rules?

PE: And, there's more than simply the craft and the skills. It's a vision, an attachment not only to the literary, but also to the artistic, which no one is empowered to teach.

FA: What books do you teach? What books are important to you?

PE: There are so many books. Teaching is different. You don't necessarily use a good book. Bad books often make the best lessons. What books do I love to read? I read *The Way of All Flesh* every year by Samuel Butler and I love Ellison's *Invisible Man. Moby-Dick* is a great novel. It's fantastic, and so is *Huck Finn.* We wouldn't be doing this if it weren't for *Huck Finn.*

FA: Hemingway called it the "best book we've had."
PE: I don't know if that's the case because there are all sorts of flaws in it, but that's the beauty of it. The idiocy of calling something the perfect novel is kind of wonderful because no one can say what a novel is, especially a literary novel. I make a bet with my students. If they can draw a picture of a novel, an archetypal novel, then find me three novels that they think are really fine and fit that picture, then I will give them an A and they won't have to do anything for the rest of the class. And they can't.

FA: Do they try?
PE: Some do, but you kind of know about them right away. (Laughs.)

FA: What bad books have you learned a lesson from?
PE: I don't name bad books.

FA: What's next?
PE: I've got a new novel coming out in the spring and a book of short stories as well. I co-authored a so-called experimental thing that is going to get me into trouble when I read out the title of it. I woke up one night, and I had a title and I was going to write this, and the title was *The History of the African-American People [Proposed] by Strom Thurmond, as told to Percival Everett.* That is the title, but now it's *as told to Percival Everett & James Kincaid.*

FA: Thanks for your time.

Percival Everett

Rone Shavers / 2004

From *BOMB Magazine*, No. 88 (Summer 2004), 46–51. This interview, "Percival Everett" by Rone Shavers, was commissioned by and first published in *BOMB Magazine*, from *BOMB* 88/Summer 2004, pp. 46–51. © Bomb Magazine, New Art Publications, and its Contributors. All rights reserved. The BOMB Digital Archive can be viewed at www.bombsite.com. Reprinted with permission.

I sat down to talk with novelist Percival Everett on the pretext of discussing his new epistolary novel, *A History of the African-American People [Proposed] by Strom Thurmond, as Told to Percival Everett & James Kincaid*, but truth be told, I was looking for any old reason. You see, Everett has three (that's right, *three*) books slated for release this year: the aforementioned *History* (Akashic), a co-authored satire about the American obsession with celebrity and our political system—and yes, the two grow closer every day—as well as the sycophantic industry that is book publishing; the recently released *American Desert*, which concerns the misadventures of a college professor who is accidently killed on his way to commit suicide, and the chaos that ensues after he sits up at his funeral, for all definitive purposes, alive; and a collection of stories, *damned if i do* (Graywolf), probably written just to complete the hat trick. In all, I desperately wanted to have a conversation with Percival that would be recorded for posterity, mainly because Percival Everett is a friggin' genius. But don't consider it odd if you've never heard of him, for although he's by no means antisocial (on the contrary, he's actually quite gregarious and generous with his time, teaching at the University of Southern California during the academic year and at various writing workshops during the summer), Everett actively shies away from the PR machinations that most other writers seek. And although he has published more than fifteen works of well-received fiction (mostly with small presses, for reasons revealed in our conversation), his books are so stylistically varied that attempts to summarize his interests or creative oeuvre prove extremely difficult. In almost every one of his works, you peel away one layer of references and meaning only to find another, only then to discover another, only to come upon another, until—well, you get the idea. Welcome, then, to an interview about everything, because in many ways, the meaning of everything is the only subject Everett really writes about.

RS: Would you consider yourself an avant-garde or experimental writer?
PE: I don't know what *avant-garde* or *experimental* means. Every novel is experimental.

RS: What do you think you're bringing to the table in terms of American Arts and Letters? Do you see a purpose to your fiction?
PE: Do I see a purpose to art? Of course there is a purpose to art, but do I see a function in my fiction? No. Is it going to feed anybody? No. Hopefully, the world is richer for more art being put into it. That's what I care about.

RS: Do you consider yourself a satirist? I say *satire* because of such works as *A History of the African-American People [Proposed] by Strom Thurmond* and *erasure,* as well as *Glyph.* All three books poke fun at one aspect of American society or another. Is it important for you to have humor in your novels?
PE: Humor is an interesting thing. It's hard to do, but it allows you certain strategic advantages. If you can get someone laughing, then you can make them feel like shit a lot more easily. I'm not interested in sentimental stuff; I'm a little too self-conscious to pull it off.

RS: I have this theory that Americans can only deal with serious work if it's funny.
PE: Aristophanes gets out a lot of great stuff because he's funny, whereas you can only read Aeschylus in so many ways. His tragedies are beautiful, but they're limited. Likewise, if you read Kafka and don't think it's funny, you're not reading Kafka very well. (Laughter.)

RS: How do you categorize yourself as a writer? Do you work within the constraints of a particular fiction category? Your works are so all over the map.
PE: No, whatever the particular work is that's what it is. I don't put myself in a camp. I want to write what works for the story at hand. I serve the story, basically. I don't think that as the author I'm terribly important, and I don't

want to be. I want to disappear. If anybody's thinking about me when they're reading my work, I've failed as a writer. The work is supposed to stand by itself. I'm teaching you to fly. When you have to go solo, hey, I'm not there.

RS: Does theory influence your work at all?
PE: Only insofar as it's a source. Anytime anybody goes through that much trouble to come up with something nonsensical, you have to have fun with it. It's hilarious stuff. It's not important that it means anything that takes us somewhere, because it's not going to. But the fact that anybody wants to *think* it is, that's fascinating.

RS: Yet *Glyph* is influenced by semiotic theory and post-structuralism.
PE: Well, I'm making fun of post-structuralism.

RS: Even *erasure* takes the piss out of theoretical positions, notably Gayatri Spivak's idea of strategic essentialism. I am wondering if you yourself have a theoretical position that you're working out.
PE: If anybody thinks they're actually going to delineate the necessary and sufficient conditions for any literary work of art, then they're greatly mistaken and would probably be better served picking up some other line of work, like computer maintenance. But if you're out to play with ideas and have some fun with them, and admit that that's what you're doing, and don't tell the regents at a university that . . . it's important to watch how ideas work and how they can be manipulated. That's probably the most important question to me in the world: What can you do with thinking? But to take it seriously, I mean, that's why the French, Derrida and Barthes, are so much fun. The fucking Americans get so earnest about this stuff that it stops being fun.

RS: Well, what about the New Critics, and their idea about the absolute autonomy of a work?
PE: Oh, they need to take a pill. (Laughter.) Just chill.

RS: But you do have that New Critical approach, especially if you say that the work is the work and that's all there is.
PE: Well I suppose, but I just don't give a shit about the artist anyway. Why should I? If I find a painting a hundred years from now, and I can't appreciate it until I find out something about the person who made it, it's not much of a painting.

RS: What would you describe as your aesthetic point of view? Do you have one?

PE: What do I like? I like stuff that's smart, stuff that challenges me and makes me think differently, that introduces me to things I didn't know before.

RS: Give me some examples.

PE: *Tristram Shandy* is probably the best novel ever written. It takes every form of literary discourse of its time and exploits it. *Huck Finn* is fantastic. Chester Himes's *If He Hollers Let Him Go* is a very sneaky book. And oddly anticipates so much of *Invisible Man* that it's frightening.

RS: I have a couple of questions about your style.

PE: Style schmyle.

RS: Your style, or lack thereof. (Laughter.) Do you have a predominant style?

PE: Style is a tool. The work will dictate the style.

RS: So you write in a manner that suits the work.

PE: The only reason I would want a particular style is so that people could identify every work of mine as mine. There's nothing at stake for me in having people recognize the work because of stylistic consistency.

RS: You tend to blend styles a lot.

PE: Well, I play with styles; I think they're amusing. I think that anybody who thinks they have a style—it's like watching punk rockers get ready to go out. It must take you two hours to get that look. How many safety pins do you need? To me there's a wonderful irony in that. To work so hard to dress your work. Send the work out there naked.

RS: What's also interesting to me is the way you use history. Much of your work is dependent on historical events, but then the events tend to be jumbled: It's not literal history, it's mixed up. For instance, in *Watershed*, there is an infamous event from the American Indian Movement, but the novel is set in contemporary times.

PE: I create a circumstance that's similar to the siege at Wounded Knee. It's interesting that you call it infamous. It's a little like the American insistence on calling its attacks *battles* and the enemies' attacks *ambushes* or *massacres*. History is like memories: It is constantly being reconstructed. History doesn't exist without the lies. We believe in some way that history makes sense, but history is an amorphous, very strange creature that's constantly changing.

RS: Why do you rely on the historical so much?
PE: Well, we live in a world. We define ourselves by the times through which we live. Everything is historical. If you read any philosophy now, you can't help but be historical.

RS: Why? I mean, I don't read philosophy.
PE: Can you understand any theory about the narrative of film if you don't know Aristotle? The answer is no. Everything's dependent on the work that's come before it. Our understanding of philosophy is necessarily historical, because otherwise we wouldn't be addressing anything. The problems of philosophy are historical: What is beautiful? What is a promise? How do we perceive?

RS: Perception, and misperception, is a central issue in your work. Take Ralph, for example, the baby genius from *Glyph*. He's so brilliant that he refuses to speak. The attempt to understand how people construct meaning leaves him flummoxed. And then there's Thelonious, the writer in *erasure*. He's the victim of misperception after misperception, until he no longer recognizes himself. And then, of course, there's Strom Thurmond, from the latest book. He actually becomes convinced he's the person most capable of writing the history of black people in America.
PE: Let me just say that I wish I could've made Thurmond up and that he didn't exist. But sadly, he did exist. I've written a lot of books. Some of them are going to be that way, others are all based in contemporary story and don't do that. I don't think anyone living in any time cannot be interested in the past and its manipulation.

RS: What if someone accused you of trying, in not necessarily a bad way, maybe a clever way, to rewrite African American history?
PE: What the hell's wrong with that? You can write anything you want to. If anybody takes anything they read, history or fiction, as some gospel, then fuck 'em anyway. Who cares? The point is, take it and then play with it.

RS: Would you say that your work is corrective?

PE: I'm not correcting anything. That would mean I know enough to correct. I'm just a dumb writer.

RS: Well then, what about a personal history?
PE: I don't write anything autobiographical. I'm private, and I hate this nonfiction shit that's out in the world. These memoirs. Oh my God! I do not care! I'm sorry you're dying, but I don't care.

RS: Or that your mom beat you with a two-by-four.
PE: And really, if you're writing memoirs, she *ought* to beat you with a two-by-four.

RS: (Laughter.) Actually, if one reads enough of your work, one could begin to trace certain commonalities, especially in terms of family. You don't want your personal life to be the basis of a novel, but do you think that there are experiences or bits of your history, your family, that inadvertently slip out?
PE: Well, I don't know if it inadvertently slips out. I understand some things, like that the relationship between the father and Monk in *erasure* is a lot like the relationship between this old woman and the main character, David Larson, who ends up living on her ranch in my early novel *Walk Me to the Distance*. But Monk's relationship with his mother in *erasure* is nothing like the relationship Suder has with his mother in my first novel. The father in *erasure* is a combination of several people.

RS: There are certain generalities in your work, to the point where you could say, Well, maybe it's drawn from personal experience.
PE: Like what?

RS: Let's just say that the mother figures are not exactly the most stable. (Laughter.) Like in *Suder* the mom is . . .
PE: Well, she's nuts. But she's the only one who has sense enough to be nuts in the world in which she lives. And in *erasure* the mother just has Alzheimer's.

RS: But also, in terms of personal experience coming through, generally your characters are of a particular class. They're professionals: doctors, hydrologists, baseball players, fiction writers.
PE: That's the world I know. I know artists and I grew up with doctors. My grandfather, father, and uncles were doctors. My sister is a doctor. And I

spend a lot of my time with ranchers, hydrologists, and veterinarians. Occasionally someone will say, "That's not the Black Experience." And I laugh and say, "I'm black, and that's my experience." I know a lot of black people whose experience is that, but it's not what people want to think is the black experience—they want their black experience to be inner-city and rural south.

RS: All that is the preamble to my next question, which is: How important is class to you, especially given that class tends to be conflated with race?
PE: I'm a card-carrying member of the ACLU and I go to the ballet and I train mules and I write fiction for a living.

RS: What does that mean?
PE: That's my point—it means absolutely nothing. People live in the worlds they live in, and they're interested in the things that interest them. That's what makes this world fascinating. I really don't think about class. Everybody should read fiction. I think everybody should read Joyce and Ellison. I don't think serious fiction is written for a few people. I think we live in a stupid culture that won't educate its people to read these things. It would be a much more interesting place if it would. And it's not just that mechanics and plumbers don't read literary fiction, it's that doctors and lawyers don't read literary fiction. It has nothing to do with class; it has to do with an anti-intellectual culture that doesn't trust art.

RS: But are you sure that class doesn't play a part? I mean, in a lot of your novels there's a particular break where a character will come out and say, "Oh yeah, by the way, I'm black."
PE: That has nothing to do with class.

RS: That's why I brought up the intersection of race and class. That tension's always there in your novels. Most of your main characters are black professionals to one degree or another, and there's always that break in the work, as though to say, "What? I can't be a professional and African American?" You relate a typical black experience, the black experience that isn't rural or ghettoized.
PE: I don't think I'm saying that. I don't understand it. But I guess it's not typical.

RS: Speak on that a bit more.
PE: When I grew up, there were three black people on TV, and they were

all porters. And so all that talk about the positive black role model that everyone wanted to see made sense because there was no other. In fiction as well. You had the inner-city novel, and the "yassir boss" role model, and it was not the experience that anybody I knew had. I grew up where the Civil War started, in South Carolina, and I have never in my life heard someone say, "Where fo' you be going?" (Laughter.) So Alice Walker can kiss my ass.

RS: What does Alice Walker say about the whole thing?
PE: One thing she says is that she doesn't write for people who can read. At least, somebody said she said that, so that might be a big lie, but I would believe it given what I have read.

RS: What do you think about the whole Oprah thing?
PE: Oprah should stay the fuck out of literature and stop pretending she knows anything about it, in the same way that people should stop giving any credence to book reviews on Amazon.com. And people should get educated so they can read all sorts of things and have their lives and society become richer. Walt Whitman, in *By Blue Ontario's Shore*, writes, "Produce great Persons, the rest follows." You produce better people by having smarter people.

RS: What if someone accused you of being anti-democratic? In the sense of art reaching a mass audience?
PE: Give me a fucking break. Art is not democratic. Why should everybody think they can write a novel? Everybody can't play violin. That doesn't mean people don't aspire to do it. That doesn't mean you can't have a violin and try to play it. But to think that everybody is going to be good at it, just because they want to—that's complete idiocy! That's why George Bush is president. Democracy has its failings, and one of them is that it allows the existence of capitalist rapists like Dick and Dubya. If you want an argument against democracy watch *American Idol.*

RS: I asked you earlier if you consider yourself avant-garde. Have you read William Gass's essay "The Vicissitudes of the Avant-Garde"?
PE: No.

RS: He lays out three types of avant-garde: the leftist, which ends up being conservative; the rightist, which ends up being reactionary; and a third type that always bites the hand that feeds it. I can see your work fitting in that last category.

PE: Anybody who succeeds in this capitalistic culture making serious art isn't necessarily biting the hand that feeds him. I mean, my God, look at *Guernica.* That's a great protest work, a beautiful painting. But it takes its meaning from the ugliness that allows its creation. It achieves its power because it's produced in a world full of ugliness. That's the nature of protest. It's wonderfully ironic, wonderfully weird, and, finally, absolutely human.

RS: What is absolutely human?

PE: The fact that the very thing that allows our expression of something is the thing that we hate. But we love the expression of it, so we get something from it. There are some people who wouldn't be happy if they couldn't complain. This world is made for them. Social injustice is not going to go away, so if you hate social injustice and love complaining about it, then this is the world for you.

RS: (Laughter.) Do you think your work protests in any way?

PE: Well, that's not for me to say. Of course I have a feeling about it, but the work is out there. If there's a protest in there that you can find, that's great.

RS: *erasure* is a big protest.

PE: Oh? (Laughter.)

RS: Yeah, I mean, come on.

PE: *Glyph* is almost a bigger protest than *erasure. erasure* is like describing a rattlesnake's bite. Am I protesting rattlesnakes?

RS: True, although most people would not see the protest in *Glyph* or commit to that protest.

PE: People rally around easy things.

RS: And there are some easy things to pick up on in *erasure.* Isn't satire a kind of protest?

PE: Not necessarily. I'm making fun of satire as well as satirizing social policies. I mean, I shouldn't even say this, but I write about satire.

RS: So you're satirizing satire.

PE: I hate hearing it back, but in some way, yes, I'm exploiting the form.

RS: Gotcha. So then there is a sort of form, or thematic, or style . . .

PE: I'm interested in all sorts of things, and form is one of them. I don't think meaning exists without form, and certainly form does not exist without meaning. Meaning and story come first. Story is the most important part of fiction. Without it, what's the point? If all you care about is form, become a critic.

RS: Let's change tracks a little bit. You're working on your twentieth novel now?

PE: It's around there. I can't remember.

RS: You've probably got two more in the hopper. Why are you so damn prolific?

PE: It's my job. I mean, if I were a plumber and I only fixed two toilets a year . . . (Laughter.)

RS: Has being prolific helped or hindered you?

PE: I don't give a shit as long as I can write what I want to write. I'm not trying to get rich doing this, and I don't care about how it's received. I just make novels, that's my job, that's what I want to do, that's what I love to do. I want to train mules, I want to fish, and I want to write novels.

RS: Earlier we were talking about the two-fisted writer, someone who works on one book while researching another. Do you work on two at a time?

PE: I work on several things at once. I don't sleep a lot.

RS: Are you one of those guys who gets an idea, goes to a typewriter, and pumps it out?

PE: No, I think a long time before I put anything down on paper. I write many drafts and I try to cut as much as I can.

RS: Being prolific brings a sense of urgency to your work. For those of us who move rather glacially, is that part of the whole thing? I mean, is there an urgency?

PE: No, it just comes when it comes. I live on a ranch, so I have stuff to do all the time. I'm always fixing and building, and I teach. So I sit down when I'm at home, ten or fifteen minutes every couple of hours over the course of the day, and slowly pages accumulate. And I look at what I have and I do it over and over.

RS: Wow, that's interesting. So you don't have a set time. Would you say that you're disciplined?

PE: I can say that I'm disciplined because I do complete works. But if my wife says, "Let's go to the beach," I'm in the car. It's never, "No, I have to do this."

RS: See, I totally had you pegged as one of those, "I have to write for four hours every day" . . .

PE: Oh, no. I'd go crazy. I've never done that in my life.

RS: The book that you're working on now, on philosophy . . .

PE: Oh, that's so unformed I can't really say anything about that.

AS: Do you have anything else coming up?

PE: Well, I just finished a naturalistic novel that . . .

RS: See, that's what I'm talking about, you work too much. This novel is the one starring Percival Everett, more or less, right?

PE: I just show up in it. The working title is *Wounded*. It's a really naturalistic novel. My interest is in the form of a realistic novel. You have to love the form you're working in, but I'm seeing what I can do.

RS: To tweak it?

PE: No, I wouldn't say that. Like I said before, I don't believe there's any such thing as the experimental novel, because all novels are experimental. I mean that to say any time I start a work, I have no idea how to write a novel. My students say, "Can you teach me to write a novel?" and I say, "No, I can talk to you about how novels have been written and what you might do to write your novel, but I cannot tell you how to write a novel." In that way it is an experiment every time. You can't show me three novels that you think are great literary works that look alike. Poetry is a lot more formal than fiction: You can talk about a villanelle, a sonnet, a sestina. But if you talk about what a short story is, there are no rules. But we all know. And that makes it very difficult.

RS: What is it that we all know? Because I don't know.

PE: That's the point. We can't talk about it. But if I gave you some works for a workshop, you might read one and say, "Well, this isn't a story." And you'd probably be right, but you'd be hard pressed to explain to me why it's not.

RS: I couldn't pick a story out of a police lineup.

PE: No one could. It's like Dave Chappelle says: Why do black people like menthol cigarettes? No one knows. (Laughter.)

RS: 'Cause they good, Percy, they good. (Laughter.) 'Cause you can get 'em loose. All right, you said you can't pick out three similar works of fiction . . .

PE: You can't draw me an archetypal picture of a novel and then go find three great books and have them all look like that picture. I can tell you what makes a romance novel a romance novel, but I can't tell you what makes *Finnegans Wake* and *The Adventures of Huckleberry Finn* the same thing.

RS: What if we bring genre fiction into it?

PE: Detective novels fit a certain group of rules. If they don't, then they're not detective novels. Literary novels don't have those kinds of rules. That's not to say one is better than the other, but one does have a set of criteria.

RS: Then define *literary* for me.

PE: I can't. That's the point. The only way to define *literary* is that it doesn't fit into a genre. But I'll give you the difference between art and commercial work, and this is it: You will never return to a paragraph of John Grisham's just to read that paragraph. You will return to *Moby-Dick* because you love the language, because there was an experience reading the book that means something. And what makes it that way? It's art, and you can't explain it. Something happens to you. The first time you actually see a Jackson Pollock, you will remember that. You see the real thing and you're like . . .

RS: Wow.

PE: *That's* experiencing the work.

RS: You're talking about the concept of the sublime. Methinks you're a damn modernist. There's a sublime moment in a lot of your works: Something happens and the character will either have that sublime moment or turn away from it or die or something. What are your ideas on endings?

PE: Things don't end on bombast. You go to war, and it doesn't end with huge explosions; it ends when you die or when you get to go home. And that's a quiet personal thing, not something with bands playing and the world being right.

RS: Or with you shooting the bad guy.

PE: That's right. It just ends. Every story can keep going. So it might as well just stop in an open-ended way.

RS: You pull the emergency brake when you end a book.
PE: I hope it feels that way, because if you're really into a world then you don't want it to stop, and any place it ends, it has to, in that way. You have to get off at some station. But I want to make novels as short as I can.

RS: Why?
PE: I love the economy. It's so easy for me to go on and on, but I don't like extraneous words. I really believe every word does work. And I don't want to duplicate effort. I hate repeating myself. I take a certain amount of pride in having the work lean.

RS: But you're tackling really complex stuff in your work. You don't think you're giving your ideas short shrift?
PE: You know, you don't have to fill a gallon jug when you give a urine sample. Occam's Razor is pretty sharp, and it cuts with both edges. The simplest explanation is usually the best, but I don't seek to explain anything, and I'm not smart enough to have a full discussion. As a fiction writer, I just want to illuminate the fact that there is something to discuss. I'm not a superhero. I'm just the writer.

RS: But there are certain books whose length is appropriate. Like *Gravity's Rainbow.*
PE: If the story that you have is that long, that's the story you have. Write your story. You don't start thinking, "I'm going to write a long novel." You write a novel and it turns out that it's long.

RS: Who are your peers? I don't mean your contemporaries, but throughout the ages, who would you like to have been your peers? Who would you like to be compared with?
PE: Well, I would love people to talk about my work with Sterne and Twain. Cervantes.

RS: Who do you like?
PE: I like such disparate writers. Gaddis. I love Howard Norman. Madison Bell. I like John Wideman. I'm interested in the boundaries between fiction

and fact that he explores and seldom successfully handles, really—but the experiment of it is marvelous.

RS: You tend to do a lot of that, too, in certain places.
PE: I don't do the autobiographical deal. I mean, I show up in the Strom Thurmond book, but that's just a different sort of work.

RS: All your stuff is kind of unreliable in that way.
PE: Well, the world is unreliable. I'm just trying to give you the real thing.

RS: Why do you publish most of your stuff with small presses?
PE: I like small presses. They keep you in print longer, they treat you better, and they talk about literature instead of money. I don't need money, so I go with places where literature is important. Plus I love my editor at Graywolf. I've been with Fiona McCrae for six books and she's a terrific editor and I like my relationship with her. I try to keep something with Graywolf even though my next novel and the last two novels didn't go with them. They're doing a book of my stories in November. *erasure* did well with the University Press of New England, which took a chance with it.

RS: It was hilarious seeing your book among titles about reconstructing womanhood in eighteenth-century New Hampshire.
PE: I loved it, it's terrific. All the other houses ran away from it because they were afraid of some backlash. It turned out there was no backlash; everybody got in line. I really wanted to piss somebody off.

RS: Well, I think you pissed off Oprah!
PE: You can't piss off illiterate people with a book. And so then the same people who had been afraid of it lined up to see the paperback run. It was stupid.

RS: You have the most interesting relationship to publishing of any writer I know. Just in the sense that it all seems to bounce off you.
PE: I really don't care. As long as I'm dealing with people I think are serious, I'm happy.

Satiric Inferno

Peter Monaghan / 2005

From *The Chronicle of Higher Education*, 11 February 2005, A18–A20. Copyright © 2005 *The Chronicle of Higher Education*. Reprinted with permission.

Percival Everett can frame a house. He also raises mules and breeds roses. And the strikingly trim and fit forty-eight-year-old professor of English at the University of Southern California can also write a hell of a novel. Increasingly, his eighteen published works of fiction are winning him notice in literary circles.

Mr. Everett's writing is "unapologetically intelligent," reviewer Ben Ehrenreich wrote in *LA Weekly*.

"He's literature's NASCAR champion," wrote the fiction writer James Sallis in the *Boston Globe*, "going flat out, narrowly avoiding one seemingly inevitable crash only to steer straight for the next."

With acclaim like that, why does Mr. Everett's sidelong stare on bookjacket photographs seem to say, "Don't mess with me"?

Perhaps it is the long road that he has traveled to win that acclaim. In the past, Mr. Everett earned a living as a ranch hand in the West and Southwest, a high-school mathematics teacher in Florida, and a jazz and blues guitarist while working his way through the University of Miami. He has also pursued an on-again, off-again career as a painter of abstract canvases.

The stare, it turns out, also has a lot to do with the way he feels about how his work and that of other African American artists is categorized.

"I don't want to talk about race," Mr. Everett says, "I just want to make art." His fourteen novels, three collections of short stories—the latest, *damned if I do* (Graywolf Press), is just out—and one children's book (with a first book of poems about to appear) make up a literary universe that flouts rigid boundaries and easy conventions. He has written a mock Western, a semi-surreal post-apocalyptic tale about the last fertile woman alive (a three-hundred-pound, oddball government clerk), a hilarious novel in letters and

71

memos that negotiate the publication of Strom Thurmond's account of his seminal role in bettering the lives of African Americans, and re-creations of the myths of Medea and Dionysus. He has spun stories of a one-legged rancher and her retarded son, lost Vietnam veterans, orphans who turn up from nowhere, a man who performs a Caesarean section on his wife so he can be the one to deliver their baby, and a cowboy varmint who mourns his dog's death more than his woman's disappearance.

Mr. Everett's latest novel, *American Desert* (Hyperion, 2004), is about a mediocre, philandering English professor whose head is lopped off in a car accident while he is on the way to his suicide, but who comes back to something like life in the middle of his funeral. With his head rough-stitched back onto his body, he is abducted into the worlds of religious crackpots, ufologists, and shadowy government scientists (who are attempting to clone Jesus). It is a scathing satire that spares neither academics nor governments— and certainly not apocalyptic nuts such as the sect leader Big Daddy, a sort of L. Ron Hubbard figure writ even larger in fictional guise.

Even though most of his work is not, on the face of it, about the subject of race, Mr. Everett is a satirist whose frame of mind will not permit him to keep that topic out of his novels. He simply resists being pigeonholed in any category, including as an "African American" author. In today's literary and academic climate, however, that is a hard battle to win.

Interviewed at his home, seventy miles from Los Angeles, Mr. Everett, though a writer of biting wit, is genial and quick to laugh as he explains how he gets so many books written while running a small ranch. He is sitting in the house that he fashioned from a ranch building, where he and his wife, the scholar Francesca Rochberg, live. He has plenty to do, today as every day, to maintain the cool microclimate he has created with gardens around the house that otherwise sits in a parched terrain bordering 40,000 acres of waterless badlands.

He has animals to feed starting at 6 a.m.—a menagerie that includes a goat, two dogs, and a cat (Eartha Kitty), as well as two mules, a horse, and five donkeys. He also has the gardens to see to, with their 150 varieties of roses, and pepper trees, eucalyptuses, herbs, and wildflowers. Often enough, he will have repairs to make on the house or various other buildings on the property.

It is a good thing, really, that it is often scorching hot outside. The heat forces him to retreat indoors every now and then. When he takes those fifteen-minute breaks, he knocks out a page or two of the latest of his novels. "I work when I can," he says.

Mr. Everett found a wider audience in 2001 with *erasure* (University Press of New England). That book and other works are earning Mr. Everett high praise. *American Desert* is "Frankenstein redone for the good old U.S.A., and another sign that Percival Everett has leaped into the front ranks of that small group of first-rate American satirists," according to Alan Cheuse, a professor of English at George Mason University, in one of his regular book reviews for National Public Radio's *All Things Considered.*

Mr. Everett's voyage to literary prominence and a job in academe included many ports of call. After studying philosophy as an undergraduate at Miami and as a graduate student at the University of Oregon, he headed to Brown University's writing program. There, at the age of twenty-six, he wrote and sold his first novel, *Suder* (Viking, 1983), which drew the attention of the *New York Times Book Review.*

Since 1985, Mr. Everett has taught at the Universities of Kentucky, Notre Dame, Wyoming, and California at Riverside. These days, he calls the University of Southern California home. He says he sleeps little, but does, sometimes, relax, while thinking about work: He spends summers fly fishing, and writing, on Vancouver Island, British Columbia. Ms. Rochberg, his wife, is a MacArthur Award–winning scholar of Babylonian astronomy and astrology. The couple met at Notre Dame. "When she told me what she did, I proposed," he chuckles.

Mr. Everett's good humor belies a distinctly anti-Enlightenment view of human nature. "I don't operate under any illusions about the world—it's a bad place," he says. "Always has been, always will be. Human beings aren't particularly admirable."

That attitude comes through in his writing, but humor keeps it from souring. Says Mr. Everett: "If the best I can do in this life is be entertaining in some way, then I'll be entertaining in that way. Still, I'll talk about the things that I think are vacuous and the things I think are evil, knowing that certainly not because of my pointing them out will they change."

He locates the origins of his wit in his voracious childhood reading. "It was shaped by Mark Twain, Groucho Marx, Bullwinkle, and Laurence Sterne," he says. "And I love Samuel Butler. *The Way of All Flesh.* I read it every year. It's hilarious."

Mr. Everett's skeptical take on human endeavor, said Mr. Ehrenreich in *LA Weekly*, ensures that "there is little celebration of the onward march of American culture in his work, and none of pop culture." Mr. Everett's disdain for those, he added, "shields him from the lures of commerce and celebrity."

"Not that I'm running the risk," quips Mr. Everett. As if to minimize his likelihood of stumbling onto either money or fame, he generally discourages journalists from visiting. "I find it offensive, in our culture," he says, "how people want to know about people that people want to know about." On a more personal level, he adds, "I don't really like attention. I'd rather have people just look at the work."

Mr. Everett is torn, then, when nominated for honors. He has received several in recent years, including a Fellowship of Southern Writers' Hillsdale Prize for Fiction, in 2001, and an American Academy of Arts and Letters Award for Literature, in 2003. But the award that almost stumped him came in 2002 when he was chosen for the Zora Neale Hurston/Richard Wright Foundation's first-ever Legacy Award, for *erasure*.

"Right up until the time I accepted it, I thought about not accepting it," he says.

Mr. Everett's primary discomfort had to do, like so much in his life as a writer, with the impositions of American conceptions of race—and of any identification of him as an "African American writer."

In some of his books, it emerges only in passing, or ironically, that a lead character is African American. In *Glyph* (Graywolf, 1999), his sendup of postmodern critical theory, academe, and much else, Mr. Everett's hero is an eighteen-month-old baby with a high IQ who reads (the classics of Western literature and philosophy) and writes (observations informed by the likes of Ludwig Wittgenstein) but refuses to speak, and who reveals his race to the reader—"Have you to this point assumed that I am white?"—only after 53 pages of daunting engagement with Roland Barthes, Friedrich Nietzsche, and many more graduate-school titans. "It is not important unless you want it to be," adds brainy little Ralph. In other works, Mr. Everett obscures his protagonists' race, or makes them raceless.

erasure, much of which he wrote with a crow he named Jim perched on his shoulder, is different. It tells the tale of Thelonious Ellison, a resonantly named writer of arcane, experimental novels—sound familiar?—who is disheartened by reviews like the one that hails one of his books as "finely crafted, with fully developed characters, rich language and subtle play with the plot," but finally objects that "one is lost to understand what this reworking of Aeschylus's *The Persians* has to do with the African American experience."

Ellison refuses to be reduced to as facile a category as race. A summa cum laude graduate of Harvard, from a family of doctors, the protagonist notes that "I am good at math," "I cannot dance," and "I did not grow up in any inner city or the rural South." When a book agent assures him (as Mr. Everett himself has been told) that his books would sell well if he would "write the true, gritty real story of black life," he retorts that he is living a life "far blacker than he [the agent] could ever know."

The character also registers his disgust with the acclaim for a book titled *We's Lives in Da Ghetto*, by middle-class novelist Juanita Mae Jenkins. The book begins "My fahvre be gone since time I's borned and it be just me an' my momma an' my baby brover Juneboy," and is hailed for its "haunting verisimilitude." So, pseudonymously, Ellison thrashes out a ghetto novel of his own, *My Pafology*, whose seventy pages are reproduced in *erasure*. In it, Van Go Jenkins, a nineteen-year-old rapist and street thug, knifes his mother to death for bugging him, and takes off on a spree of mayhem interspersed with reflections on his achievements, which include fathering, by four women, four children with names like Aspireene and Dexatrina.

Ellison intends his novel as a scathing attack on false, underclass-dialect fiction and, beyond that, all the reductive stereotypes that dog African America. But it ends up winning a handsome literary prize for which Ellison is himself a judge. He shudders at the thought of revealing that he wrote the book; but, worse, he cannot persuade his (white) fellow judges that the book is not "the real thing."

In *erasure*, wrote Robert MacFarlane, a lecturer in English at the University of Cambridge, in a review in the *Evening Standard*, "Everett neatly kebabs one after another of contemporary America's race clichés." And yet, Mr. Everett insists that his book is not really about race, finally. In a review in the *Observer*, Sean O'Hagan agreed, saying that as "funny and provocative" as *erasure* is on American race mores, it is "a much bigger book than that, and, as such, is as much about blackness as *Lolita* is about prepubescent female sexuality."

erasure's real focus, he says, is the work of writing, and its multiple difficulties. Ellison has no doubt, before and after he writes *My Pafology*, that critical reception is a rat's nest. He also is beset by personal difficulties—by erasures: his mother's Alzheimer's disease; his sister's murder; his brother's divorce. Meanwhile, in Ellison's English-department world, writing and reading have themselves been erased, or at least smudged, by Roland Barthes and his fellow post-structuralists. Ellison delivers a conference paper in which he burlesques postmodernist obfuscation and mocks his colleagues for enshrining post-structuralism rather than taking it (as Mr. Everett does) as playful provocation. One colleague is so affronted that he punches Mr. Everett's protagonist.

The irony of winning the Hurston/Wright award for the novel "was not lost on me," says Mr. Everett. But there is no avoiding the fact that in writing about an author who is trying to assert his individuality over race, Mr. Everett draws attention to the very prejudices he wishes to dismiss. Nowhere is this more poignant than in the *My Pafology* section, which is an exaggerated retelling of Richard Wright's seminal 1940 novel of disenfranchised, angry black urban life, *Native Son*. Mr. Everett says he chose to mimic *Native Son* because it was marketed to a white audience as a sensational novel by a black writer, and that, he believes, "had an impact on what the market would seek after that."

Mr. Everett says he wanted *My Pafology* to express "the power of story." It certainly does that, as Van Go Jenkins runs riot only to end up being captured in front of evening-news cameras while exclaiming, "Hey, Baby Girl. Look at me. I on TV." The book does so well that it attracts a megabucks movie contract—and just as well, because Ellison needs money to care for his mother. (In an amusing resonance, Mr. Everett jokes that he agreed to a book tour for *erasure* only because his Vancouver Island cabin needed a new roof.)

Given the way the publishing and criticism industries operate, Mr. Everett will probably be read as a "black writer" by almost everyone, despite his careful construction of reasons not to be. In a June letter to the editor to the *New York Times*, he responded angrily to one element of Sven Birkerts's review of *American Desert* and *A History of the African-American People [Proposed] by Strom Thurmond, as told to Percival Everett & James Kincaid* (Akashic, 2004) (he wrote the latter with a USC colleague). He objected to the "insidious racism," as he saw it, of Mr. Birkerts's identifying him high in the review as African American: "I am sure that Birkerts in previous reviews has not found it necessary to identify other authors as European-American or white." He added: "I simply am tired of people connected with publishing and art in this culture being so amazed that anyone not white can create a work, that race is all they can see."

"These debates have been going on since the Harlem Renaissance," says Alexander G. Weheliye, an assistant professor of English at Northwestern University and one of many instructors now assigning Mr. Everett's novels to classes in African American literature and culture. "Countee Cullen said the same thing—that he wanted to be thought of as a writer, first. People like Langston Hughes criticized him for that. Today that has a different valency. A lot of authors want to render African American identity a bit more complex than it has been, without abandoning it."

In that sense, Mr. Weheliye agrees, Mr. Everett's stance is rhetorical: He knows, of course, that he will be defined as black, no matter what, but that makes him only more determined to challenge the definition.

Even if unhappily, he sometimes accepts that identification. He decided to take the Hurston/Wright award because he feared what observers would do with any controversy that surrounded the foundation that gives it. Last year he was even a judge.

At times, Mr. Everett is willing to engage questions of race quite bluntly. Upon winning a South Carolina Governor's Award in the Arts in 1994, he was invited to address the legislature at the State Capitol.

"I don't really like that kind of public appearance, but I really couldn't pass it up, given the Confederate flags that they had there," says the South Carolina native. "I essentially just stood up and said I couldn't talk because of the flags, and sat down. There was a reception following, and . . ."

"You went to the reception?"

"Oh, yeah. What was interesting was how many members of the legislature came up to me and said how happy they were that I had done that."

The reticent public speaker observes: "At least I finally got to say something that seemed to matter to me. It wasn't just some boring reading."

An Interview: May 3rd, 2005

Alice Mills, Claude Julien, and Anne-Laure Tissut / 2005

From *Reading Percival Everett: European Perspectives*, eds. Julien and Tissut (Tours: Presses universitaires François-Rabelais, 2007), 217–27. Interview conducted on 3 May 2005. Reprinted by permission of the Presses universitaires François-Rabelais.

CJ: Thank you for agreeing to spend time with us. I have prepared a set of questions in agreement with Alice and Anne-Laure who are of course welcome to bring up other questions of their own on the spur of the moment.

We would like to start by asking you about your beginnings as a writer, the moment you knew you wanted to be a writer, the moment you knew you were a writer.

PE: My move to write fiction was, oddly, a natural one. I was studying philosophy. I was studying Wittgenstein and J. L. Austen, but what that work consisted of was the construction of scenes in which people spoke to each other and addressed philosophical issues. So, I was writing scenes, anyway. I wrote a story which I submitted in my application to the writing program at Brown University where I was accepted and where I wrote my first novel. That's how I moved into fiction. It was kind of an organic move, so I don't know if I had some actual realization that I was a fiction writer as much as I still saw myself as attempting to address philosophical concerns.

A-LT: So *Suder*, your first novel, was born of philosophy?

PE: Basically, all of my books come out of a desire to explore something about language and how language works, even though I do write stories that deal with other things, maybe.

AM: *Suder* moves from east to west. How do you explain leaving one's roots?

PE: All things move from east to west geographically. The sun does, and so should we. I have frequently come across that situation as a teacher of the

American experience. Mark Twain has Huck Finn say he is going to "light out for the Territory," and I see myself following the same path.

CJ: We next would like to open the field of literary models. What writers, by and large, have been an inspiration to you?

PE: There are a great many. I need really start with Laurence Sterne and *Tristram Shandy*, the most important novel to me. For no other reason than his use of every type of literary discourse available to him in his time. And he exploits and comments on that discourse, which, however, remains quite recognizable in a story. The book also has in it that wonderful marbled page, collections of asterisks. And there's the blank sheet, a page of no words, just color. It's wonderfully experimental. My sense of humor has been influenced by that novel, and also Samuel Butler's *The Way of All Flesh*. And of course Mark Twain. And I love the work of Angela Carter, Zora Neale Hurston, Ralph Ellison. There are so many contemporary writers I love that I can't possibly mention them all.

CJ: We would now like to ask a question about your motives for writing. Where does the urge to write come from? Charles Johnson has answered he writes because writing an idea into existence is the only way to deal with it. Like his mentor, John Gardner, he argues that moral issues pertain to literature, that writing provides a mode of knowledge: a mode of understanding others and, by virtue of that understanding, understanding oneself. Would you place yourself in the same line of thought?

PE: I certainly understand that. I don't want to sound ironic, but I believe personally the opposite. Every time I finish a book, I know less than when I started. I think I know something when I start writing and, as the problems I approach become more complex and interesting, I realize that everything I thought I knew was wrong. And that's the exciting part about writing novels. After eighteen books, I know considerably less than most people. I'm well on my way to knowing nothing, which is my goal, I guess. (General laughter.)

CJ: I now come to the diversity of your writing that struck me when I discovered your first thirteen books, which I read one after the other over a couple of months. Some writers seem to be constantly reworking the same material—which does not mean they are poor writers. On the contrary, inventiveness characterizes your work. I sometimes have the impression you like to go from one challenge to another in order to explore the possibilities another mode offers. I'm just guessing. What does this diversity bring you?

PE: I love to study. There's so much I don't know anything about that any time I get an opportunity to study and learn something, I will. For instance, the main character in *Watershed* is a hydrologist. When I wrote that novel, I read twenty-five or so books on geomorphology and hydrology and actually went out in the field in the company of a hydrologist. Not simply so I could learn about hydrology and sediment movement through watersheds, but so I could learn to think and talk like someone who does that for a living. My aim was to have Robert Hawks come across in the novel not as if I had studied hydrology to write a story, but realistically. The same is true of the Greek stories of Medea and Dionysus. The exciting part is that I was attracted to the stories. Those two books, though similar, come from different places, different needs. The Medea novel comes out of my longstanding dissatisfaction with the slant of the existing story—that the excuse for her killing her children was that this woman had gone mad. That seemed too simple. There are all sorts of other tracks. She is a hero in my estimation, and my story came out of that kernel of dissatisfaction. The Dionysus novel proceeds from a desire to understand some notion of deity. I read many translations of *The Bacchae* but couldn't own the material. So, I read more translations and finally did my own. It was awful, a terrible result, but it gave me entry into that material and I finally possessed it in such a way that I could use it. The first version of the first half of the novel was in verse, which was truly poor, but, again, just that stuff helped me to control the material. I get to study something with every novel and that's what I like.

A-LT: At the beginning of *erasure,* Monk speaks about his books that are on the wrong shelves in bookstores. Does that refer to *For Her Dark Skin* and *Frenzy,* or is it personal?

PE: It is personal. But, despite the glaring similarity between that character and myself, he's not me. It's not an autobiographical novel. My experience of having novels that have nothing to do with African American literature falters with the Medea novel, whose character is black. But finding *For Her Dark Skin* and *Frenzy* in a section marked "African American Studies" seems wrong-headed and runs counter to my work. Someone interested in Greek mythology might not think to look for those books in the African American section, and someone interested in African American studies probably is not so interested in Greek mythology. Anyway, it's a loss of sales to me! (Laughter.) Besides the fact that it's culturally offensive.

CJ: You have brought up your desire to learn and to protest as motives for writing the Greek novels. Can you describe moments when you realize an event, or an idea, can develop into a story?

PE: I wish I could because then I would do it more often. I do not know. It is magic, a wonderful thing. Those moments come differently with every book. Sometimes, I'll hear a story and tell it to myself over and over until I can change it enough so that it becomes mine. With my latest novel, *American Desert*, I knew I wanted to write a novel. I mean I felt something was brewing inside me. I was driving back to my ranch in the desert and noticed an exit sign to Theodore Street. That name struck me. I pulled off and the novel fell into place with Theodore Street for its main character. I cannot say why but I do not question such things. I just did as I was told: went home and started working.

CJ: So, that's where the name Theodore Street comes from! I had built up an onomastic game opposing this character's first name, 'Gift of God' in Greek, to the banality of his last name, 'Street.' It appears I was in a blind alley.

PE: That's fun. That's what literature can do for you.

CJ: The three of us have a hunch how one can proceed from writing *Cutting Lisa* to writing *Zulus* (at least from a very loose thematic standpoint: the body, motherhood). But how one proceeds from *Suder* to *Walk Me to the Distance* is an evolution we cannot begin to fathom. Can you help?

PE: Those two novels are really different, but there are ways in which they are similar. Both characters are looking for a sense of familial integrity, dealing with the feeling of alienation within the culture. And, finally, both move from the South to the West. They are similar in those ways, but are totally different as persons.

CJ: We would now like to come to satire and humor. The *Playboy* magazine blurb on the back cover of *damned if i do* praises your "sharp satirical voice only predictable in its provocation." I suppose they may have had a story like "The Appropriation of Cultures" or the earlier *God's Country* in mind. . . . Satire is present, but I also feel, side by side with it, a sense of fairness to your characters. A French word comes to me, *tendresse*. Would such words as kindness or considerateness do in English? As if satire was aimed at society at large, not individuals.

PE: I have never been interested in building straw men simply to knock them over, though, of course, I do introduce in my fiction ideas or persons

I disagree with. But I don't approach fiction—or, more generally, writing—with the notion that I know what's true and right. I raise questions. That's what I'm smart enough to do, and the fact I write fiction for a living is more than ample evidence that I'm mentally deficient. (General laughter.) So, you can't take what I say, but I can ask questions and that's what I do in fiction. Kindness? I don't know if it's kindness, but I try to be fair since I'm not trying to say that I'm right. And I find it interesting to try to approach or represent people I would not care for in real life. It's a real challenge for a writer to take a character she or he dislikes, even despises, and be able to occupy that character's space in a way that's fair and allows the reader to understand why that person can think that way. I'm interested in that aspect of my work.

AM: Does that apply to Strom Thurmond?

PE: Well, maybe especially to Strom Thurmond. (General laughter.) You know, I read a lot about Thurmond before writing *A History of the African-American People* and finally determined he probably never was really an evil man, though the results of his actions often were. Interestingly—though I am not saying it really means much—there's no instance (at least that I know of) of his being recorded or marked as having used the word *nigger*, and I suspect he wouldn't have. I don't see him as hating black people. He just liked white people a lot more than he liked blacks. (General laughter.)

CJ: Our next question has to do with textual genetics. I have often wondered how you moved from one slice of life in a story to another level in a novel, and back to the same character in yet another story. What I have in mind is "Still Hunting," that developed into the Reskin episodes in *Watershed*, while Robert Hawks resurfaces later in "Alluvial Deposits"—all three of them in different locations. I am interested in this kind of recurrence, another instance being the cousinship between *The Body of Martin Aguilera* and "Warm and Nicely Buried." What made you discover the potential in "Still Hunting" with respect to *Watershed*? What made you decide there was potential for another story in Robert Hawks as a person and a hydrologist in a different setting?

PE: The true answer is I don't know. The answer that makes sense in an interview (laughter) is that so much came with the first story that I knew I wanted to use it again at some point. So, to me, "Still Hunting" was more or less a note. It was a story, but also a mental note. Then the Robert Hawks character came after considering, not the present story of his life, but the past events that went on with his father and his grandfather in South Carolina. And then he reappears in the story "Alluvial Deposits" because I find it interesting to have what I consider ghostly echoes of characters popping up throughout my work. I never really wanted to say this but I will: I don't consider any work singularly. I think I am writing an entire body of work, as diverse as its pieces are. I see it as one very long work that will finally make sense together. So, I hope all these things tally with each other and that the ghostly echoes I'm referring to—this recurrence of characters and situations—is finally a function of playfulness rather than an obsession with a particular person, a particular idea, or a particular kind of relationship.

CJ: The Robert Hawks in "Alluvial Deposits" is different from that in *Watershed*. On the one hand he comes to the story without a past, as you said, and, on the other, he is not as racially militant and relies on the help of the local police.
PE: Well, his past doesn't come into play. Just as race does not explicitly surface in every story, which does not mean it isn't there. Robert's blackness—if that nameless character is Robert—is not visible in "Still Hunting." He turns militant more or less by accident in *Watershed* and is more subdued in "Alluvial Deposits."

CJ: Let us turn to another aspect of your career. When I attended the last session of your creative writing workshop at College Station, your students described you as a "slave driver"—obviously meant as a compliment. (General laughter.) What does teaching creative writing bring you as a person and as a writer?
PE: I get paid relatively well to hang out with smart young people and there's absolutely no reason for me to complain about that. Of all the things these kids want to do, they want to make art. Most of what they produce is not very good. But that's OK. They want to make art and that's absolutely wonderful. Even though their compositions are seldom outstanding, I like to sit with these bright young people and talk about their work. I learn a lot from them. I'm privileged. I learn as much from them as they learn from me. But I don't care about the students' work as stories, I care about them as writers. Stories are mere tissue.

AM: Creative writing is not taught here. What would you tell French students interested in enrolling in such a class? Could you describe your teaching practice?
PE: I would first tell them I'm lucky because my students want to be in the

class. We have classes that are required and my colleagues and I engage in this kind of torture. But my creative writing students want to be tortured and I appreciate that because making art is not easy. I have my students first relax in the beginning workshop, and I tell them they must realize they are all going to be treated equally badly, that it is going to be a painful but enjoyable experience they are going to appreciate for the rest of their lives. Then we launch into the class. My advice to everybody is to read—and then read some more. And to love literature. If they don't, they might as well leave the room. There is not a lot of variety to the exercise itself. The class consists in teaching by immersion. They write something and we talk about it. If they have an idea for a story, they go ahead and see how it works out and hand it in. Then, we talk, dissect the text and I try to help. Writing . . . Rewriting . . . The process is repetitious.

CJ: I would like to go back upon your earlier definition of stories as "tissue." I have in mind Gilles Deleuze's theory that writing is not an end in itself because it is anything but personal. Deleuze seems to invite readers of fiction not to think in terms of themes, but of an activity where fluxes fuse with other fluxes. If that is the case, what can—what *does*—literature do for the writer, apart from providing an opportunity to learn? Must readers dispense with what Michel Foucault calls the "authorial function"—readers looking for themes in order to build their fantasies of who the writer is into meaning?

PE: If the reader is reading to uncover some meaning about me, then there is little hope. We read because we love language. We learn about ourselves by the way we understand the working of language, the nature of meaning, the importance of making meaning.

A-LT: A question comes to me on the topic of art and politics. Your novels can be anything but militant, and the narrator in *erasure* refuses to write the epic novel of the ghetto or indulge in racial protest. Still, race is an important factor in his life. So, where do you stand between the militant novel and the exclusively aesthetic one? Could you enlarge upon the interaction between art and politics?

PE: All my novels are subversive and militant, but none is social protest. The notion of a novel of the ghetto is a construction of white America. Publishing is an industry controlled by white America. You can easily pigeonhole or categorize a people and control the perception of others. In fact, it's amazing how often people are going to see themselves as fitting this or that category, this or that description. So, *erasure* for example is, I think, quite important in that it rebels against the established practice of pigeonholing the black experience. Black people in America are as diverse as white people. They live in each and every part of the country; they practice different religions, or none at all. I didn't have a clichéd religious upbringing because my grandfather was an atheist, my father is—was—an agnostic and I am what I call an "apath." I simply don't care. And so, I don't fit the stereotype of the black American church-going, gospel-singing person. And I think this stereotyping is unfair. I have never heard anyone ask a white American, and certainly not personally, "Who is your leader?"—but they will ask blacks that all the time. Truthfully. And we are all supposed to say the same thing, "Jessie Jackson." (Laughter.) It's not a fair question to start with. So, I see art as being far more political than so-called political discussion.

CJ: I would now like to bring other forms of art into the discussion. I was privileged to visit you in Moreno Valley, where I was introduced to another aspect of your creative life: painting. What does painting bring you? And why did you choose not to draw the illustrations for *The One That Got Away* yourself?

PE: I'll address the part about the children's book first. I personally can't stand any kind of representation in visual art. I produce nonrepresentational paintings. My drawings for that book would have been meaningless to a seven-year-old. I'm not an illustrator. I paint because I love spreading color and not because I'm attempting to construct an identifiable scene. And that brings me to why I do paint. The relationship with visual art is a more immediate visceral, emotional one. When I look at a canvas and start spreading paint on it, it's physical. There it is in front of me and it's exciting in a very different way than writing. Starting a novel is like entering a bad marriage. No matter what I do, it's going to end badly, to be full of emotional ups and downs. It's going to alienate me and I'm going to be alienated from anyone I know—family, friends—and it's going to last a lot longer than I want it to. The relationship is shorter with a painting. Though it's thoroughly emotional, too, and fraught with ups and downs, it's not that long year-after-year intellectual connection with things that wakes you up, saying "I have to think about this again." With a painting it's something more—I guess immediacy is the term that comes to mind.

CJ: Going back to collaboration between artists, how did the idea for *A His-*

tory of the African-American People burgeon into your mind? We are asking that because such collaboration is rather unusual.

PE: I wrote that book with James Kincaid, a Victorianist in the same English department as myself. I sat up one morning in bed and this title came to me: "A History of the African-American People by Strom Thurmond." My first thought was to write a parody of an actual history text. I mentioned this to Jim and was just sort of playing with the idea when Jim asked, "Can we write it together?" I answered "Sure" and we started. We did not write what I thought we would. It organically became this epistolary thing, letters going back and forth. Jim is a work maniac. (The interviewers laugh.) Yes, I know. (Laughter.) I must elaborate on that. He's a raving maniac who writes in longhand with his left and is typing with his right. And so he was going, having lots of fun and growing wild, and it was really hard to keep up with him. So, we sort of split the labor. We came up with this book which only by the longest stretch of anyone's imagination is actually a novel, but it was a lot of fun for us.

A-LT: Allow me to be provocative. What about your collaboration with Richard Wright and Ralph Ellison in *erasure*?

PE: Oh! Well . . . I turned a deaf ear to their complaints. (General laughter.) I was probably somewhat unfair to Wright in the way I exploited *Native Son* when creating the novel within the novel, and perhaps to some extent probably paid too much tribute to Ellison. But I don't think so. I love *Invisible Man*. Though, interestingly, my tribute to *Invisible Man* is supplanted by my tribute to Chester Himes's novel *If He Hollers Let Him Go*. My references to Himes are scattered throughout the book in a lot more subtle way. That's my quiet tribute to Himes who, I suspect, would have liked that sort of thing.

CJ: We also thought we would ask you to name your favorite among your own books.

PE: I love all of my children, idiots and geniuses alike. I don't think I hold one over another. Perhaps *Glyph* is my favorite, only because it was the easiest for me to write as it is closest to my own voice. I didn't have a lot to do to change the rhythm of the thinking, which, I know, is terrifying to Anne-Laure, who is starting on the translation.

CJ: You turn Roland Barthes into a ladies' man in *Glyph*. (Being a Frenchman . . . the stereotype says he should be—just as a black man must be a natural-born dancer.) Then there is the hilarious pastiche of *S/Z* in *erasure*. Is this satire, or celebration?

PE: I only made him a ladies' man because it is a citable preference. I love Barthes. The *S/Z* pastiche I intended more as a comment on the way Americans, and perhaps the British, apprehend his work. When you put Barthes in the hands of Americans it all of a sudden becomes very earnest. They miss the playfulness of it all, while I think it's a lot of fun—and Barthes must have been enjoying himself too. The ideas are important and sometimes completely nonsensical, but that's what's amusing. So, as I'm making fun of that character I create, Barthes, I believe I'm also making satire—though not necessarily of Roland Barthes himself. There's more than just one level to satire. In *erasure*, I'm certainly satirizing the publishing industry and a certain kind of novel, but I'm also making fun of myself and the entire endeavor of making a novel.

CJ: Derrida appears briefly in *Glyph*. Are you going to put more French theoreticians in a future book?

PE: So weird that you should mention that! I've been reading nothing but Lacan's work for the past year. Reading all the Seminars again has been a lot of fun. Derrida does show up in *Glyph*. But that character is actually reappearing in a novel I have sort of started. He is writing this novel, a history of Western philosophy starting with the Greeks, that has several narrative threads. Right now I'm on the Italians, but he will go all the way up to, at least, the Enlightenment. And, in there, I hope he gets into an argument with Lacan about what in the world he is doing. Not about philosophy itself, but about what it means, what he finds himself figuring. This is part of the landscape.

CJ: We also thought we would ask you a question about the outdoors, only occasionally dangerous for your characters and in many cases a refuge from society where they can be safe in the company of animals.

PE: I won't say anything about my need to go outside. I'm very lucky these animals allow me to live with them, and I simply love the outdoors. I couldn't live and write if I didn't spend a lot of time outside, on the streams and in the desert. Animals teach me patience. I don't have a schedule while I work. I don't wake up and write for three hours, and then do something else and come back to my desk. I've never done that. I get up, mend fences and feed the horses, move a lot of manure. What working with the animals allows me is this opportunity to trust myself. As I realize they trust me, then I can trust myself. I know that I'll get the work done. I don't get excited about it. I don't get nervous, I don't become anxious about work. I just do it. I guess that's what I get from them.

AM: A lot of your characters have a passion for trout fishing. Does fishing have anything to do with patience?

PE: It does, but, more than anything, you need a reason to stand out in the middle of an ice-cold stream with waders on. Fishing seems to be the best reason. Fishing requires patience but also an understanding that it is not only about catching the fish. It's about putting yourself in the place where you can catch a fish. It's about loving the place that will allow you to catch a fish. And there's a lot of detective work involved in fly fishing. The first thing you have to do when you show up on a stream is to read the river to find out where trout are likely to be, and which kind of insect to select. Is it an insect in its larval or adult stage? An aquatic, or a terrestrial one. All that is rather tentative stuff when you realize that in some places a hungry trout will bite on anything. It doesn't matter whether you have the right insect. It's only a desire to somehow re-create those elements of nature that come together in that one place at that time of day.

CJ: Am I right to say you seem to go fishing on your own? Many of your characters have a fishing partner (I am referring to Warren Fragua, a recurrent character in your fiction located in New Mexico)—except Robert Hawks, who had rather be on his own.

PE: I never noticed that.

CJ: Maybe I am too curious.

PE: Is that possible?

CJ: One last question, maybe. I don't know about my two colleagues, but when I read *American Desert* I thought it could make a wonderful scenario for a movie. Has it occurred to you, or had you rather be in the same anti-Hollywood league as Rawley in "True Romance"?

PE: That's a bad neighborhood I don't feel like going in. If someone wants to make a movie of it . . . great . . . send me the check . . . . But I don't care about it. If they make it, then I can buy more hay for the horses. Otherwise, just leave me alone. There is no artistic interest in it. I don't anticipate this kind of thing. I don't desire it.

CJ: It has happened once, has it not?

PE: That was a terrible experience. My novel *Walk Me to the Distance* was made into a film whose title I won't tell you because you might happen upon it. Even if you read my novel and then watch that film, you will not recognize it. Let's not talk about it.

CJ: I agree that movie is poor compared to a book I find deeply moving. . . . So, unless Anne-Laure or Alice has another question to ask, let us close this pleasant and instructive time together. We are glad more fiction is being composed to find its way to the printing press. Thank you very much for your time.

"The South"

Alice Mills and Jack Lanco / 2005

From *Reading Percival Everett: European Perspectives*, eds. Claude Julien and Anne-Laure Tissut (Tours: Presses universitaires François-Rabelais, 2007), 229–31. Interview conducted on 4 May 2005. Reprinted by permission of the Presses universitaires François-Rabelais.

AM: It is a pleasure to welcome Percival Everett, who is the author of eighteen books of fiction and who also teaches creative writing at the University of Southern California. Though a Southerner by birth, Percival Everett has been living in the western United States for many years. He was born in Georgia but grew up in South Carolina from age five to seventeen. We also know, because it was widely reported in the press at the time, that in 1989 he was invited to give a speech at the state legislature of South Carolina. As he was speaking, he noticed the Confederate flag in the room, interrupted his address, and walked out.

PE: Um . . . actually I knew the flag would be there. I showed up and then refused to speak.

AM: Sorry for my mistake! Let us remember that you started a controversy that eventually led to the removal of the Confederate flag from the Capitol building a few years later. We would like to hear you on the South, on your memories in general, and whether you have considered going back. Did you leave voluntarily to go west, or under other circumstances? We would be very much interested in any thoughts you might like to share with us.

PE: Thank you for inviting me to speak here. As your introduction suggests, I have a troubled relationship with the South—and with the United States in general, I must add. First of all, I would like to dispel some of the stereotypes of the South. I have a "white" great grandfather, a Jew who lived in Texas, where he married a former slave. He sent my grandfather to medical school in Tennessee, which he left eventually to become a practitioner in South Carolina. I don't think I have a Southern accent. This is an expectation with

90

people in the United States. I am tired of hearing "You don't sound like you are from the South," whatever that is supposed to mean. My entire relationship with the South has been formed by this family background. I believe I sound like anyone I grew up with. Maybe I don't, but I really believe that.

I left South Carolina for Miami when I was seventeen. I remained a Southerner there, considering Florida is as far south as you can go in the United States. But it was there I got a foreign accent, in college where everyone around me was actually speaking Spanish. The character of Miami was not at all like South Carolina, where the Civil War started and where I had had a high-school teacher who taught us the Civil War was a war of aggression. I did not first go west when I left South Carolina, and there are other places I lived at before I settled across the continent.

After I published three novels and my first collection of stories (by the way, all four books are set in different locations across the country), I was invited back in South Carolina to address the state government on the subject of art—as if they had some idea what art is. I did know the flag was flown above the Capitol and in that chamber, but when asked if I would come and speak my immediate response was "Yes," though my immediate feeling was "Are you kidding? No. I don't want to speak to you." However, I kept that to myself because I knew what the right thing to do was: start my address and quickly come to that awful symbol, the basis of my troubled relationship with the South. So, I stepped to the lectern and said that I was there to speak to them on art, but that art and politics are inextricably bound together and that that flag, a symbol of exclusion, was unacceptable. And I left. Having said that, I now believe that flag ought to be there, ought to be flown atop the State Capitol, ought to be in that chamber for the reason it tells you what the United States really is. You know, when you walk into a minefield, it helps to have a sign that warns: "Minefield." It's a good thing and that's how I feel about the United States. Now I have been in many places in the country, I sometimes tell myself they ought to keep a Confederate flag in hotel rooms, just as a reminder.

The United States has used the South as a wonderful scapegoat. If you have a really awful member in your family, anytime you do something bad you can point to that member of the family and feel good about yourself— think you have done better. That's what the United States has used the South for, not when just about everyone thought there was nothing wrong with slavery, of course, but later when it became practical to criticize exploitation and segregation. The North and the large Western urban areas have excused their behavior toward minorities, the American word for downtrodden and disenfranchised peoples, by blaming the South for all the evils in the land. But the most segregated city in the entire United States is not in the South: that's Chicago, Illinois; and the only place in the whole United States where I have ever been called a "nigger" is Cambridge, Massachusetts. I grew up where the Civil War started but no one ever called me a "nigger" there, though I know my father was. This is what America means to me, and this relationship with the United States supersedes my relationship with the South. I am a Westerner. I don't think about the South. I don't want to return and live in the South. I want to see the sun set on the ocean.

JL: To move beyond the South and the Civil War, I'd like to know how you look at America today. Do you see it in terms of factionalism, or of unity based on the motto "United we stand, divided we fall"?

PE: It seems to me America has made a career of being fractured. The Civil War is a white-on-white fracture, among many others. I have to address this question on today's situation by prefacing my answer by saying that when George W. Bush became president I went to Canada and bought a house. I actually live in Canada part of the time now. I think that the situation, the political game created by the Bush administration, is hinged on fracturing—on polarizing—American society. In fact, we have an ongoing conversation about Red and Blue states, the Blue states having voted for John Kerry and the Red ones (including the notoriously litigious Florida) for George Bush. We have maps with all the Red states in the middle and the Blue ones on either coast. And, sadly, this Blue and Red language has been embraced. For the truth of the matter is that the margin of victory in terms of seats in any of those states was negligible. And the more the Republican Party and George Bush can underscore the alleged differences between those states, the more distinct people will feel, the more fractured a society we will have, and the more paranoid people will be.

JL: How do you see the future? Communities, ghetto and non-ghetto, living apart?

PE: Oh, the future . . . the same bad way that it is now will continue. For whatever reasons you can think of, the rich will get richer and the poor poorer. That's America. I do not perceive any change coming.

Mules, Men, and Barthes: Percival Everett Talks with *Bookforum*

Kera Bolonik / 2005

From *Bookforum: The Book Review for Art and Culture*, 12.3 (October/November 2005), 52–53. Copyright © *Bookforum*, October/November 2005, "Mules, Men and Barthes: Percival Everett Talks with *Bookforum*," by Kera Bolonik. Reprinted by permission of *Bookforum*.

Percival Everett is one of America's most imaginative and industrious contemporary fiction writers, publishing fourteen novels (and three story collections) in as many years. But his devotion to craft is matched only by his aversion to the business of publishing. This has earned Everett a cult following, praise from his peers and critics, innumerable awards, including the PEN/Oakland-Josephine Miles Award for Excellence in Literature, the New American Writing Award, the Hurston/Wright Legacy Award, and an American Academy of Arts and Letters Award. This recognition hasn't deterred his satiric impulse. Everett ridicules the publishing industry's tendency to ghettoize and fetishize writers of color in his novel *erasure*, when an obscure black experimental novelist named Thelonious "Monk" Ellison hits it big with *My Pafology*, a pseudonymous parody of a bestselling memoir, *We's Lives in Da Ghetto*, written by an Oberlin graduate. Indeed, the joke proves not far off the mark: When Doubleday launched its African American imprint, Harlem Moon, the publisher made him an offer for the paperback reprint rights for *erasure*. The irony and money were both tempting, but Everett turned Doubleday down. Since the beginning of his career, he has almost exclusively published with independent presses. As a result, Everett has been able to be as audacious, inventive, sardonic, and honest as he wants to, as is evident in such literary endeavors as *God's Country* (1994), a hilarious Western picaresque; *Frenzy* (1997), a lyrical venture that turns Greek mythology on its ear, featuring Dionysus; and *Glyph* (1999), an academic satire about a baby with an IQ of 475.

Wounded is far more somber, a novel that returns Everett to his favorite landscape both on and off the page: the beautiful western desert of Wyoming. In it we meet a middle-aged widower named John Hunt, who is a black horse trainer sharing his ranch with his septuagenarian uncle Gus in Highland, a small rural town near Laramie. Their white and Native American neighbors revere the two African American men as integral members of the community. But John and Gus haven't witnessed discrimination in their home until a gay University of Wyoming student is brutally murdered and John's new ranch hand is arrested for the crime. The national media descend on Highland, putting the town under the microscope, and the events that follow threaten John's safety and that of everyone dear to him.

Everett was visiting the East Coast from his home near Los Angeles and came to the *Bookforum* office to speak with me in mid-June. Raised in South Carolina and educated on both coasts, Everett has been teaching American studies and critical theory in the English department at the University of Southern California since 1998. Though he is too modest to elaborate on such things, I did gently press Everett into revealing the ways in which his versatility extends beyond his pages: On the ranch he shares with his wife, Chessie, he trains mules and, at one time, horses. He also shyly admitted to being an accomplished jazz guitarist, fly fisherman, woodcarver, and painter, and has studied biology and philosophy. With interests this plentiful and a literary palate as broad as Everett's, it's little wonder that he flinches at the mere notion of being pigeonholed.

KB: *Wounded* opens with the savage murder of a gay University of Wyoming student. You taught at the University in the '90s. Were you inspired by the Matthew Shepard case?
PE: In part, though I'd already returned to the University of California at Riverside, where I was on the faculty. Interestingly, aside from its physical beauty, Wyoming is probably the one place in the United States where I feel the most comfortable. I never felt the kind of racism I have felt on the East Coast. I was living on the One River reservation at the time. Shepard's murder was an unfortunate crime committed by a couple of aboriginals of the area, but it's hardly an indictment of the place. The media deals with these crimes in such a strange way, as if these things only happen in rural areas or small towns, implying intolerance is simply the way of life in these places. Brutal crimes happen all over the country. Ours is an intolerant culture.

KB: John, the enigmatic protagonist of the novel, is a horse trainer; it's a perfect career choice because he's an expert at reining in his emotions, especially rage, desire, and sorrow. I've read that you were a ranch hand as a young man.

PE: Yes, and I spend a lot of time with horses. I've trained them. But for the past few years, I've lived on my ranch with mules, training them.

KB: I didn't know you could train a mule. What does it take?

PE: Patience. (Laughs.) They're very smart, and any second they think they're smarter than you, all is lost, and unfortunately, they are smarter than I am. Seriously, you can train them to do anything but race. They have to have a reason to do something. Mules don't see much sense in running in a circle, so they just run in all directions.

KB: When John is riding a horse he's training, he lets his mind wander, and when anxious thoughts emerge, the horse responds. Does a rider really have to have a clear conscience before mounting a horse?

PE: Horses can tell when you are nervous. They can read people pretty well. I had to train myself to not react around them because they'd react to me. John has to control his anxiety. The horse he's riding in that scene, Felony, is an extremely exaggerated case, of course. (Laughs.)

KB: One quibble I have with *Wounded*, however, is that all of the gay men in the novel—David, Wallace, the dead college kid—are represented as physically defenseless. They need a burly straight man to come to the rescue.

PE: I don't view these characters as representative of any group. They're individuals. The gay men I have in this novel are young and naïve, so I only meant it as a function of youth, not of their sexuality. Since there are no other gay people in the novel, I can see why it would appear that way. I recount a story that happened to me in a bar in *erasure*, where this redneck came in and started harassing a gay couple. In the novel, Monk interferes and a fight ensues, and then the two gay men get up and they're these huge, muscular men and they're laughing at the scene. In life, I ended up sitting down and having a meal with them. The irony of it was wonderful.

KB: Had you ever considered toughening one of the gay men in *Wounded*, maybe making David a little more thuggish? We see a very sick old man like Uncle Gus with more physical strength and defensive know-how than David or Wallace. Were you worried about portraying a gay man as emasculated?

PE: No. I really wasn't attempting to offer a political perspective as much as to tell the story of these particular characters. David is a gentle person. He suffers from a kind of estrangement from his father that makes this gentle person suffer the way any of us would. I don't see him as representative of anything but himself. Gus, on the other hand, is more experienced. He's perceptive. He's someone I aspire to be.

KB: Gus and John make good parents to David. John would even seem to have a womb, of sorts: that cave he likes to explore. It's the site of epiphanies, intimate encounters, rejuvenation. It's there that he makes love for the first time after his wife's death six years earlier. He also brings David into the cave to save him from life-threatening frostbite. The cave conjures up all sorts of psychoanalytic implications here.

PE: Caves are really fantastic. They're physically beautiful, they're dark—you can't see anything in them. I went through lots of caves when I was writing this book. I didn't know why I was studying caves, initially. But as I went through them, I became interested in that threshold where the cave stops being a place to get out of the weather and starts being, well, a cave—that tension between safety and fear and the unknown. I understand being safe and I understand being afraid, but it's that gray area between them that the cave offers, and the more familiar you become with the cave, the deeper that zone goes, but it's still there.

KB: I was struck by the fact that John and Howard had been college friends. The two couldn't be more different: John studied art history and collects art; Howard majored in business and became a tax attorney living in Chicago, choosing big cities and the corporate animal. John prefers big skies and real animals. Is he disillusioned with the capitalist world, or is he just a modest guy?

PE: The thing about rural people and ranchers that urbanites don't recognize is that many ranchers are quite cultured. Living away from cities doesn't diminish one's interest in the arts and life in general. Maybe it's because I live on a ranch, but to me John isn't so extraordinary in that way. I think it's fair to say of John that he simply wants that life. He's not going at it as a negative reaction to the world, but as a positive attraction to one.

KB: You have almost exclusively published with small independent presses on principle. Are they better publishers?

PE: In my entire publishing career, I have been looking for a great editorial relationship, and I found it with Fiona McCrae at the Graywolf Press.

She's like my Maxwell Perkins. I followed her from Faber and Faber. I love everything about Graywolf—we've done seven books together; I even love my copy editor. And Fiona and I have developed a strong bond—we don't always agree, and we each seem to get our way a fair share of the time, but I always trust her. And Graywolf lets me do pretty much what I want to do knowing that I'm not going to make a whole lot of money. I never think about the marketing. I just want to make my art; that's what makes me happy. I feel very fortunate just to be able to work. I do have a very hard time going out there and doing publicity, but lately I have done a lot more interviews and publicity. Well, more than I used to.

KB: You've earned many awards and garnered a lot of praise from your peers and critics. A few years ago, you were offered a rather ironic opportunity to help inaugurate Doubleday's African American imprint, Harlem Moon. They wanted to reprint the paperback of *erasure*. Now, that's funny.
PE: Yeah, they offered me more money than I'd ever been offered in my career. But I couldn't do that to my book, even though I was tempted by the idea of invalidating the imprint with this particular book. (Laughs.) I couldn't bring myself to do it.

KB: Each of your fourteen novels is different from the next. Which, if any, was the hardest to write?
PE: They're all hard in different ways. I should say that none of them was easy to write. I think *Glyph* was probably the easiest novel for me to write because it was closest to my heart and my sense of humor. I had so much fun rereading Barthes's *S/Z* and parodying it in *erasure*. It might have been the most fun writing in the past few years. *Frenzy* may have been the hardest. That was my novel about Dionysus, and the language is so different than my language.

KB: You're a graduate of Brown's writing program, and you have taught creative writing for a number of years. What are your thoughts about these programs?
PE: I have mixed feelings about them. I don't think that they ever really hurt anybody. I think that if you're going to write, you're going to write. But a lot of the work seems derivative to me. Everybody is worried about getting published instead of worrying about making art.

KB: Last year you published *A History of the African-American People [Pro-*

posed] by Strom Thurmond, as Told to Percival Everett & James Kincaid (2004), in an epistolary format. What was it like to collaborate with another writer like James Kincaid, who is a literary theorist?

PE: It was a very different kind of book. We actually approached it with the same seriousness we approach all of our other work. I came up with the idea. I just kind of woke up with the title one morning. The epistolary part came more out of Jim's head than mine. But the concept for the book came from me.

KB: So, how did you set up the collaboration?

PE: It was a division of labor. Jim wrote many of the letters and I wrote a few, and I wrote all of the interactions with Strom Thurmond and the contracts—all the prose parts. So we just divided it up. Jim writes fiction, as well. He's probably my closest friend in Los Angeles. It was fun for us. There's no point doing anything unless it's fun.

KB: You've sent up academe and publishing, using satire as a way to examine, among other things, race relations in American culture. How do you manage to keep satire engaging, funny, and relevant without veering into the didactic realm?

PE: I think the way to make satire easy is to keep as close to the truth as possible. We choose things because they bug us, and they bug us because of the way they really are, and when you really start to examine these things, they're just funny. One of the most ironic things about some of my satire is that I'm fairly earnest about it. There's a lot of irony in the fact that I take the things I'm talking about seriously. I actually like literary theory, for example, so to write my novel *Glyph*, I had to believe I understood enough of it to write about it, and to make fun of it. I found that I had to respect it. It doesn't mean I agree with it. I just think that it's funny.

KB: So, you train mules. You write an average of a book a year. I've also read that you are a fly fisherman, a musician, a painter.

PE: I used to be a musician in college. I played jazz guitar.

KB: Did you study painting?

PE: No, not formally. I look at a lot of paintings. I paint in oil.

KB: You're a Renaissance man of the American West. And you balance all of that with a full-time teaching job at the University of Southern California. That's a lot.

PE: It sounds like a lot more than it is. I teach two classes a semester, writing and theory.

KB: It can be hard to teach and write at the same time. How about for you?

PE: It can be exhausting. Luckily I have good students who want to work and read. Of course not all of the work is good, but working with them is exciting. I get paid relatively well. It's intellectually stimulating. I think it helps my work, ultimately. I never feel rushed about work; I don't feel pressured to make art. At the same time, I don't have a guru mentality. I don't want to teach people to write the way I write.

KB: Have you had the gratification of seeing your former students' work hit the bookstore shelves?

PE: Yeah. Chris Abani was one of my students, and his novel *GraceLand* did extremely well.

KB: I'll say. It was selected for the *Today Show* Book Club back in January. Well deserved, too. It's an incredibly good novel.

PE: I just read the manuscript for Abani's new novel, and I liked it quite a bit. I also really like the work of Emily Raboteau, who was a student of mine. It is satisfying seeing their work. In a way, it's more satisfying than seeing my own.

Interview with Percival Everett

Jeffrey Renard Allen / 2005

Transcript of interview recorded on 7 November 2005. Copyright © 2005 Jeffrey Renard Allen. Published by permission of Jeffrey Renard Allen (www.jeffreyrenardallen.com).

The following interview was conducted before a live audience at The New School in New York City on November 7, 2005. Following my introduction, Percival Everett read two excerpts from an early version of *The Water Cure* (2007), after which we began our exchange.

JRA: Tonight I have the tremendous honor of introducing Percival Everett, who will be engaging in a conversation with us. Percival is the author of nineteen books, which should put us all to shame. These books include a book for children, two books of stories, and sixteen novels, including *Wounded*, his most recent novel, which was published by Graywolf Press. His twentieth book is scheduled for publication either by the end of the year or by early next year; this will be his first book of poems, which is called *Regarding a Function of Gesture* [*re:f (gesture)*], and that will come out from Red Hen Press.

Mr. Everett was born in 1956 in Georgia, but grew up in South Carolina. His first novel, *Suder*, was published in 1983. Presently he teaches at the University of Southern California in the writing program. He has studied philosophy at the University of Miami and also at the University of Oregon, and he has a master of arts from Brown University. Among his many awards are an award from the Hurston/Wright Foundation as well as a Lila Wallace-*Reader's Digest* Fellowship and an award from the American Academy of Arts and Letters. He's also an editor at *Callaloo*, a prestigious literary journal, and in addition to his numerous publications, he is a painter. So, that should also put us to shame. (General laughter.)

I think what's really remarkable about his work is that in some ways it totally defies categories. Among his many novels, he has two which can be described as Westerns or anti-Westerns. He has probably three books which could be described as traditional, kind of realist narratives. He has a couple of novels which are essentially riffs on Greek mythology. He has other types of novels, which I guess we would consider more experimental, playing with types of form and metafictional ideas and such, so there is tremendous variety in what he's done. In fact, it seems as though he is trying to do something new with every novel. So it's a tremendous honor to have him here. And without further ado . . .

(Applause.)

PE: Thank you for having me. I make a mistake when I'm traveling of watching CNN, and last night—I just have to share this with you—I was watching the news and there was the anchorperson sort of talking about the rioting in France. And I'm here to inform you that apparently, according to her, the riots were started by African American youths. (General laughter.) Because that's synonymous with black in the world now.

I'm going to read from a new novel, and it's a novel that's been giving me some trouble because I don't know what the hell I'm doing. (General laughter.) And fortunately it's a feeling that's not foreign to me, so I haven't canned it yet. But it's in process, this novel, and what I mean by that is that it's really in fragments and I want it to really be in fragments. I don't want it to ever connect up. But what I will read to you are two fragments of it which unfortunately will give you the idea that there is some kind of cohesion to this text—and it's all a lie. The title, as it stands, is *Other Languages Are All We Have* . . .

(Applause follows the reading.)

JRA: It's sort of hard to know where to begin with you because you do defy classification in many ways. I was wondering if you could perhaps talk a little bit about the very, kind of eclectic nature of your writing. I'm not going to ask you where ideas come from, but you know, where do they come from? (General laughter.)

PE: I appreciate your not asking that question. (Pause.) I don't know. I just want to make art, and I don't think about what it's going to look like before I start making it. And I don't think about what it's going to do once I turn it loose. It just starts happening, and I guess either I'm dumb enough or crazy enough to let it happen.

JRA: I've read, at least in one previous interview, where you said something like you have an image of the book before you start writing it. Could you maybe talk a little bit about that?

PE: Only insofar as I can say that exact same thing again. It's a really hard thing to articulate. When I start a book, I can't say that I'm working on a book until I see the shape of it. And when I say that, I have no idea what I mean. I just . . . I know what the book's going to look like. I don't mean the cover or anything like that. I know how it would feel. I know what the paragraphs will feel like. I have an understanding of the negative space on the page. But it's more a really private impression than it is something that I could ever articulate.

JRA: So in terms of the novel you just read from, which is in progress, do you have an overall sense of where it will end up, that kind of thing?

PE: God, I wish I did. The thing about this, and I usually don't talk about novels at all, you probably know that from reading, but this one is . . . I've been talking to myself a lot, and that's been fruitless so maybe this will help. (General laughter.) What I want to achieve with this, and it will probably change because it might be impossible, is I truly . . . I have this theory that Heraclitus's fragments were written as separate little pieces and that they are, in fact, fragments, and that they are not pieces of a whole. And what I want to create is a novel which sort of obstructs the reader's, even *my*, desire to create a chronological, linear, or understandable narrative—and yet somehow at the end of it understand the life.

JRA: I see. Well you just mentioned Heraclitus, and you studied philosophy as an undergraduate and I guess even did some graduate work in philosophy as well. To what degree does philosophy shape your work? Or to what degree might you be described as a philosophical novelist? I mean, even though your work is quite varied, are you working out philosophical issues?

PE: I think all writers are. And it sounds awfully highfalutin to say that I'm working on philosophical issues. I mean, there's a whole lot of stuff I don't understand. And not all of it is philosophical, it's just stuff of people, and so I started writing. And the beautiful thing about novels is I think I know something when I start one, and by the time I'm done with it I realize I didn't know anything at all. And that's the beautiful experience.

JRA: Kind of a process of discovery in some ways?

PE: Yeah, discovery of my own ignorance. And it's kind of a contradictory thing: On one hand, we write and expect people to want to read what we write, and on the other hand, it's the most humble-making process I can imagine. I like to view my career as this: I know less after each book. And I think I'm well on my way to knowing nothing. (General laughter.) But my friends at least confirm this for me. And I think that's right. I think that's what art's supposed to do for me. To answer your question about philosophy, the philosophy I did early on was mathematical logic and I do that to sort of relax still, but it's not something to . . . I sure hope it doesn't show up in any novels.

JRA: (Chuckles.) Okay. I think, in at least one interview, you mentioned how when you were studying philosophy it didn't feel quite right for you, and you started to write scenes and that's kind of where the first fiction came from. I don't know if that's the case or not? (Chuckles again.)
PE: Who knows? It might be. It's probably some bullshit I told them. (General laughter.) You know. Sure. (More laughter.)

JRA: Okay. One thing you've been very vocal about is this whole question—I hate to use a term like *identity politics*, but for lack of a better term—but the whole question of you or anyone else being labeled an "African American writer" and, you know, you've been very vocal about the fact that you're not an "African American writer." Can you talk a little bit about your view of that term, and this whole question of labeling writers in terms of their ethnicity or racial identity or whatever?
PE: I try not to talk about that. So it's funny that people think that I've been vocal about it because I try . . . um . . .

JRA: Well maybe you've said something once or twice, and it becomes a whole big thing?
PE: I said it really loudly; that's why. (General laughter.) Well, first of all, as much as this culture wants to carry on this notion of race, though there really is no . . . anthropologists gave up race as a category in the beginning of the twentieth century, but our culture hasn't, so race exists. Speaking logically, I am an African American novelist. I'm also a 5'11" novelist. I'm, at this point, a California novelist. But I've gone to a lot of bookstores, and I see this section "African American," usually it's "Studies" or "Literature," and, you know, I don't see "White Literature." And I don't know what that means. And, I *do* know what it means. It means the same thing it means when I pick up an art book that wants to call a certain art "folk art" or "naïve art." It wants to put art in a separate category to make it seem as if somehow it is not quite

art. And that's the problem I have. I don't have any problem with identifying myself with any number of groups, races, people, and, I suppose, given my great-grandfather was Jewish, I'm a Jewish novelist. (General chuckling.)

JRA: Let's stop there. (General laughter.) So, I think I agree with you in certain respects. I mean, my sense of what you're saying is we often have a ghettoizing of certain writers. I mean, for example, there was an article about, you know, poets and writers, and it starts out by saying something like, "Percival Everett is one of the most prolific African American writers," and that you published nineteen books in, I think, twenty-two years or something like that. That makes you one of the most prolific writers period, doesn't it? But even there it seemed like that was a way of someone else saying that your achievements were only important in a certain arena.

PE: I guess that's the important thing to . . . and I don't care how I'm perceived, I really . . . again, I just want to make books. I don't read reviews. I don't look at sales figures. But the interesting thing about that article was that the writer was African American. It's not a symptom that's unique to white Americans. This is cultural. And he falls into the same traps that any of us can. It's sad. You know, he's a smart guy. But as he's writing this, he's thinking and this language just happens. And that's the frightening thing: The language just happens and so art suffers.

JRA: And I think also in some ways the term brings with it certain expectations. What I want to do is try to get more into your actual process, if that's possible. I mean, a number of commentators have noted that you often don't identify your characters in terms of race. Or at least in certain books you don't. Race isn't a way of, you know, building character on the page. Is that a conscious decision on your part?

PE: Well, it was initially. But it's an interesting thing. If I don't have my character comb his Afro or cross Lenox and 125th Street someplace in those first ten pages, then that character's white. That's not true. And then we see it on the news. I don't know if we see it as much as we used to see it. You know, when they identify bank robbers it used to be that . . . I can't get this right. It's something my parents pointed out to me when I was a kid. If the robbers were black, they would say they were black. If they were white, they wouldn't say anything. And that has an effect on a kid watching the news. I'm not sure what my point was with that. But I just don't think that the designation of race is something that has to happen in the ways prescribed by the culture and by cultural expectations and by readers' expectations.

There are all sorts of things that you can read in which you can identify the characters as belonging to different groups. And I have one novel in which the only thing that would, sensibly, have you know that the character was black, unless you really pay attention to certain rhythms . . . and even then rhythms vary from place to place. People of African descent in this culture are as diverse as people of European descent. They don't share all the same experiences. They don't all talk the same way. They don't all have the same concerns. But in this novel, this funeral happens at an AME church. If anybody cares to take note of that, well it's there. If they don't . . . . It's curious to me that somebody wants to make that distinction and understand that person's being this or that.

JRA: Okay. It's kind of curious that your, I guess we could say, most successful novel in some ways, *erasure*, is the novel which offers up parodies of notions of race, and . . .
PE: I can't tell you how much that pisses me off.

JRA: (Chuckles.) But do you think that's just a matter of people simply not knowing how to read the novel? They didn't know that you were making fun of some of these issues and such?
PE: I don't know how they could have missed it. You know, people are worse than anybody. (General laughter.) They get everything wrong. And the irony of the reception of that novel wasn't lost on me immediately. And it's very sad and it's also very funny. It was funny, first of all, to have the major houses running from it for all sorts of reasons and being afraid of it—at least that's what I was told. I don't know if that's actually true. And then when it did well, having them line up to buy the paperback rights. Well, they lined up to buy the paperback rights, and the first in line was an imprint—I don't remember which press it was—and they wanted it to be the inaugural book of an imprint called Harlem Moon. And my first question to my agent was, "Have they read this book?" And briefly I toyed with the idea that, you know, it would be great to have a press publish a book that immediately invalidated the press itself. (General laughter.) But forever my book would have "Harlem Moon" written on it, and I couldn't do it.

JRA: That's quite funny. I'm wondering, you know, given that your work is so varied with respect to style, is every book for you an individual kind of thing? Maybe I've asked this question in some ways already, but I guess I'm curious to know if it's been a conscious career choice to try to do something different in each book, and if in some ways that's been some attempt to defy being pigeonholed as an African American writer, whatever the label might be?

PE: If it is, it's unconscious. I don't know. It makes me sound awfully smart and I don't think I am. And I view all the novels as a part of a whole, but I'm not thinking about anything except making the book in front of me and style is just a tool. So as I start thinking about stories and style, the style that it needs becomes apparent to me. But I never think about audience, which, if I look at my bank account, is pretty apparent. But it's true. I just don't think about whom I'm writing for. I just think about making the book.

JRA: So you're very willing to take chances and risks as a writer, which is perhaps unusual in some ways or not typical, if I can say that?

PE: And, again, you're making it sound kind of brave, and that's just the way I work. I don't think a lot about it. I just go to work.

JRA: With a given project, is there a stated amount of time that you usually like to have the book completed in? Is it, like, a year, or however long it takes?

PE: However long it takes. Same with the length—however long the book's supposed to be is how long it will be. I like shorter novels, and I tend to write a lot more than I need and then I chop aggressively.

JRA: That's kind of surprising. In one interview I read you said that you don't work every day or you have kind of lazy . . . you describe yourself as lazy, in fact, if I recall correctly.

PE: No, I don't write every day. I spent the last twelve years training horses, and I don't have time to mess around with novels all day. (General chuckling.)

JRA: It's quite amazing that you manage to finish so many books if you don't go at it every day. I mean, how long do you work in a given day when you're actually working on it?

PE: I call it work amnesia only because I really, truly don't remember working. I know I work through the day and I take breaks. I go in and I jot things down, and then I'll have these explosions of work where I'll stay up three or four nights in a row. But I don't stress over this stuff. It's just books.

JRA: You make it all sound so casual.

PE: Ain't nobody shooting at us. (General laughter.)

JRA: Not yet at least. But maybe I'll change the direction of the questions just slightly. I'm curious about your development as a writer when you studied at Brown and what that was like in terms of pushing you on and such.

PE: Well, I was never a student in the workshop at Brown. I guess I tend to be a little bit cranky, and so I when showed up, I said I didn't want to go to any classes. And Brown, then, was kind of interesting. They said okay. And so I just wrote and lived in Providence basically. Which was, I guess, penance enough. (General chuckling.)

JRA: So did you develop any relationships? Were any particular structures or writers there helpful?

PE: Well, Robert Coover was there at the time, though we got to know each other later. He wasn't teaching then. But I liked him. And I played chess every night with a writer named R. V. Cassill, who used to edit the *Norton Anthology of Short Fiction*. I'm not a fan of Cassill's work, but I actually liked him as a person. And part of it was . . . Verlin just liked to mess with you. And he was also just a terrible chess player. (General laughter.) So I would always beat him. And I'm a terrible chess player too, but he was even worse. And finally he got so upset that I was always beating him that he took me into his basement and put a BB rifle in my hands and said, "Shoot at that box over there." I thought it was a strange enough request, but I did. Days later he came to me at the mailboxes near the department and said, "You know"—his hands would shake when he talked—"when you figure out why as a right-handed person you shoot left-handed, this novel will fall into place." (General laughter.) What do you say to that? I said, "Thank you, Verlin." But I already knew why I shot left-handed. I was left-handed. (General laughter.)

JRA: Actually, he blurbed your first novel, if I recall correctly.

PE: Yeah, and I was very grateful to him. It was Verlin, who was not my professor, who took my first novel and sent it to his agent without telling me, and I received a call from her. And she asked if she could represent me, and that was the start of my career. It was very generous of him.

JRA: Like most writers, I'm sure you know plenty of other writers, and I'm wondering if any of them serve as your readers, or do you tend to work on your own and when the book gets done it goes off to your agent and such?
PE: I've never given any book to anyone to read, and I just send it to my agent. You know, I've been living on a ranch. Who's out there? I can give it to my mule to read (general laughter), but he's a harsh critic.

JRA: So, you teach writing. How do you approach teaching? What is it that you try to get across to your students?
PE: Well, some of them are in this room, actually, and so I should be honest. I don't know about teaching writing sometimes—because of these students, actually. I think occasionally I can help, and usually I think I'm helping a student who probably is going to find it anyway. But maybe I can accelerate things just a little. I have graduate students now who look at me and say, "Can you teach me to write a novel?" And I look at them and say, "Honestly, no. I can't. I don't know how to write a novel." I don't. I've written novels and apparently evidence suggests that I might write another one, but I don't know how to do it. Every time I do it, it's something completely different, something completely new. And, in that way, I can't tell them how to do it. I can prepare them for that discovery, in some way. I can teach them how to read, and I can teach them how to be critical, and I can teach them to step away and look at their work in different ways. But that's really all I can offer.

JRA: And I know you teach a course on theory for writers. What's that about?
PE: We kind of laugh about my take on theory. My students call it "The Big-Game Hunter's Rule of Philosophy." We cover everything from the Russian Formalists to deconstruction, but you sit on a high perch and every time the philosopher pokes his nose out you simply blow it off. (General chuckling.) You just don't give him any room at all, and then we make fun. And I say this in all honesty: I find it fun if I can teach someone to rewrite what they've read and expose it for its absurdities, because then you necessarily understand it. I like theory, I actually do. But it's bullshit. It's ridiculous but it's wonderful. I like thinking about it. I love that somebody has thought it, and I get excited about it. I get excited about Lacan. But it's all supposed to be fun. And that's how I teach it.

JRA: And so what do the students get out of it? (Chuckles.)
PE: Oh, who cares? (General laughter.)

JRA: I guess I was trying to pose a serious question. (More laughter.) I mean, are you trying to establish connections between theory and writing, or is it a way of teaching students to think about writing or think about their own work, or . . .

PE: Well, I think anytime that you get students thinking then you're helping with the writing—and seeing that there's all sorts of stuff that can be source material for your work. I think after they've studied it with me they understand when I tell them that sometimes I can start reading a book about the history of calculus and I will understand a chapter I'm working on. It happens all the time, and that's why I have a library. That's why most of my working is reading.

JRA: It's kind of serendipitous then?

PE: Yeah, well . . . certainly. It's just making connections in the world. I was thinking about the simple functions of addition, subtraction, multiplication, and division earlier and how they don't apply to infinite decimals, and I came up with the first section of this novel. No one else might see it, but that's how it worked.

JRA: Interesting. And is it true that, given the many books you've done, and I'm sure there are a couple others that are already finished that we'll be seeing, but . . .

PE: I wish.

JRA: Is it true that it doesn't get any easier for you? Is that a fair statement? That you find every . . .

PE: It's never easy, but . . .

JRA: Do you work quicker now than you used to, you think? Or anything like that?

PE: I don't know, depends on the work. What's hard is giving an injection to a 1,200-pound animal that doesn't want it. That's hard. It's not hard to sit around in my living room thinking about novels. (Laughs.) But also, writing a novel is the hardest thing I've ever done because there's an investment of self. There's a lot of fear associated with it because you're putting yourself out there, no matter what you think about being removed from the material. Your stuff is in the world, and that's a scary thing. But . . . no, I'm not any better at doing it than I was. I think I'm a better writer. Interestingly, I don't know if I'm a better artist. But I'm a better writer. I hope I'm a better artist, but I don't know.

JRA: In one of your interviews, you mention how sometimes in readings you read something that you've done in the past and you actually start revising as you read it.
PE: Well, part of that is because I have a reading disorder. I can't read line by line, and so I kind of read chunks and I forget what it says, and so I revise.

JRA: I'll just ask a final question. I'm curious about your painting and, you know, what role that plays in your life as an artist—and when you started painting and how often you do it and how you balance the various things— the painting and writing and your horses and all that, you know?
PE: Again, I just do it. I've been painting seriously for about fifteen years, but I had a real long gap. And I had to move off that because I became productive with the novels. I like the painting because it's a completely different experience with art than a novel. It's something that's physical, and it's a really emotional response to the canvas. A novel is like knowingly entering a bad marriage. You can't really justify it to your friends or your family or to yourself, really. And no matter what you do, it's going to end badly.

JRA: You mean in the terms of the time it takes you away from other people?
PE: No, the time, what it's going to do to your personality. You know, there's going to be all these ups and downs. Half the time you're not going to understand the thing. It won't understand you. And it's a long haul. It's there every day. You wake up and there it is. When you hate it, you wake up and there it is. When you love it, you wake up and there it is and it hates you. (General laughter.) And it's this intense intellectual drain and exercise, and it's all in your head. There is no release in your body for it. So the painting is a completely different experience. They do inform each other for me, but though the paintings can give me a headache and drive me, you know, sort of crazy every now and then, there's a certain amount of physical joy that goes with making them.

The Wicked Wit of Percival Everett

Shashank Bengali / 2005

From *USC Trojan Family Magazine*, Winter 2005. Reprinted with permission from *USC Trojan Family Magazine*.

There might not be a more fertile mind in American fiction today than Percival Everett's. In twenty-two years, the USC English professor has written nineteen books, including a farcical Western, a savage satire of the publishing industry, a children's story spoofing counting books, retellings of the Greek myths of Medea and Dionysus, and a philosophical tract narrated by a four-year-old. He has given us a galaxy of vivid characters—an art-loving horse trainer, a disillusioned hydrologist, a big-game hunter, a baby genius, a slumping major-league ballplayer who learns to fly, even the late Senator Strom Thurmond. Pigeonholing Everett's "style" seems as futile as predicting what he'll write about next.

So it's maddening to him when the literary establishment tries to fit him into easy categories. The easiest, of course, has to do with skin color. Last year, an article in the *New York Times Book Review* on his novel *American Desert* identified Everett in the second sentence as an African American. Everett had to respond.

"I feel confident in stating that the color of my skin has little to do with that novel," he deadpanned in a letter to the editor. (*American Desert* is a Frankensteinesque farce about a suicidal college professor decapitated in a freak car crash who returns to life at his own funeral.) Such veiled racism, he concluded, "makes one appreciate the overt brand of bigotry practiced by the likes of the late Strom Thurmond."

That letter was a rare public outburst from a private man who assiduously avoids the business side of fiction. "I don't read reviews, and I don't look at sales figures," he says over a lunch of eggs Benedict and apple pie at a downtown Los Angeles diner. Dressed casually in a black polo shirt and jeans, the lean, fit-looking professor says he'd rather just write and let the books speak for themselves—and largely, they have.

Through two decades of producing diverse, demanding, award-winning fiction, Everett has earned a devoted readership and wide respect for his uncompromising approach to writing despite the book world's ever more commercial leanings.

"Percival Everett is, for me, one of the best American fiction writers producing now," says Charles Rowell, a professor at Texas A & M University and founder of the literary journal *Callaloo*, which recently published a special section in tribute to Everett's work. "I appreciate his willingness to write about any subject that he wants, not to be restricted by whatever publishers and tradition dictate."

The *Washington Post* has called him "one of the most adventurously experimental of modern American novelists."

"He's literature's NASCAR champion," the *Boston Globe* praised, "going flat out, narrowly avoiding one seemingly inevitable crash only to steer straight for the next." Reviewing Everett's send-up of post-structuralist academic theory, an *LA Weekly* critic wrote in 2000: "If only one novel of *Glyph*'s wit and intelligence is written in Los Angeles every year . . . this new millennium may just prove itself bearable."

Everett probably didn't read that review, but if he had, he'd have been pleased, because of all his books—and he typically doesn't play favorites— the voice and humor in *Glyph* are closest to his own. Set in the 1970s, the novel is a critique of the impact of French literary philosophy on American academia, narrated by a four-year-old linguistics prodigy named Ralph Townsend. Having grasped sophisticated language by the age of ten months, Ralph (whose IQ is 475) gets annoyed when his mother reads to him the tale of Goldilocks—"some drivel about bears and a blonde girl," Ralph sneers. He perks right up when she gives him *Tractatus Logico-Philosophicus* by twentieth-century linguistic philosopher Ludwig Wittgenstein.

Over-wise and hyper-fussy, Baby Ralph distrusts the spoken word and, while still in his crib, begins to communicate via hastily scrawled notes to his astonished parents: "lips look ugly to ralph when they are moving ralph needs books in his crib." When the outside world gets wind of the brainy babe, a succession of kidnappings ensues, with physicians, academics, government operatives, and a prison guard scheming to get hold of Ralph.

Glyph is classic Everett—challenging, relentlessly imaginative, filled with high-flying intellectual acrobatics, and often flat-out funny. But in this commercial age, there's an immediate problem with such a book: How to market a satire of French post-structuralism with footnotes on every page and an appendix labeled "Ralph's Theory of Fictive Space"? It's not surprising that *Glyph* didn't win a wide audience; it was described even by some admirers as too smart for the room.

None of this fazes Everett, who has never shot for the bestseller lists. "I write to make art. I don't really care about making a lot of money," says the author whose face graced the cover of the May/June 2004 issue of *Poets & Writers* magazine. "I don't think about the audience. I don't want the work to be inaccessible, but I don't mind if someone finds it difficult."

He says he writes about what interests him, which explains his prolific output and the range of subjects he has tackled.

He reads voraciously—probably more than he writes. Take the array of books he was reading last summer: a history of geometry titled *Euclid's Window*; *The Birds of Heaven*, a naturalist's story of his global pursuit of cranes; a book about the Indonesian volcano Krakatoa; *A History of the Arab Peoples* by distinguished Oxford scholar Albert Hourani; and one or more volumes on French psychoanalyst Jacques Lacan, the father of postmodern thought. Reading widely is essential to his writing, Everett says: "I put everything in and see what comes out."

"His genius, possibly, lies in the variety of work that he has created," says Fiona McCrae, director of St. Paul, Minnesota–based Graywolf Press, which has published several Everett books. "From work to work, you never know what he's going to do next. That's partly why he's been slow to get the recognition he deserves," she adds. "He's not building up a consistent profile. Just as soon as people understand who he is, he goes and does something different."

Everett says he can't help it. "I have no idea where the stories come from," he says. "It's just whatever I'm interested in." The perpetual student, Everett is someone who revels in intellectual inquiry; for him the extended experience of creating a novel is endlessly fascinating. "I like studying," he says. "I'm always reading, and it starts me researching some subject. I don't do that thinking I'll find a book. It's just magic."

"Magic" is Everett's shorthand for his writing process, something he admits to having difficulty describing. After he finishes writing a book, he likes to put it aside entirely and move on. It's not uncommon for Everett to begin public readings by announcing to the assembly of fans: "I'm sick of this book."

"I'm terrible at talking about my work," he explains. "It's flattering to be asked the questions. I just wish I was a better interviewee. I've always been really reserved, always avoided doing interviews. I'm trying to be better at it."

Colleagues cite Everett's great modesty. "He's completely unpretentious," says James Kincaid, a close friend and fellow USC English professor with whom Everett co-authored last year's satiric show-stopper *A History of the African-American People [Proposed] by Strom Thurmond, as told to Percival Everett & James Kincaid*. "He's a celebrated novelist—and he talks about it as if he were tearing off little notes to the teacher," says the distinguished scholar in Victorian studies and childhood sexuality.

In person, Everett is soft-spoken with a ready laugh. While he's laconic about his work, he quickly animates when the subject turns to politics or life in his adopted home of Southern California. As a child growing up in Columbia, South Carolina, the son of a dentist, Everett used to sneak into the book stacks of the local university library and while away hours reading. He left Columbia at age seventeen to enroll at the University of Miami, playing jazz and blues guitar to help put himself through college. Later he taught high-school math and worked as a ranch hand.

Everett has enjoyed something of an extended love affair with the West since he first drove cross-country in his early twenties. "I like the space, the landscape, the characters, the many different geographies," he says. "It informs a lot of my thinking and my work."

A decade ago, he and his wife, Francesca Rochberg—a professor of Assyrian history and astronomy at UC-Riverside—bought a ranch on fourteen acres of desert foothills in Moreno Valley, seventy miles east of Los Angeles. Everett is an animal lover. On the ranch he tends to a small herd of mules, horses, and donkeys. ("There's always some sort of donkey issue," he complains cheerfully.) He's also got a goat, two dogs, and a cat. And a two-story studio where he paints abstract canvases.

Running a ranch doesn't permit Everett much time for writing. "It was a lot of work at first, when we had to kind of rebuild the place—putting up fencing, clearing chest-high brush," he recalls. "It's less now that the place is kind of established, but there are still periods of heavy work." Everett wakes at 6 a.m. to feed the animals; he spends his days repairing fences and fixing water lines. When he needs a break from the blistering heat, he ducks inside and bangs out a few pages.

The steady pace of farm life helps Everett keep a level head. "Shoveling manure puts things into perspective," he quips.

During the school year, twice a week he makes the seventy-minute commute by train to USC, where he has been on the faculty for six years. After three years as English department chair (his colleagues call him a "gifted administrator"), he returned to full-time teaching, or as he puts it: "I get paid relatively well to hang out with smart young people."

Having previously taught at the University of Kentucky, Notre Dame (where he and his wife met), and UC-Riverside, where he ran the program in creative writing, Everett says he particularly admires USC for embracing the surrounding community and for enrolling students from varied backgrounds.

"My last undergraduate class was almost a model of ethnic diversity," he says.

His students say Everett is tough, but for those who can take his criticism and the silent glances that practically scream "You can do better than that!" the rewards are great.

"He's probably the only person who's read everything I've ever written," says Bridget Hoida, a doctoral student in USC's creative writing program. "As a writing student, a lot of people pat you on the back. Maybe sometimes you'll hear a few things about what's not working. Percival will have you turn to the last page and say there is one redeemable paragraph in the whole thing. He's the first person I've had to lay it all on the line with, and he will tell it like it is."

When he isn't teaching, Everett divides his time between the ranch and a summer home on Vancouver Island, British Columbia. This year, he spent less time in Canada and more time trout fishing in Idaho and Montana— traveling alone, driving along riverbanks until he found a secluded spot he liked, and camping out under the stars. "No one wants to be with a smelly, cigar-smoking fisherman," says Everett, justifying his hermit ways. But the truth is, "he's very much a loner, despite being such a warm person," says Kincaid. "He has adjusted to a kind of geography in his mind of being alone a lot."

As fetishistic as some writers are about their work schedules, Everett's less-structured methods may reflect the fact that he came to writing relatively late. As a philosophy student at the University of Miami, he was interested in Wittgenstein and in what is known as ordinary language philosophy, an approach that tackles deep philosophical problems through close analysis of everyday speech.

Because this kind of study depends on posing hypotheticals involving everyday conversation, Everett found himself writing a lot of dialogue. Gradually, as he grew disenchanted with philosophy, he began writing stories. He ended up in a master's program in writing at Brown University, where he wrote his first novel, *Suder*, about a third baseman whose major league slump sends him skidding into self-awareness. The book was published to acclaim in 1983, when Everett was twenty-six.

But during the past twenty years, the West's vast landscapes, culture clashes, and sense of isolation have increasingly marked Everett's fiction. In recent novels, Everett has trained an unsparing eye on today's wide-open spaces, with characters no one would recognize from *Gunsmoke*. The 1996 novel *Watershed*, for example, features a young hydrologist, who happens to be black, getting mixed up in a bloody showdown between Native Americans and federal agents over water rights.

"I certainly write the West I see," Everett says. "The West of movies, television, and much literature is a West that never existed. It's a fascinating, complex place, like any place, but it so often falls into that category of cowboys."

With *God's Country* (1994), he parodies pastiches of the Old West with aplomb. Gleefully turning the genre on its head, Everett gives us the worthless cowboy Curt Marder, a racist Union Army deserter, and Bubba, the tracker hired to help find the bandits responsible for kidnapping Marder's wife (whose loss evokes less emotion in Marder than the bandits' killing of his dog). Everett uses the pair's journey to skewer every shibboleth about daring cowboys, know-nothing Indians, and the "Manifest Destiny" that drove America's expansion in the nineteenth century. It's Bubba (a black man) who turns out to be the quiet, strong hero of Western lore. Even George Armstrong Custer, that old warrior, makes a cameo as a crossdresser.

There's serious intent behind all the humor and high jinks, reminiscent of Twain (whom Everett cites as an influence, and whose mark is evident in Everett's best satires). In a recent issue of *Callaloo*, USC English professor William R. Handley observed in his essay on *God's Country*: "The formula Western (in its most popular version and with little sense of irony or parody) often responds to the history of American expansion and colonialism with reductive typologies, Manichean morality, and neat plot resolutions—all of which Everett's work dramatically eschews."

But Everett is at his deftest with the highly charged issue of race. In *Glyph*, Everett waits until fifty pages into the novel to have Baby Ralph pause his stream of commentary on post-structuralism and abstract-impressionist painting to ask the reader:

*Have you to this point assumed that I am white? In my reading, I discovered
that if a character was black, then he at some point was required to comb his Afro
hairdo, speak on the street using an obvious, ethnically identifiable idiom, live in
a certain part of town, or be called a nigger by someone. White characters . . . did
not seem to need that kind of introduction, or perhaps legitimization, to exist on
the page.*

It's a trick that Everett uses elsewhere in his fiction—obscuring the race of
his characters or, as in *Glyph*, springing it upon readers in a way that forces
them to confront their preconceptions. It can be disorienting, even disturbing. In an essay in *Callaloo*, the writer Madison Smartt Bell recalls coming
to the end of Everett's third novel, *Cutting Lisa*—about a doctor who performs an abortion on his daughter-in-law. Only then did Bell notice Everett's photo on the back of the book. "I . . . thought, before I could stop myself,
'Oh, did it say somewhere those characters are black?'" As it turns out, the
race of the characters isn't mentioned at all.

But Bell's knee-jerk reaction raises what, for Everett, is the greater question: Has popular fiction conditioned us to make European features the default in any work of art? Everett certainly thinks so. "In this culture, readers
assume that if there are no other clues, then the narrator is white," he says.
"That's an assumption no one can make."

It's just one form of what Everett calls the "insidious racism" that infests
the public's response to art. He thinks again of the *New York Times* review
that made a point of mentioning his race. "I get reviews like that all the time
that just don't make sense," he says. "Even if the novel had African American characters, I don't know why it makes a difference that I'm an African
American writer. Reviewers feel they need to say, 'By the way, the writer is
black.' I've never seen, 'By the way, the writer is white.'"

Out of a career's worth of frustration with this apparent double-standard
sprung *erasure* (2001), Everett's best-received book to date—but one he was
somewhat saddened to write. It features an Everett-like protagonist named
Thelonious "Monk" Ellison, a writer of esoteric fiction whose latest effort
has been rejected by seven publishers, the last of whom calls it "too difficult
for the market." Ellison has been told that he should put aside his intellectual
leanings and "settle down to write the true, gritty stories of real black life."

Meanwhile, the runaway bestseller of the moment—breathlessly trum-
peted by an Oprah doppelgänger—is a book titled *We's Lives in Da Ghetto.* Penned by a middle-class Midwesterner, it begins: "My fahvre be gone
since time I's borned and it be just me an' my momma an' my baby brover

Juneboy." Fawning critics praise the book's "real" language and "true to life" characters, while its pandering black author lands a lucrative movie deal.

The scholarly Ellison is incensed by the book's success. In response he dashes off his own expletive-laden ghetto rant: *My Pafology*, written under a pseudonym. (In presenting this novel within the novel, Everett wickedly mimics *Native Son*, Richard Wright's legendary 1940 novel credited with first laying bare the violence, poverty, and injustice of ghetto life.) The fictional author intends *My Pafology* as a broad satire of the book world's persistent appetite for urban stereotypes. To his horror, the slim novella winds up a bestseller and winner of a major literary prize.

In real life—and here's a bitter twist of irony—*erasure* won the Zora Neale Hurston/Richard Wright Foundation Legacy Award in 2002. At the awards ceremony, Everett couldn't resist a bit of sarcasm. Asked by the *Washington Post* what the event meant for African American fiction, he shot back: "I don't know. Have you been to the bookstore lately? Have you seen the 'white fiction' section anywhere?"

Everett says he used to get much angrier at that sort of thing, but he's mellowed a bit. "Maybe it's age"—he's forty-eight—"but what comes along with that is growing tired of it."

Tired of reporters and critics he may be, but tired of writing he clearly is not. The last two years have seen a flood of publications: an absurdist novel (*American Desert*) and a contemporary Western (*Wounded*); a collection of short stories (*damned if i do*); his first volume of poetry (*The Wall*); an introduction to *The Jefferson Bible*, the Founding Father's famous re-edit of the gospels; and an epistolary novel (*A History of the African-American People [Proposed] by Strom Thurmond*).

Upon reading the last—a wicked lampoon of the publishing trade presented as a series of (fictional) letters and memos negotiating the terms of publication of an account, by Strom Thurmond, of the segregationist senator's seminal role in bettering the lives of blacks—one begins to understand why Everett stays far away from the book world's politics and prejudices, instead devoting himself wholeheartedly to his wife, his ranch, his teaching, and his writing.

Uncategorizable Is Still a Category:
An Interview with Percival Everett

Anthony Stewart / 2007

From *Canadian Review of American Studies*, 37.3 (2007), 293–324. Reprinted with permission from University of Toronto Press (www.utpjournals.com). Copyright © *Canadian Review of American Studies/Revue canadienne d'études américaines* 37, no. 3, 2007.

AS: It is my great pleasure to be talking to Percival Everett, the author of fifteen novels, three collections of short stories, a volume of poetry, and a children's book. Professor Everett is distinguished professor of English at the University of Southern California, where he teaches creative writing and critical theory.

So, thank you again for agreeing to do this. One of the aspects of your work that fascinates me most, at least right now, has to do with what looks to me as a contradiction between the reception of your novels. Every review I read is very positive about your work; my students love your work when they encounter it in my classes, invariably for the first time, and, of course, they're always surprised that they've never heard of you before. So, I'm hoping we can talk at least a bit about that.

I said to you when we were chatting yesterday, first of all, that I should admit that I've gotten the impression from published interviews with you that you don't particularly like being interviewed. Is that a fair assumption?
PE: Yes, that's fair. I'm not an antagonistic sort, but I tend to be pretty reserved.

AS: Because you work in an English department, you sort of have a split perspective on the world of literary culture, let's call it, as both an academic and an artist. And this split perspective sometimes appears in your fiction. I have often thought that most artists hate academics or, at least, hate critics, maybe because critics try to limit and pin down the necessarily expansive view of the artist and, in a sense, I'm guilty of such an enterprise in being here and interviewing you. Do you agree with that assessment of critics or, for that matter, of the artist? That is to say, maybe you don't think most artists have an expansive vision.

PE: I don't know whether I think of artists as having an expansive vision. What's interesting about artists usually is that they have a fairly narrow vision, and that's what makes us interested in what they create. I mean, a painter is not trying to paint the whole world. They're just trying to paint a piece of it. If I were trying to write an everyman story, it would be terribly boring and stupid. I'm trying to write an individual story about an individual person, about an individual life, and as far as critics limiting what I can do, they see different things in my work than the things I would see. So, if anything, it makes my understanding of my work expand. Now, it doesn't mean I agree with it, but it also doesn't mean that they're wrong.

AS: That's interesting, because when you think of something, and I want to get back to Ellison in a bit, but when you think of something like *Invisible Man*, one of the things that seems most attractive to a lot of people about *Invisible Man* is, in fact, that the unnamed narrator is characterized often as an everyman figure.

PE: After the fact, certainly, but there was no way for Ellison to work on that thinking of him as an everyman. If he had, then the life would never have emerged as a real one. He has experiences that are unique to that character, but from reading and extrapolation, they become those that we have all experienced, and that's true of any fiction.

AS: I'm thinking of the relationship between, on the one hand, the everyman figure and, on the other hand, the individual. The working title, as you probably know, of Orwell's *Nineteen Eighty-Four* was *The Last Man in Europe*. And so, on the one hand, there's that figure who is worried about being a minority of one, as he says, and worries that the figure who is a minority of one is, by definition, insane. And, on the other hand, if he does not represent something that other people relate to, then, in fact, he does look insane. Or at least non-representative of anything that matters to anybody else.

PE: Yes. That connection is made because we all live individual lives. We look at stories and we supply the extrapolation to the general. If you read a biography or an autobiography, those things have lessons for all of us. They become stories that are more expansive necessarily. This is what we do with stories. Otherwise, we wouldn't be interested in them. But that person liv-

ing her or his life cannot live it thinking, "I'm going to live this for everyone."
Nor are they telling it in that way.

AS: It ties in with another point, which is maybe a more central problem in
the relation between critics and artists, that a lot of critics assume that writers see their own work as sort of an overall project. And I know, from our
brief conversations, you really don't, do you?
PE: Well, I see all the works as fitting together, as an overall project. I'm
writing one big novel.

AS: How do you see it? What is that one big novel about?
PE: I can't tell you that. If I did, I'd have to kill you. But it's constantly growing. These books are in a dialogue with each other. It's a conversation that
I'm having with myself, and the work is having with itself, and I'm having
with the work. It's my way of understanding the world. And that's what it
does for me, personally. Then, once it's outside my experience, who knows
what it does? I can't control what it does, or whether anyone will see it as a
project, or as a literary life.

AS: You did say before that maybe what holds it all together is the line between the signifier and the signified.
PE: Well, philosophically, that's what interests me. Trying to understand
how that line between the meaning that we might intend and the meaning
that we do perceive or receive, how that line at once divides it and holds it
together.

AS: The line of the fraction.
PE: The line of the fraction.

AS: I've said this to students, in fact, that the hyphen between *African* and
American can be seen as a hyphen or as a minus sign.
PE: I love that. That's great.

AS: And I guess the oblique stroke, the slash, in the same way that you're
describing the line between the signifier and the signified, works in the same
way.
PE: Yes. Or it can be a break in the stanza.

AS: As I've mentioned already, my students have thoroughly enjoyed your novels, and when I have given conference papers or lectures on your novels, people have been very quick to ask about other work by you that I might recommend. What three books of yours would you recommend as an introduction to your work? And why these three?

PE: I wish I could take credit for this line. "I love all my children, geniuses and idiots alike." I feel closest to the book I'm working on at the time, and I really divorce myself from the books when I'm done with them. There're some that I haven't read in their entirety after they've been published. In fact, a bunch. I don't think about it. And, I don't know what I think at any given moment, what I will think, or what I have thought, and so to say that one or the other is representative of my work, well, I just feel is being unfair to the work as a whole. I can tell you that *Glyph* was probably the easiest book for me to write.

AS: *Glyph* was the *easiest* book to write?

PE: Yeah. It's the closest to the way I think, and the connections I make. And so, in a way it just kind of came out. Structurally, it was a challenge to make. But it was, for me, not even the most fun, but the easiest.

AS: Because it's a very complicated book!

PE: Then you can imagine what it's like to live inside my head! That's not necessarily a good thing!

AS: Is *Glyph* still your favorite? You had said in another interview, you said two things and this is part of the reason I asked the question. It was an interview at a very specific time and it had to do with giving readings of *erasure*, which you said you hated doing, and you said that you got to a point where you really didn't like the book anymore.

PE: Well, that's true of all the books, though.

AS: But you did say as well that *Glyph* was your favorite.

PE: To read from. It's just easier to read from. Again, it's just the rhythm of my thinking. Also, I can't read line-by-line. I pretty much see the page and I really recite it from memory, and so I change things all the time, and for some reason it's easy for me to memorize those pages, though I can't do it now, but when I look at it, it just kind of comes to me.

AS: Your French translator, Anne-Laure Tissut, has told me about two con-

ferences on your work that she has attended, in Tours and in Grenoble, both
of which you also attended, I think.

PE: Yes.

AS: And I also noticed, a couple of years ago, on a trip to London, that *Glyph*
was just being released in paperback, and it was in pretty much every London bookstore I went into, as usually was *erasure.* That has not been the case
in Canada, certainly, or in the United States, I'm thinking, and so, as I said,
while pretty much every review I've read of your work has been positive,
what do you suppose accounts for your higher profile, or what looks like a
higher profile, in England and in Europe than in North America?

PE: I don't know. I don't think about those things too much. I think they're
more reading cultures than our own. Word of mouth is a different thing in
England because it's such a small country. And in France, there's a love of
books that we just don't have here. Every town has a book festival. French
people like books.

AS: Just what you said about reading cultures, you said this in "Signing to
the Blind," about black writers specifically, "I do not believe that the works
we produce need to be any different; the failing is not in what we show but in
how it is seen. And it is not just white readers, but African American readers
as well who seek to fit our stories to an existent model. It is not seeing with
'white' eyes, it is seeing with 'American' eyes, with brainwashed, automatic,
comfortable, and 'safe' perceptions of reality." And so, on some level, what
you were just saying about French and English reading cultures, which don't
seem to exist in America, at least not to the same extent, I guess that's what
you're getting at in this passage from "Signing to the Blind."

PE: Of course the writer benefits from the fact that more people read. But
I don't know if they, in those countries, escape the same acculturation that
we do. I think often their expectations do mirror ours, or at least their experience with expectations is the same as ours. Their expectations might be
different. And one can't deny that they have a fascination with American
authors often. So, once again, I'm the exotic, which is not exactly a comfortable space to inhabit, but I recognize, I'd be stupid to not recognize, that's
part of the appeal.

AS: And yet, the exoticism seems to work differently there than here, insofar
as there, to the extent that you're the exotic, it seems that that causes people
to read you, and to provide your books in their bookstores, whereas here . . .

PE: Being black in America, you're exotic in certain places and certain times. You're exotic if you're in New York and you're brown and you happen to be a Cheyenne Indian. But if you're black, "you're not exotic, we're used to you." You're exotic in that awful way if you show up at a fancy party and you're the only black person there. But on the street, you're not exotic. And the same would be true of white Americans who wander into a party full of black people. But they're not exotic. They're simply out of place. And that's how it's perceived, by everyone. It's a wonderfully fucked up culture we live in.

AS: The difference between being exotic and being out of place. Being exotic is something that somebody else can put to use. Right? You can sell exoticism in a way that maybe you can't sell being out of place.
PE: Exactly, which is why the easy road for American publishing has been to publish novels about black farmers or inner-city, you know . . .

AS: Slaves.
PE: And slaves. Because these are pictures that are easily commodified. But if it's the black middle class, and it's not so different from someone else, then what's exotic about that?

AS: And, more to the point, what's saleable about that? Well, the hotel I'm staying in provides the *USA Today* every weekday morning.
PE: Oh. A fine newspaper!

AS: I was going to say, it's a nice hotel anyway! And, the *USA Today* has produced a list of twenty-five books that "leave a legacy," as it says. And the two books on the list by African American writers are *Beloved,* by Toni Morrison, and *Waiting to Exhale,* by Terry McMillan. And, the little blurb with the Morrison book has to do with "Morrison's masterpiece," "Pulitzer Prize," "propelled her to Nobel Prize for Literature in 1993," and points out—this is something I did not remember—she is the last American to win it. But the blurb for McMillan says, among other things, "Terry McMillan's groundbreaking novel about black women looking for satisfying relationships was a wake-up call for the publishing industry. Readers of all races were hungry for entertaining stories about African Americans." And it's clear that you don't buy that, do you?
PE: No. And it's a sort of amusing little comment on the culture. I cannot imagine—ever—someone saying that the culture is going to "awaken to the

needs of white women for relationships." Or "the groundbreaking work that exposes white women's needs for satisfying relationships."

AS: It's remarkable to me, and one of the things that I think is really great and really important about your work on some level is that it thematizes that kind of ingrained expectation. The comment that Ralph makes in *Glyph*. It's about page fifty-six into the book where Ralph makes the comment that "up until this point in the book, dear reader, I'm assuming you figured I was white." And, I remember reading *Glyph* for the first time and feeling kind of caught out in a way because . . .
PE: Well, it made you feel like shit.

AS: But I knew what you looked like and yet I found myself also doing that, wondering at least, whether or not Ralph . . .
PE: That's the way we're trained to read. You step in water. Your shoe gets wet. It's not a good thing. It's not a bad thing. It's just a thing. This is the culture in which we live. This is the way we're trained to read. It's not a good thing. It's not a bad thing. But it's a thing. But it doesn't mean it has to remain that way.

AS: And yet at the same time, implicitly at least, the publishing industry seems almost to prefer that it remain that way.
PE: Now, see, that's a bad thing.

AS: But on some level, it's the difference between going into a grocery store, and you're in the canned vegetable aisle and you see cans of peas. And so you know that if you go home with this can that's marked as having peas in it and you open it and it doesn't have peas in it, you have a right to a complaint.
PE: Yes.

AS: And on some level, the publishing industry as a whole, with a few exceptions—namely, the people who publish your work—are willing to say it doesn't always have to be peas. Or, at least, it doesn't always have to be this particular brand of peas. And, who knows, try it, and you may like these as well.
PE: I love your analogy, but no one's going to complain if you open the can and it's diamonds.

AS: And that's been my experience and my students' experience in reading your work.

PE: That's nice of you to say.

AS: Sherman Alexie, in his really enthusiastic introduction to *Watershed*, says of you, ". . . everybody, including other African American writers and scholars, is ignoring him. And I think Everett is being ignored precisely because he is so threatening." Now, especially in light of what we were just talking about, the difference between exoticism and being out of place, I'm wondering what you make of Alexie's comment, and whether or not you see yourself as threatening.

PE: I don't think about stuff like that. I make books. That's all I care to do. What would I be threatening? The stakes are so wonderfully low.

AS: But are they? I mean, after a fashion I can't help speculate, at least, about what North American society might look like if specifically black men were not characterized as invariably, almost by default, occupying one of three positions—athlete, entertainer, or criminal. And if expectations changed that much, it seems to me the stakes could actually be quite high.

PE: Well, I suppose that's true. This is America, and we'd fuck it up somehow! George Bush is president. We're not a bright people. But, of course, what you're saying is true. If we had some ham, we could have ham and eggs. If we had some eggs.

AS: I wonder also how frequently you attend the MLA annual convention. I ask because it comes up in *A History of the African-American People [Proposed] by Strom Thurmond* and it also comes up in *American Desert*. It's just mentioned in passing in both books.

PE: I'll never go.

AS: Have you ever been to the MLA?

PE: Sadly, yes. That was years ago, and I was directing the graduate program at Kentucky and we happened to be hiring, so I went. I actually went because my best friend was chair of the department at the time and we just went together. I have no interest in any kind of conferences, any kind of conferences.

AS: I know what the answer to this is but I'm going to say it anyway. It does

seem to me that if you were to go to the MLA, it would be one of the fastest ways to increase your profile as a writer.
PE: Oh really? Oh no. I wouldn't do it, then.

AS: It's either that or being a feature for Oprah's book club, obviously.
PE: I love the irony in that.

AS: So you've never been asked. Oprah's book club, I mean.
PE: Oh no. After *erasure*? I'm artistically offended by that kind of thing. That anybody can claim to vet art and then feed it to the public seems to me pretentious, portentous, and probably pernicious and vile. And I won't participate in it. When I say I make books, I have an old-fashioned and maybe arcane sense of myself as an artist. And that's all I really want to do. I don't care about fame. I don't want to be famous. I want to be comfortable. I want my family to be comfortable. But I don't need to go to some conference and have people recognize me as the author of a certain book. I'd much rather go and see somebody else recognized as the author of a certain book. That's not why I do this. I do it because it's the artistic life I want.

AS: And I have to say, you hear people say that from time to time, usually very famous people who are doing things to make themselves more famous. I have to say that with you, I actually believe you.
PE: I've been so successful at avoiding fame, up to now.

AS: On that subject, in a way, not being better known actually allows you a certain degree of freedom in your writing, doesn't it?
PE: I have nothing to compare it to. And I like to think that it wouldn't matter at all. That my work wouldn't change, one way or the other.

AS: A lot of commentators refer to your work as "uncategorizable." And it seems to me that the freedom to create on your own terms, which results in this sort of uncategorizable variety in your work, must be aided by not having to "represent" African Americans and just being able to write what Percival Everett is interested in writing.
PE: Well, first of all, I can't represent African Americans. No one can.

AS: But people are put in position to try.
PE: Yes, and you see how the work suffers for that. I don't pretend to rep-

resent anyone but myself. Now, does that mean I don't think that I can possibly be a decent role model for a kid someplace? Well, no. That idea is thrilling to me. But I would think that if I were a really good carpenter, I could be the same role model for that kid. But a carpenter doesn't go to work thinking he's representing anyone when he builds those cabinets.

AS: Orwell seemed to feel quite similarly about his position as a writer and, as I mentioned to you, his tombstone doesn't actually mention even his pseudonym, let alone that he wrote. And he most prided himself, it seems, on being a farmer and somebody who was in touch with the simple things in the world.

PE: Good. Yeah. I think that's wonderful. I hope my tombstone doesn't say "writer." One thing I did like is that the word *uncategorizable* is a category. Which I resent.

AS: On the subject of what you want to write about—when religion appears in your work, as it does from time to time, and I'm thinking of the grace Mr. Reskin tells in *Watershed*, for instance, religion usually looks ridiculous, hilarious, or at least highly contentious.

PE: I'm just reporting the facts.

AS: But one thing, on that subject, and I'm not quibbling with you, but I am quibbling with you, I have noticed that the same verse—Isaiah 38:1 ("Set thine house in order: for thou shalt die, and not live")—appears in three of your novels. It's the epigraph of *Cutting Lisa*, and it's stated in *Watershed*, and also in *American Desert*. I'm wondering why that passage specifically?

PE: Well, it fits in those places. It's less about religion than it's about getting things straight.

AS: Which describes what we're all trying to do, just being here.

PE: Yes.

AS: But I guess it describes your work. But it also describes your work in the way that it describes all of our work, I suppose. Anybody's work.

PE: Right.

AS: What theorists do you tend to teach in your theory classes? And also, I was hoping you could go over briefly what you're doing in your class this term. What you're asking of your students.

PE: Well, recently, the last few years, I've talked a lot about Wittgenstein. And, of course, Wittgenstein isn't a theorist, and for me this isn't as much about critical theory as it's about philosophy and language. The course I teach to the writers here has ranged from a survey of literary theory from the Russian Formalists to deconstruction to a more direct focus on Derrida and Wittgenstein together. I think what I mostly try to teach students is not to be afraid of theory. And I guess I think about a lot of it more like the French. I don't take it all that seriously. American scholars, and I think British as well, become so damned earnest when they start talking about this stuff, as if there is some right answer, and it stops being fun. Half the time, it's fairly clear that Barthes is not serious. And that's what is interesting. When is he serious, when is he not? Why is he not serious? He's having fun. The idea of play becomes really important. There have been classes where I've taught Robert Scholes and we've talked about semiotics. And that's always fascinating. And, certainly, Lacan and Habermas, and people filter in. But basically I'm not teaching this to give them theories as much as I am to demystify the reasons we have them. And to teach them to make fun of it, and I do mean to make fun of it. To ask the question that Wittgenstein would have us ask of any philosophical premise or treatise or statement, which is "What do you mean by that?" And it's just surprising how often that question leads to the falling apart of a philosopher's stance.

AS: The great, almost slapstick moments in *Glyph*, since Barthes is a character in *Glyph* and appears almost as a buffoon when he appears, with his silly, empty background disclaimer whenever he does something that seems odd, "After all, of course, I'm French." That sort of demystification of one of these really central theoretical figures. Somebody mentioned Ionesco among the figures that your work reminds them of. And I wanted to ask you, have you found Samuel Beckett's work an inspiration or influence to yours? I ask because one of my students noticed a Beckett-like quality to some of your dialogue. So I was wondering if Beckett ever comes up, or has come up as an inspiration or an influence for your work.
PE: Well, I love *Waiting for Godot*. And interestingly, I find it to be the most plot-driven literary work I can imagine. And that's the fascinating thing to me about it. But, whether it affects my work, I don't know. Stuff goes in.

AS: I teach it, when I teach *Godot*, as being about progress. Because, as you said about it being plot-driven, people talk about it being circular and nothing happens, and one of the characters actually says that, and, of course, that's not actually true. There are two really key points when they actually learn something in the first act that is applied in the second act.

PE: They also get to the point when they can say that it's circular!

AS: Yes, exactly. Like "uncategorizable," which becomes a category. But I also teach it as a story about love. It's the smallest society that you can have, right? Two people. Me and not-me. And it seems to me what's central and what's most beautiful about *Waiting for Godot* is their relationship and, at a couple of key moments, they decide to cooperate instead of to compete, which is a simple, basic choice that we get when we interact with other people. We can either cooperate or we can compete. And they unrelentingly decide to cooperate.

PE: Or we can focus on the word *pusillanimous*, which is, just that sound, something that you stop and focus on, and it's fascinating to me.

AS: How so?

PE: The basic units of communication. There's really no reason for that word to show up right there. Which makes it an interesting choice of words in that place. I can't believe this is in my head. I haven't thought about *Godot* in so long. But when you come to that word the play stops and it becomes about the sounds. The most basic units of meaning. And to fail to attend to it might be informed by the word itself—cowardly, or whatever. And that's, to me, the moment of genius in the play.

AS: While one way to characterize your work—getting back again to the idea of what is categorizable and what isn't—would be to call a lot of your work "postmodern," for lack of a better way of putting it, you don't play postmodernism in a glib way, as is often one of the criticisms of postmodernism. That there's nothing at stake, and that it's all just play, but play in a bad way. This is especially true of your allusions to Ralph Ellison's work, which, in your work, almost come across as homage. Ellison, the consummate modernist. His work comes up repeatedly in your work. In another interview, you said that you often re-read *Invisible Man*. And I'm wondering what about Ellison's work brings you back to it so frequently, in your reading and in your work?

PE: Well, I like the novel. And to say that I like it is to say that I like a lot of novels, because in the same way that I make playful reference to Ellison in many places, I think there's a failure to see how much he makes reference to Chester Himes, in *If He Hollers Let Him Go.* The entire "battle royal" scene is done in maybe a page—the woman with the flag on her belly, and every-thing—she's painted in Himes's novel. I can't remember her name. She's the welder who accuses Robert of rape. But the description of her, with the red, white, and blue face, is that character. I just happened to land on Ellison as a way for me to accept the fact that I work in a tradition. And it could have been possibly another book. It could have been *Tristram Shandy*. There are different references to *Tristram Shandy* in my work and it's no less impor-tant to me. It's just that those are the ones that are easy to see and the ones that are more fun. Maybe it's postmodern. I don't know what postmodern means. If anything, I'm a modernist. Not that I want to be, but in the new work, in the novel that I've just finished, that's coming out in August, nearly every reference in the book is either to Lewis Carroll or James Joyce. I'd be hard-pressed to find Ellison in there. I'm trying to think. But, of course, he is, because I can't escape that.

AS: Because he's part of the tradition. As is Carroll and as is Joyce.
PE: And Carroll certainly is part of *Glyph*.

AS: If you don't mind my asking, what's the new novel called?
PE: *The Water Cure.*

AS: In Palahniuk's *Lullaby*, there's a description of a water cure, and it's a nurse who starts murdering people on a geriatric ward in a hospital she works at. And she "cures" them, as the novel describes her, by holding their noses closed and pouring water down their throats.
PE: Well, the water cure is what they called the dunking, or the torture, in the Inquisition. If you died during it, then you were cured. "Confess. I am a witch. Okay, we'll kill you. And if you don't confess, you're obviously a witch."

AS: In another interview, you mentioned *The Way of All Flesh* as another book that you go back to. But since one of my principal interests is Ellison, I'll ask you this, too: What in Ellison's work, either in his fiction or his non-fiction, are you critical of?
PE: Critical of? I don't know if it's my place to be critical of anyone's writing. I'm fascinated by the things he writes and thinks, whether I agree with him or not. Any day I might agree or disagree with a lot of stuff in his nonfiction. I don't really walk around remembering a lot of that. I know the novel really well. One thing I'm critical of is that I wanted more work from him. And

that's just a selfish desire. And I think that it's just awful that *Juneteenth* was published. I think an artist should have control over his or her work, and he didn't choose to publish it. I don't mind if it was left archivally for somebody to go look at, I think. But I certainly don't think it should have been published as a novel because his hand didn't get to finish it.

AS: Because, you've mentioned this to me before, since the artist can't control it once it's finished, can't control reception, can't control what happens to it after that, the artist should at least be able to control it until then.
PE: That's why we do this.

AS: One thing that has been brought up to me more than once about your work—came up again at a conference recently—was that the female characters in your novels are not drawn particularly sympathetically, is the argument. This came up at a conference I was at recently when somebody mentioned what she saw as a conflict between Monk Ellison and Juanita Mae Jenkins, for instance, and also Kenya Dunston in *erasure.* What do you make of this?
PE: Well, I think there are people who might read badly. Or at least only count the characters they want to. I think some of my stronger characters are women—Sixbury in *Walk Me to the Distance*; the mother in *erasure*, though she suffers from Alzheimer's, is, I think, sort of the base of his stability. As if men fare any better with me.

AS: A related question is that the more central point—this is as much a statement on my part as anything—but it seems to me that the more central point about your characterization is that most of your characters (whether male or female) are just complex, unsympathetic in some ways and sympathetic in others.
PE: They're all flawed. We read fiction because people are fucked up. That's basically it. We don't read about happy families. We might, but that's a newspaper feature article. We read because there are problems, whether they're overcome or not. That's why we're interested. So, yes, people are complex. People have problems. At some point, in someone's life, things aren't good. And that's why we're interested.

AS: And I was thinking, specifically, of three different things that three different writers have said. Hanif Kureishi makes a point that it's not his job to create virtuous Indian characters and vicious white or British characters.

Rita Dove says that it is not her job as a writer to produce strong, virtuous female characters just to satisfy some sort of ideological program. And, of all people, E. M. Forster, making the statement about his production of *A Passage to India*, indicates that one of the simple things he realized was that both the Indians and the British were just shits.

PE: And it's true. People are people, and they're worse than anybody.

AS: This comes out of the idea that people are people. Monk Ellison, in *erasure*, has a similar experience to one Robert Hawks has in "Alluvial Deposits." And it's something that I don't think he admits to in *Watershed*. Both characters express their sorrow and their embarrassment for underestimating someone based on their superficial preconceptions of them. I know I'm not supposed to ask a writer about similarities in his own life to what he writes, but I can't help wondering, and I can't help thinking of examples from my own life, if you've had a particularly memorable experience in which you have done that?

PE: I've had an abstract one that comes to mind, only because I was talking about it just recently. When my friend Jim Kincaid and I wrote the Thurmond book, I realized, when we started researching Thurmond, that I didn't dislike him as much as I thought I did. Not that I would ever champion him at all. He's a racist asshole, but he became a little more human for me, and he became interesting to me. Became a more rounded flat character. You know, I realized that it wasn't that he hated black people. He just liked white people a lot more. And there's a distinction to be made there.

AS: I have to admit, the distinction is kind of lost on me, just because the effect works out to be the same!

PE: Yes, the effect works out to be the same.

AS: I'm thinking about the Thurmond book. I taught it this past year, and I don't think—because I'm Canadian and my class is Canadian—I don't think my students found the book nearly as amusing as I did. I read the section in the restaurant at the end of the book to a colleague who is in the office next to me, and she laughed to the point where she had tears in her eyes. And so, when you're talking about Thurmond, who's just a cartoon character anyway . . .

PE: He was in life, yes.

AS: In the days after Thurmond's death, Aaron McGruder's cartoon *The*

Boondocks, if you're familiar with it, the main character is a ten-year-old black boy named Huey Freeman, and Huey is reveling as he walks around . . . Huey never smiles. He's a very serious little boy. But in this context he's reveling in the quality of the sunshine and the freshness of the air and the fluffiness of the clouds, all of this inspired for him by the news of Thurmond's death. Especially since you grew up in South Carolina . . . you've sort of answered this, but I'm curious nonetheless . . . do you ever feel anger towards those who might historically (or even contemporarily) hate you because of your own ethnocultural background? I ask this question as a Canadian because, as a black Canadian, I have sometimes found myself marveling at the mixture of what looks like allegiance, on the one hand, and animosity, on the other hand, between many African Americans and the United States, and specifically the American South.

PE: I'm more amused by it than anything. I mean, I think when I was younger, both by feeling and fashion I was angry. But now I really do find it amusing. I'm mostly amused by the importance given to something like Thurmond's death. It just didn't mean that much. First of all, the man's a thousand years old. He died long before his death. But the relationship of black Americans and someone like Thurmond in a state like South Carolina is so complex. It's so fascinating. There are lots of black people who voted repeatedly for Thurmond. They weren't stupid people. Maybe in some ways they'd been seduced, or whatever. A lot of them were, like the white people who voted for Thurmond, simple people. And he was a consummate politician. Here was a guy who took the time to write condolence cards after reading the obituaries in South Carolina papers to every family. In fact, there's a story of an aide going into his office, telling him he was wasting his time doing that. And he just didn't listen to the guy. A couple of years later, a man came up the steps while the aide was standing there with Thurmond, with his whole family, and said, "Thank you for writing us that card two years ago when our son died," or whatever. "No one important had ever done anything like that for us and we'll vote for you forever." There's a weird kind of proletarian beauty to that, that's not dismissible just because he was a racist idiot. There's something interesting about that.

AS: I have to admit, you make a great case. I have a very difficult time grasping that.

PE: It's hard to grasp. But it's fascinating. And so it's difficult to just dismiss a figure like Thurmond. And it's probably more difficult to dismiss him than it is someone like Jesse Helms, just because of the period in which he came up. I don't understand a lot of it. But I am fascinated by it. But obviously I'm not fascinated enough to go and research Thurmond any further.

AS: Several reviews of the Thurmond book at some point will mention that Thurmond is drawn in a quite sympathetic way. I have to say, I don't see that when I read the book.
PE: I find that amazing that anyone would say that. I mean, the man stands on his head and dies at the end of the novel.

AS: What do you suppose they mean?
PE: I don't know. I suppose they're just surprised that he's presented with any kind of kindness in him. Which says more about them than it does about Thurmond or me. And, again, Thurmond isn't important enough for me to vilify him so greatly. He's interesting to me historically and culturally, but he's just kind of a sad man, in many ways, who did have a very full and strangely important American life.

AS: And "American" with all of the inherent contradictions in that word.
PE: Exactly.

AS: Because Thurmond was a real person, more or less, it's more difficult for me to grasp than in the world I work in, which is imagination and metaphor. Because the example that comes to mind has to do with the film *Crash*. There's a moment in *Crash* that, on some level, sums up all of the contradictions that emerge from being black in North America. Matt Dillon, the racist cop, who basically molested Terence Howard's wife in that earlier scene, rescues her from the burning SUV, right before it explodes. And, there's a great moment, after he has gotten her out and she's wrapped in a blanket by other police and she's being led away, and she looks back over her shoulder at him. Nothing's said. And in that moment, what we're basically being told is "nobody is a racist all the time." And on some level, that's the really confusing thing of dealing with racists or racism. Nobody's like that all the time, because we're complex. Even the worst person, on some occasion, is still capable of doing a really good and selfless and noble thing, irrespective of their otherwise bigotries.
PE: Most people. There are some racists who are pretty good at it!

AS: But that's why they stand out. They're anomalous.
PE: And someone like Thurmond, in Edgefield, South Carolina, when he

came back from law school . . . I don't know where he went to law school. He offered people in his community to teach them to read if they would come to his house on Sunday. And people did, and some of them were black, and he was teaching people to read. You know, that's amazing. And if he hadn't been Thurmond, that would be something we would say, "This was a really great person who did this." So it is very confusing. And again, interestingly . . . I honestly don't know if this is true of Thurmond in his private dealings . . . there's apparently no instance of anybody ever hearing Thurmond say "nigger." Now he might have said "nigras." But no one ever heard him say that. And I come back to that very strange distinction between liking white people better and hating black people. It's a weird, weird American thing.

AS: And on that subject, I think one of my favorites of your short stories is "The Appropriation of Cultures," from *damned if i do*, where Daniel Barkley takes back the rebel flag by calling it, among other things, the "Black Power" flag and buys a used pickup truck with the flag across the back of the cab and starts driving it around Columbia, South Carolina, where he attends university. We've been talking about this a bit, but I still want to pursue it. Is this story about the prospect of progressive change, is it about the law of un-intended consequences, or is it, as we've been discussing, about the bizarre and contradictory nature of life in the South?

PE: Well, I'm not so optimistic as to think things can change, but I do think that the symbols can be taken. In the same way that white people take slap-ping five. Or when you hear a used-car salesman rapping his deal on televi-sion. And it takes the power out of those things. It defuses those things. So, it's about the possibility of defusing symbols just by embracing them. But again, I don't know what I was thinking when I wrote the story.

AS: But the idea of taking back symbols, especially in the way you were describing. This is something Ellison actually reveled in. Ellison liked the idea of black people getting whiter and white people getting blacker. And he saw that as central to being American. I think it's very peculiar to Ellison. When Ellison used the word *American*, as opposed to the way you use it, for instance, Ellison sees it as hopeful and optimistic and syncretic, and all of these great, productive things. You see it inherently, and so do I, as some-thing problematic and contradictory.

PE: Well, Ellison's experience is formed, really, pre-Civil Rights, pre-Viet-nam, pre-Watergate. And *Invisible Man* comes out after that "unifying victory" over the Nazis, over the Fascists. For us, that's wonderfully naïve, amazingly naïve. But again, we have the benefit of time, after his thinking. And in that naïve way of thinking, just the thinking of meeting in the middle ground and forgetting differences as a way to become closer, is, well, it's insane.

AS: And you said you couldn't think of anything you were critical of him for!
PE: But that would be a little like criticizing him for the cut of his suit, given when he lived.

AS: I find, especially teaching his work alongside yours, one of the things that I point out to my students and one of the things that I really get fixed on when I teach Ellison's work, is a tone of earnestness in his work that you don't have in yours, and I've said to my students it's the difference between being born in 1914 and being born in 1956. That there's a safety in your confidence, a confidence in your personhood, to put it as awkwardly as I can think, that Ellison doesn't have, even all the time that Ellison spends in his nonfiction arguing against having to argue that he is a person. Again, it gets back to the notion of "uncategorizable" being a category. Even as he is arguing, really quite stridently at times, about not having to make an argument about being a person, he is, nevertheless, backing into making an argument about his being a person.
PE: And it's because of his arguments that I get to assume this position of some ease.

AS: And on the subject of ease, some of your work, and here I'm thinking specifically of *erasure, Glyph, American Desert, A History of the African-American People [Proposed] by Strom Thurmond*, and your introduction to *The Jefferson Bible*—they cut pretty close to various bones. The publishing industry, the literary academy, and a couple of important American political figures, and they come in for some very pointed satire in these books. Do you ever worry about biting any hands that might be feeding you (particularly the academy and the publishing industry)? Or is that just part of the fun of writing fiction?
PE: I never think about audience at all. I just think about trying to be as truthful as I can to my experience and the culture.

AS: We've talked about that you work on your own terms, and I think that's one of the really hopeful and inspiring things that I get from your work, especially because most of the conferences I go to I'm the only black presenter, and so if I say "race" once in the title and then don't mention it again, it's still going to come up in questions. Is part of your own terms publishing photos of yourself on your books? After all, you could have your novels published as Thomas Pynchon does, for instance, without any pictures at all. And I'm also thinking about the picture of you on I think it's the British edition of *erasure*, where you are posed to look like a sixties black radical.

PE: Oh, no, that was on the American one, and I chose that on purpose because it worked with the book. But the other times, the publisher wanted a photograph . . . and that's why they're all snapshots . . . here's a photograph. I don't care. They like having photographs. They can have a photograph. And then it becomes a kind of ironic thing for me. Sure, have at it. This'll confuse you. But in that particular photograph, I was twenty-two years old in that photograph, and a completely different person. And so I liked the whole thing in *erasure* of his becoming a completely different person.

AS: This idea of having been a completely different person is sort of fascinating and really portentous in a way because I find myself thinking that one of the many problems of being exotic or out of place is that you don't get to change. Because you know all of this, because you know that those expectations, even if it's the ironizing of giving snapshots because they want pictures, that still at least acknowledges the relationship between expectation and audience.

PE: Oh, sure. I acknowledge the relationship. I just don't think about audience when I'm working. And I don't deny the importance of audience. The work isn't complete until somebody reads it. The circuit of art isn't complete until it is received. And meaning's not made until that happens. But my job is not that. My job is making it.

AS: And that's again, getting back to where we started, the difference between being a critic and being an artist, for instance. Your job and my job are different. I recently had a conversation about you in preparation for this interview, and I said that your sometime reluctance to talk about race was based on your knowing that if you open the door unproblematically to a willingness to discuss race, then that would be what all people would ask you about. And, while I recognize that I've asked you more than one question to do with race, I'm wondering if you think that evaluation is a reasonably accurate one? In other words, isn't the main thing for you to be able to discuss race on your own terms, or not, to the extent that's possible?

PE: I discuss race when it comes up.

AS: What do you mean?

PE: Well, listen, I live in a particular place at a particular time. Even though, I, with every anthropologist in the world since the beginning of the twentieth century, dismissed race as a category, it is a bogus yet *real* category that's perpetuated by the culture. By everyone in the culture, and I'd be stupid to ignore that. I'd also be crazy to not think that I can go out and by virtue of my skin color get into a lot of trouble in certain parts of the world, and especially in this country. So I can't dismiss that. But at the same time, when I wake up and I brush my teeth in the morning, my thought is not, "Hey! I'm not white!" And I think that astounds a lot of white people. Race comes up sometimes. Sometimes it does not. Sometimes I'll bring it up. One of my favorite scenes is in *If He Hollers Let Him Go*, where Robert . . . I think his last name is Jones . . . is sitting behind the wheel of his car and this white guy looks at him as the white man's walking across the street. He looks at him and reminds Robert Jones he's black. And just the invasion of that look. And that's when it comes up. Or when it's a beautiful day. It's sunny. You're walking around with Barbara, your partner, and you're in Vermont. You've made a short trip down to the U.S. and you walk into an antique store, and you're strolling around, and it's a wonderful time. You're laughing at something you've just remembered, and you turn a corner and there's a pyramid of mammy jars. And it kind of hurts your feelings, a little bit. And you think, "In this store, do they know that this is offensive?" And then it becomes complex again, because these things exist in the world. People collect everything. And you have to think the person who built this pyramid of mammy jars wasn't thinking, "Boy, I'm going to get these black people when they come in here." They like mammy jars. And, now, it's problematic that they would like these things! But nonetheless, they do.

AS: I often think that when I see white lawn jockeys on people's lawns.

PE: Yes. As if painting them white changes what they are.

AS: Well, not just lawn jockeys. But white lawn jockeys or the little boy fishing, or whatever it's going to be. Those don't offend me, except, obviously, for my sense of taste. But they don't offend me racially in the way that the *black* lawn jockey or the little *black* boy fishing off the same imaginary pier, somebody's front step, normally, offends me. And I have wondered, getting back to what you said about that's when it gets complex, that's when I've said to myself, "Okay. What's bothering me when the kid's black and what is different about what's bothering me when the kid's white?"

PE: Yes. Because one, somebody knows and they're throwing it in your face. The other, they must be so stupid that you're not worried about them. To have a lawn jockey painted white means you're so out of touch with this world that you don't know the history of the thing that you're choosing to put in your yard. That, and added to that the taste thing, and you see this and you think, "I want to have this in my yard." That's a dismissible person.

AS: I have said to more than one person about your work (and I've said it in classes I've taught on your work), that if you were white, you'd be Thomas Pynchon, someone well-known for challenging and complex fiction, and not as an anomalous black writer who—for some unknown reason—doesn't write principally about race. I'm wondering what you think of that.
PE: That might or might not be true. It's just a thing.

AS: You have tended to present solitary characters at the center of your novels. And here I'm thinking of somebody like John Livesey from *Cutting Lisa*, as the still point in a turning world, so to speak. Why do you suppose you are so interested in figures who thrive and find meaning in isolation? And I ask that especially because of what you've said about the cooperative enterprise of finding meaning in terms of art, that a book isn't complete until somebody reads it. But a lot of your protagonists actually seem to find meaning on some level by making a gesture of isolation or a movement away from the societies they live in.
PE: Well, writing is solitary work. Regardless of what completes the circuit, it's done alone. There are lots of gregarious and social writers who spend a lot of time with people. I don't. My experience with the world is pretty much solitary. I'd much prefer to be with a horse than a pack of people. And so that's part of my experience coming into the work. It's how I understand the world.

AS: This is related: You say, in fact, in "Signing to the Blind," that *Walk Me to the Distance*, for instance, is about alienation. And it seems that alienation is an undercurrent in a lot of your work. In fact, it would be fair to say that a lot of your books are about love, violence, and suffering, and on top of that varying degrees of redemption. And based on what you just said, these are expressions of how you experience the world.
PE: Everything in the work is, and that's the frightening thing about writing fiction, is what's in there is something that I can find in me. Good and bad. And when you start realizing that as an artist, as a person in the world, all

of this stuff is coming from one source, it's a sobering thought. But as far as what the works mean about love and suffering, I don't know.

AS: Your relationship with your work is, I find, very interesting. It's consistent with what you've said about having no interest in being famous as such. You seem to stand, not in awe, but you do seem to stand in a humble, subordinate position to your work. That is to say, you create the work, but you don't seem to characterize the work as creating a more important Percival Everett.
PE: I don't know how it could.

AS: Well, you live in Los Angeles, for goodness' sake. Los Angeles is central to that circuit of production. At the Lakers' game I was at on Sunday, the reason the people applauded when Tobey Maguire was shown, in part, was that they just finished showing on the same screen the trailers to *Spiderman 3*. All those people who are applauding aren't applauding him because they all know him and think that Tobey Maguire's a great guy.
PE: I suppose. That's something that can be available. But how can that change me as an artist, unless I choose to write the same book over and over again, that has garnered me that kind of attention?

AS: *erasure 2*!
PE: *erasure 2*, yeah, or the prequel. And I would much rather be interested in my life and in my artistic life than have anybody know me or recognize me. That's not going to do anything for my understanding of the world except fuck me up in some terribly uninteresting way. Now, if doing that would make horses listen to me more. Then that's useful! If the horse said, "Ah, this is Percival Everett. I think I'll do a side-pass."

AS: Regarding the terms of your presentation to your readership: I'm wondering if you prefer small presses? Akashic Press, for instance, that published *A History of the African-American People* and *The Jefferson Bible by Thomas Jefferson*, for which you wrote a really great introduction—they characterize themselves on their website as contributing to "the reverse gentrification of the literary world."
PE: I've never seen their website.

AS: I looked them up, for this purpose. Getting back to the original question: Do you prefer working with small presses?

PE: In some ways, yes. The only difference is you don't get large advances and you get to deal with smart literary people at small presses. That hasn't always been the case, and it's not that many people in larger houses are dumb, but a lot of the decisions are now generated by market. I have the great fortune of having Fiona McCrae at Graywolf as my editor. She is my editor. That's how I think of her. And I like being at Graywolf. I don't know if "small" characterizes them anymore. It's an independent publisher, a non-profit publisher. Ironically, they're under more pressure to turn a profit than for-profit publishers, but I've never had a talk with them about marketing. I don't want to talk about marketing. I don't know anything about marketing. Nothing could bore me more than marketing. I want to talk about books. And that's what we talk about. When she reads my work, it's great that she gets it. I love that. But she wants to make it the best book she can make it, and so edits it seriously. Albeit I do a lot of self-editing, so there's not a lot that she does. But she's done far more than anyone in any large house has ever done as far as understanding the work and trying to understand the work. So, that means a lot to me.

AS: Now this is a question about market, on some level, but from a very specific and somewhat selfish perspective. Do you ever consider going with a larger, let's say for-profit, press, if only to safeguard the availability of your books, especially in North America?
PE: Small presses keep the books in print longer. Large houses remainder books so rapidly it makes your head spin.

AS: I did not know that. I ask this, though, because this past year for the class that I was teaching, I couldn't get a copy of *Glyph*. And I still have yet to find a copy of *The Body of Martin Aguilera.*
PE: Well, that was a very small press that went out of business. That was Owl Creek Press and they folded years ago. *Glyph* was published in 1999, and I just don't think there are any books left. And there's been no paper-back of it here. So I think they just sold out of their run.

AS: That is a cause for concern, although this explains some things to me. I am what you could call a very motivated consumer, at least where your books are concerned. The idea that some of them are becoming more and more difficult to get also means that it becomes all the more difficult some-times to teach certain books of yours. So that's why I ask the question . . . This gets back to the question of tradition. There are moments in your books where the only thing I can call it is slapstick appears in your work. Some of the names that you give characters, Stan Dutch (which to me ended up sounding like "stay in touch," I don't know if it was supposed to, but it did), and the scene in "Age Would Be That Does," when Rosendo does not realize that the cougar that he and Mauricio are searching for is actually sitting next to him, and he speaks to the cougar without turning his head. And, of course, Barthes's repeated explanation . . .

PE: His pratfalls.

AS: Yes, his pratfalls. And his "And, of course, I'm French" remark. But your books also work a lot like puzzles in that they tempt people to look up or read meaning into some of the names that appear in your novels. For instance, I mentioned Lucius Brockway before. And he's mentioned only once in *American Desert*, but if you haven't read *Invisible Man*, then that's a reference that you're going to miss. And I guess I'm wondering if you approach your novels or at least conceive of your novels, again, as you're working, with a kind of, let's call it a pedagogical purpose? Insofar as your books will sometimes make gestures to the tradition that you're describing.

PE: Pedagogical impulse? No. I have to work with these things every day, all day long. So I have fun sometimes. People buy CDs and they listen to them a thousand times. They read a book and they give it away. And I feel, well, you ought to read it a thousand times. And every time you read it you'll get something different and new. The same way you hear an oboe you hadn't heard before in a piece. I'm never trying to get someone to go read something else. I mean, it's great if they do, but I do expect a reader to study. If you want to get through the layers of meaning, it requires some work. The works I love to read require that and that's the kind of literature I'm interested in, and that's what I make. The difference between literary fiction and genre fiction is this, and I tell my students this all the time. I have nothing against John Grisham novels. I'll use him as an example. They're probably fine novels. I personally have no interest in reading courtroom . . . whatever they are. But, I have looked at them. You will never re-read a John Grisham novel, unless you forget everything that's happened. You will not walk into the room with the book open to your friend and say, "Listen to this paragraph." You will not pull the book from your shelf on a day when you're bored and open it to a random page and just read a couple of pages. You do that with *Moby-Dick*. You do that with *Invisible Man*. And you do it because these are different kinds of works. And I'd like to make that kind of work.

AS: That's a really good answer. How did the introduction to *The Jefferson Bible* come about? Did Akashic ask you . . .
PE: Yes, they just asked me.

AS: And why did they ask you? I ask the question because of the difference between Strom Thurmond and what you said about Thurmond as a character who is, harmless is too strong a word, but on some level, he's difficult to take seriously. And you make the point in the introduction that there's a lot of credit that still has to go to Thomas Jefferson—Monticello, the University of Virginia, etc., framer of the Constitution. These things matter. And so, the trajectory between those two figures is just kind of interesting to me. And so that's why I ask the question, because your dialogue with Jefferson is hysterically funny but it's also really pointed. I mean there are passages in there where Jefferson ends up coming across looking kind of stupid or mean-spirited.
PE: As he would have. They were doing a series of books with things written by presidents, and I knew of the *Jefferson Bible* and I asked to do that. It was either that or George Bush and they aren't going to get to him for a while.

AS: But you did!
PE: Yes, I did!

AS: Your point about how everything seems to have evolved except American presidents. When I said parts of it are pointed. I mean, being critical of Bush is sort of like shooting fish in a barrel. I don't enjoy doing it, although a lot of people I know do. Maybe I would more if I was an American citizen. But I'm not, so I figure it's like beating up on any of my C students. I just don't really take any fun in that.
PE: You think he's a C student?

AS: Well, yeah, rightly or wrongly. Maybe I grade more easily than you do! But at the same time, with somebody like Jefferson, somebody who matters, you do get a sense of a lack of evolution, right? The idea that giraffes' necks are getting slightly longer, but actually the other way, a diminution in presidents over the course of time, which is kind of sad, in a strange way.
PE: But American. And now we "dispire" to be president of the United States!

AS: Speaking of role models! It reminds me of something Chris Rock said about Marion Berry and he was saying how one of the things that Berry's legal problems did was to confuse the idea for kids about what they can aspire to. You know, their parents telling them, "Don't do crack. Don't do crack. Nobody who's ever done crack has amounted to anything." And the kids' response could be, "Well, I could be mayor!"
PE: I like that.

AS: He was booed for it, actually, when he delivered the line. I just thought it was funny.
PE: I like the fact that he was booed and I like the line.

AS: We talked about this but can you tell me a bit about USC's Neighborhood Academic Initiative program?
PE: I don't know a lot about it, to tell the truth. It's a program that identifies middle-school students in the neighborhood, South Central Los Angeles, and gives them the opportunity to participate in a tutoring program. If they stay with the program through high school and are then admitted to USC, they attend for free. And it's a beautiful program. I don't know really if it's affected the relationship of the university with the neighborhood, how many people actually walk around knowing about it. But it's affected the lives of these kids really profoundly.

AS: When you told me about that it's really stayed with me. I think it's a great idea and it strikes me as the sort of program that more universities could emulate.
PE: I would love to see that.

AS: Especially because universities are always telling us about all the progressive things that they mean to do. That they'll eventually get to. Is there any writer whom you study or plan to study?
PE: I study everybody.

AS: If you could imagine yourself writing a scholarly book on a writer.
PE: You see, I always think of works. I never think of writers. I think of individual books. And I'm trying to think what book I would use today. Today it might be Kurt Vonnegut's *Breakfast of Champions*. But I only say that to say something helpful to you to answer the question. I never think of writers. In fact, I always draw blanks about writers' names. I remember books.

AS: That's a better answer than you think, as much as anything else, because it draws my attention to something that I experienced in talking to a friend of mine, who is a documentary filmmaker. And he and I would talk from time to time about what he was doing, but I hadn't seen the film, and so I was thinking about what he was doing in the way that we do. I was translating it into the world I work in, which is a relatively flat, some would argue almost sterile, world. And then at some point I saw his film, the film that he was working on. It's called *Race Is a Four-Letter Word*, and it's a fascinating documentary, and he appears in it at a number of points, and it's sort of about him, but it's sort of not about him. And there was a reception after the film, and I sort of half-acknowledged and half-apologized to him that up until this point I didn't really know what he was talking about. I didn't really get what he was talking about because, in that way that we're all limited, I could only understand him from my own perspective, from my own working perspective. And the sorts of things that you've said to me, for me create that same feeling that I right now am working on your work. But when I tell people what I'm doing, I say "I'm working on Percival Everett." It's a metonymy. I'm working on you. But I'm not working on you, am I? And what you said draws my attention to that. Because when I first started reading your work, somebody said, and I don't remember who it was, but somebody said, "Well, you should interview him." And my first reaction, if you want the truth, was, "Well, why would I do that?"

PE: And that's back to the fame thing. The works are what matter. I mean, I appreciate that you want to get a better understanding of them by talking to me, though you know by now that I believe that you're not going to get a better understanding of *anything* by talking to me! But I appreciate the attention to the work, your misguided attempt to understand them notwithstanding.

AS: Right. But I think I appreciate that more clearly than I did, and so there's a lot to be said for that. I'm going to ask you this anyway, even though it doesn't actually follow. But, if you could ask one writer one question, which writer would you ask, and what would the question be?

PE: I'd ask Tom Wolfe, "What's with the suit?"

AS: That's not bad! And finally, what do you hope people get from your work?

PE: That's a really good question. Because I have nothing to tell anyone. I hope that they experience something. That in reading the work, it opens this world or their world to them in a way that hasn't been available before. And not even on the level of changing anyone, just making thinking available that moment. I want to confuse someone. And if possible have them, on some level, whether it's fun or irritating, find some enjoyment in that confusion. By *enjoyment*, I mean that in the very technical sense.

AS: For what it's worth, that may be the moment of coalescence between what you do and what I do. In the classroom, I think, at its best, that's what happens. That there isn't a bristling or a withdrawal from that sense of confusion, but that it becomes a constructive thing.

PE: In the classroom, the last thing I want students to think is that I have something to tell them. I really want them to think they're allowing me to discover the moment and the work. And unfortunately, with the book, I turn it loose and I don't get to share those things. But that's what I hope for.

AS: That's great. And again, thank you very much for doing this.

Interview with Percival Everett

Barbara DeMarco-Barrett and Marrie Stone / 2007

Transcript of "Writers on Writing" program, KUCI-FM (UC-Irvine), 12 December 2007. Printed by permission of Barbara DeMarco-Barrett and Marrie Stone.

MS: Percival Everett is the author of twenty books, including *Wounded, erasure,* and *Glyph.* His writing has earned him the PEN/USA 2006 Literary Award for his novel *Wounded,* the Academy of Arts and Letters Award for Literature and the Hurston/Wright Legacy Award for his novel *erasure,* the PEN/Oakland-Josephine Miles Award for Excellence in Literature for his story collection *Big Picture,* and the New American Writing Award for his novel *Zulus.* He served as a judge for, among others, the 1997 National Book Award for Fiction and the PEN/Faulkner Award for Fiction in 1991. He is also a distinguished professor of English at USC. His latest novel, *The Water Cure,* is available now and published by Graywolf. Percival, welcome.
PE: Thank you.

MS: Thanks for coming on. There's so much to talk about and parse through in this latest novel, and I really had the clichéd onion sort of experience with this book, of pulling back layer on layer, and it just revealed more layers. So I was hoping first we could talk about the novel, the basic premise of the book, and where the idea for it originated.
PE: I'm not very good at drawing my ideas for novels. It's all magic to me, but it originated with my embarrassment about our involvement in this war and especially the Abu Ghraib and like instances of torture.

MS: It's interesting to me that we're discussing this book the day after a frenzy of media attention on the topic of waterboarding and its endorsement and authorized use as a technique by the government. For those that don't know the practice—I can't imagine there are too many out there—but for those that don't perhaps you could give us a little definition of what it entails. And there are a lot of wonderful political asides in here in the book, and I'm interested in your use of this technique throughout the book and the reasoning behind it. But let's start with waterboarding and what it entails.

PE: Waterboarding—often known, as the novel says, as the water cure—is really a very old practice of human beings. We're bad to each other, and this is from the Inquisition, much like the Inquisition. Now, what it entails is inclining a victim—I think people who employ the practice like to use the word *subject*—inclining the victim and tying him to a board, and inclining him so that his head is lower than his loft, wrapping the face in a burlap sack or some other kind of material, and then dripping water onto that so that the person feels like he's drowning.

MS: And so you said the main motivation was watching what was happening during this war and applying that to the book. So that was the driving force behind coming to write the novel?

PE: Well, that's difficult to say. There are all sorts of reasons why one starts writing something as crazy as a novel. That's one of the things that surfaced for me quite clearly, but there are many things at work. That's among them.

MS: The other huge component of this novel is philosophy, and I came to think of this as sort of philosophical fiction, sort of a very dark, very twisted sort of *Sophie's World*. Tell me about your interest in philosophy and how it drives your fiction and whether or not it's prevalent in other novels you've written.

PE: I suppose it is in some. It's more an interest of the character of this novel. I certainly study and read many subjects, philosophy among them, and I know as little about philosophy as I do about the others. It's an exploration for me, but here in this novel it's a way for the character to address a lot of different concerns of his own.

MS: I was particularly drawn in to a lot of the identity theory that you talked about and the concept of whether or not an individual exists throughout time when they're made up of different experiences and, you know, different cells and whether or not they are the same person from the beginning to the end. As you grappled with that when you were writing, did you feel like you came to a conclusion in your own mind, and did you feel like your characters came to a conclusion on that?

PE: The fascinating thing about writing novels or making any art is I think I know something when I start, and what I'm taught by the time I reach the end is that I didn't know *that*. It's a way of exposing my own ignorance and teaching me that knowing less is better. I enjoy the opportunity to study, so that's there for me but I really can't say that I know any more about identity, except for the fact that it's clear to me that, in writing novels and entering a different world each time, my own life becomes fragmented in that way and so there's an identity crisis that goes on like that. And not necessarily in a negative way but sometimes a positive way where I feel close to the identity that I'm assuming in a way that I understand it better.

MS: That kind of brings me to another question which was, it was hard to live in this world for the two or three days I lived in it, and I was wondering what that experience was like for you on the deep level—that you have to enter a dark place like this—and what that does to you over the course of a year or two years, however long it takes you to write it? How it shapes your world view to be and live in such a dark place for so long.

PE: There are many days I didn't want to go to work and it felt bad, and it's scary stuff. But it would be easy to overplay the emotional or psychological significance of working on fiction. It's much like someone who works in an emergency room. You see a lot of awful things, but you really can't take them home with you or you'd never go back.

MS: The *Washington Post* has called you "one of the most adventurously experimental of modern American novelists," and according to the *Boston Globe* you're "literature's NASCAR champion going flat out, nearly avoiding one seemingly inevitable crash only to steer straight for the next." I'm wondering when you're writing at this level and in this way so close to the edge, what are the principles that guide your decisions? When do you know you're on safe enough ground, and when do you sense perhaps that you've gone off?

PE: Well, I never think about audience, for one thing. And those are very nice comments about my work, and what they're coded as and what they mean is I don't sell a lot of books. I don't think about anything except the work. I just make the novel I'm going to make. And as with any experiment, at times it can go badly. But that's the exciting thing about making art, and that's really all I'm interested in doing. I don't really care about satisfying anyone—and this is probably a bad thing to say—but my own artistic need at the time.

BDM-B: Percival, you're an instructor at USC, and I'm so curious how you teach writing, especially if you're dealing with students who are very interested in, say, commercial fiction and if you teach any differently those writers of commercial fiction as opposed to, say, literary fiction.

PE: I don't have any students who really write genre or pop fiction. There's certainly literary fiction that's more commercial than mine, and I like to think that I can recognize when someone's doing it well. I don't expect students to write like me or have interests similar to mine. I try to help them, and I think all of my colleagues do, with their own particular brand of writing. I cannot help someone with genre fiction; I just don't know enough about it. If someone comes in writing a romance novel, maybe on a sentence level I can say, "This reads badly," but even there I don't know enough about the form to say anything. It's not a knock on romance novels; it's just I don't know enough about it to help you. And in that way we don't really look toward students who are writing that kind of fiction. I think learning to write literary, and maybe more difficult, fiction—less formula-based fiction—will help you if you want to write other kinds of fiction. But I don't think the reverse is true.

BDM-B: Along those lines, when you are teaching, how does teaching inform your own work, or does it?

PE: As far as my work, I'm around energetic young people who infuse me with some energy and desire to go back to work. That's the most important part. It's an artistic and intellectual stew that it's nice to be around. Finally, I do tell my students, as I believe pretty strongly, that this is a solitary activity, and the best thing you can do is get away from writers and just go do it.

MS: The other thing I liked about this novel, you had a lot of drawings in the book. Several drawings that are interspersed throughout the novel, mostly a picture of what emerges over time as a cat, that begins as a single line on a page; the book is written in fragments and it over time emerges. I thought of this as another commentary on perhaps wanting to communicate outside of language. I was thinking of the cat and its symbolic significance. But I thought maybe you could talk about the drawings for a moment and how they serve the novel.

PE: Again, it's something that the character that I conceived does and how he understands his own world. I think we communicate in many different ways, and obviously drawing is one of them. Though I put a lot of thought in on whether to include the drawings, I don't think it's fair for me to comment on the work, on what the presence of the drawings means. That's there, and all meaning in any work is something I stay out of completely. That's the reader's job.

MS: And within that, and in writing in fragments, and every fragment having its different texture, was the placement and structure of this—putting it together—how difficult was that for you and how difficult was it to juxtapose the fragments against each other?

PE: Well this is difficult for me because I didn't write a chronological story or even conceive it chronologically and then shuffle the scenes. I wanted it to truly be a non sequitur, and so I went to work on each section independently, and they are in the order that they were written. I think maybe I moved one section at the end of it, but aside from that, this is how it was constructed. I referred to it in our house as a physics experiment for a long time, because it remained sixty-eight pages for weeks, no matter how much I wrote. It kept getting heavier without becoming longer, so that I had to use a dolly to move those sixty-eight pages. But finally it did burst open and started to become a novel.

MS: I'm curious about structure, and in terms of your novels, do you know the structure before you begin or does the work tell you as you get into it what it's going to be?

PE: I personally can't start working on a novel until I see its shape. I wish I could articulate what I mean better than simply that. I have a feeling about the way the novel will appear sentence-wise, paragraph-wise, section-wise, but then the novel begins to speak for itself. As you know, nothing can get you lost faster than a map, so you have to reflect upon and look at the terrain and figure out where you are in spite of the fact that you have reference points.

MS: I was also curious about the cover, because the cover shows a man who's bound and whatnot, and to me he looked more like the captor that was described in the story and certainly not at all like the man who was being held in the basement. And I was curious whether you were happy with the cover, whether it was an ironic play on who really was being held captive here, or if you had no involvement in that whatsoever.

PE: I was given choices about the cover, and I tend to be fairly bad about these things. Once I finish writing the book I really have little feeling for it. I do like the ironic part of that; the person on the cover is darker, as you would expect the main character to be, and it creates that, but I can't take responsibility or credit for the cover. They offered me these choices and I said I liked this one the best, and they agreed. But I have to admit that once I'm done with the book it's very difficult for me to generate a lot of enthusiasm about it.

MS: Do you have any last-minute comments? Most of our listeners are writers themselves. Do you have any last-minute advice or things you tell your own students when they're embarking down the path?

PE: Marry money. Which I didn't do so I . . . (laughs). No. People ask for advice for two reasons: One is to accept it and have someone to blame, and the other is to ignore it. And so I don't give advice. I do find with this book especially, that in our culture—and this something that I think all writers need to at least adjust with themselves so they can relax on it—readership seems to be very literal-minded now, and so some of the reaction I heard about *The Water Cure* is, not because it's anti-Bush—I don't know why anyone would knock that—apparently there are some who can't read a figure as insignificant as George Bush as a significant metaphor for the ills of our present society. That's the thing I've noticed so far. Otherwise just try to read and write and try to stay away from other writers.

MS: Percival, thanks for taking the time to be with us.
PE: Thank you very much.

How We Mean: An Interview
with Percival Everett

Andrew Medlin and Trevor Gore / 2008

From *The Pinch* (U of Memphis), 29.2 (Fall 2009), 95–100. Interview conducted in February 2008. Reprinted with permission of *The Pinch*.

Percival Everett is the author of more than twenty books. He has received, among other awards, the PEN/USA Literary Award (2006–2007), the Hurston/Wright Legacy Award for *erasure* (2002), and the Literature Award from the American Academy of Arts and Letters (2003). His most recent novel, *The Water Cure*, was published by Graywolf Press. He teaches creative writing at the University of Southern California.

This interview was conducted by Andrew Medlin and Trevor Gore and transcribed by Matthew Peters as part of the 2007/2008 River City Writers Series at the University of Memphis.

Q: You've been known to take issue with critics and academics who label writers as too "contemporary" or "experimental." How do you feel about that?

PE: The only reason I have problems with being called an "experimental novelist" is that I don't know what that means. When you do an experiment, you try to see what makes something work, and I think any time you step away from a novel or any work, you have to wonder, how is this functioning? How does this mean something in the world? It's a terrifying and beautiful idea that you can put together sounds and have them mean something to somebody, but when you release those sounds you can't control what they're going to mean to that somebody. My wife comes home with a new haircut and I say, "Gee, I like your new haircut," and that means something completely different than if I wait three hours and say the same words delivered the same way. So, that's meaning, and how we mean is fascinating.

Q: Your novel *The Water Cure* is composed of short, non-linear segments. What informed your selection of structure for this book?

PE: It wasn't a matter of selection. Every work comes differently and I don't really know at the time how I'm creating it. There's a thing that we all do that I'm constantly exploring. It's how our brain assembles stories so that no matter what you write and no matter what order the words go in, people reorganize the words to make some sense of it. I can't control what sense anyone is going to make of any story. That's a very freeing concept. I simply play with the story enough so that I think the reader will have some fun reconstructing it. That's the way stories come to us in life—the way the world comes to us—and that's what I was trying to do with *The Water Cure.* We never get a narrative running in front of us. We're bombarded with stimuli and we create the narrative, and that's what I wanted this book to do. The reader would be bombarded with the thoughts of this man and then create his narrative.

Q: How do you come to the storylines themselves?

PE: Storylines also come to me in different ways. Sometimes it will start with a chunk of a story and other times it will all come at once. But I can't start any work until I have a shape and it comes to me. It sounds like I'm speaking about magic, and I am. You think that you start with a blank piece of paper and end up with a story. That's magic and I never want to forget that part of it. Sure, it's hard work and all, but there's something magical that happens. I can't explain it and I don't want to explain it.

I have a novel called *American Desert*, and it's about a guy whose head is chopped off in a car accident in the beginning. He sits up at his funeral with his head sewn back on and that's the beginning of the novel. It's a love story. It came to me when I was driving home one night. I thought I had a novel brewing, but I didn't know. I was still living on a ranch, and my exit off the freeway was Theodore Street. I get migraines and I had a really bad headache. I remember thinking, If I could only chop my head off I would feel so much better. I drove under the Theodore Street sign and the novel came to me. The character's name is Theodore Street. I can't explain what I mean by "it came to me," but all of sudden I was working on a novel.

Q: How does a writer make short, non-linear segments such as those in The *Water Cure* work?

PE: With this book, I didn't want to write a straight chronological story and then merely shuffle everything so it was out of order and in smaller segments. Each section was written in a non sequitur fashion as a piece, and the book appears in the order that these things were actually written. I imagined this character and how his tortured brain might work.

As for how you make the segments work, you can't ask yourself that question while you're working on it, because you don't know what it's going to do until you finish. It's a bit of a push of faith, but you have to stay with it and get to the end. Then you can look back to see what it's doing, if it works, and you can fiddle with the sections. I don't ever want to feel so bound to a conventional narration of the story that I can't interfere with it. That's why I enjoy teaching undergraduates more than graduates.

Q: Why is that?

PE: Because they're nuts. They will literally try anything. If I say, "Why write it like that? Why not write the story as a list?" they get all excited. I had a so-called "experimental workshop" where I said, "I don't want to read anything I've ever read before. You don't have to write this on paper, but make me a story." One woman wrote a story on cubes that fit into each other and you had to read it by turning them around. I had a student write a story where the character was the story and some of the pages were crumpled and you had to go through it. In another story you had to read the scenes in certain locations in the neighborhood of the campus. We walked about two or three miles during the workshop period to the location, and it was amazing, because reading it there in front of the grocery store with certain things being described affected how we received the story. We really learned how stories work. I learned a lot from my students that semester and that's what's kind of thrilling about it.

Q: Would you say that they are more willing to engage with nontraditional ideas about writing?

PE: Yeah, and that's what I'm trying to shake out of my graduate students. I had a course like that with them last year where—my classes are very small—there were four graduate students and myself. The students had to vet their proposals for an experiment. They wrote a really conventional story, and then offered a proposal of how they were going to make it different.

But we had to approve, so they had to pitch this to us like we were producers and they were pitching a movie. They came in and told us what they wanted to do, and we would say, "No, that sucks. Who's going to give you money for that?" You know, that kind of thing. One student's story started as a fairy tale, which became a huge blog. In the blog, a fictional woman was writing a fictional story, so it was a fiction within a fiction, and there were comments that she had constructed that were a part of it, but there was also room for the reader's comments. It was really nice and the exercise freed her fiction immensely.

Q: How does the use of other artistic mediums, such as playing guitar and painting, inform your writing process?

PE: Well, I'm not certain that it does, except that it's another way to express myself that I have to explore. I think that any kind of relief from writing fiction is good. Any time you can express yourself and make some art that doesn't require sitting there staring at words for hours can only help you. I find it freeing to work in different forms, but in the same way that I find hiking, climbing, and working with animals freeing. It's just a way to have your mind work a different way.

Q: How about studying the classics? In several of your books you draw significantly on Greek mythology. What sort of impact does that have on your work?

PE: It probably affects it in ways that I don't recognize, but mostly I see it in my notions of the construction of story and how stories work together in a web of tales. In mythology there are connections that may not be direct, but if you go down a few steps and move over, you realize that the story of Ariadne is somehow connected to the story of Dionysus in a way you hadn't thought. It informs my work a great deal, but mostly my structure. Yes, structurally, it's been a huge influence.

Q: Is research a large part of your process? Is it something you set out to do?

PE: Ninety percent of my work is research. I only write books because it allows me to study. I can go out and learn about something I didn't know, and then promptly forget it, but still I love finding out about the world.

I have a novel, *Watershed*, which is about a hydrologist. I didn't know anything about hydrology. So I read twenty-five or twenty-six texts on geomorphology and hydrology and went out with a hydrologist in Wyoming to do some stream studies before I wrote a word. I wanted to be able to write and sound like a hydrologist without sounding like someone who had read twenty-six books on geomorphology and hydrology. That required me to know enough to stop speaking about hydrology and start thinking about it. It's like learning a language. When I finally started working on the novel, I actually drew topographical maps of an imagined watershed in northern

Colorado and wrote hydrologic reports about that watershed. I was imagining myself doing the research that the character from my novel was doing. One or two of the hydrologic reports actually became a part of the novel. All of the rest was simply me finding this character's internal space. I had to do all of that studying just to get the character.

Q: With research being such an important part of your process, do autobiographical events ever get into your books?

PE: There's a scene in *Watershed* that actually happened to me, but I don't consider it autobiographical. The character goes into a Native American church. I went to a few meetings there, and I've eaten the peyote every time and nothing ever happens to me—I'm really upset about that. But, the first time I went was with a man named Abraham Spotted Owl. The teepee was set up in his backyard, and in the novel there's a huge description of the clearing of the area. We're sitting there in this meeting and the peyote comes around. I had asked Abraham before the meeting, "Should I take the medicine?" And he said, "Yes, I've seen many visions taking the medicine," and I said, "Well, of course you have, you're drugged."

I sit down in the teepee and then had to stay up all night, which is apparently not hard for me. As we're sitting there waiting for the medicine, they begin to sing. Arapaho songs don't have lyrics. They're chanting a phrase, but it's not lyrics and it's played on a drum filled with water. The drummers drink through the skin of the drum and they find this tone. It's one tone and they sing. So, I'm listening and I'm sitting between Abraham and this big guy named Hiram and I hear chanting. "Happybirthdayhappybirthday," and I think *Wow I haven't even taken the medicine and I'm creating words for the song.* They're singing "Happy Birthday." And I look over at Hiram and he says, "It's my birthday."

After I ate the medicine, I sat there waiting, looking at the fire, and listening to the songs thinking at any second I'm going to see a little station wagon of coyotes come driving around. Nothing happens. I look over at Abraham and his eyes are saucers. His pupils are completely dilated, and he looks at me and I know that he's seeing all sorts of things, but I'm seeing nothing. The morning comes, and I walk out. In the novel the character walks out of the meeting not having seen a vision or having hallucinated and he tells this to the old man who's invited him into the meeting, and the old man says to him, How do you know? And so for all I know I'm still sitting in that teepee, and I'm just imagining that I'm here. That was research, but I didn't even know it then. I was just living there. I didn't know then that novel was coming to me.

Q: You're working on a piece, how do you know when you've done as much as you can and it's finally publishable?

PE: I don't ask whether something is publishable. All I think about is the work and the life that the work has. It's very easy for me to sit here having been published and talk about how unimportant that is but—it *is* unimportant. There are so many beautiful works of fiction that have not been published and so many truly shitty works of fiction that have been. And that's good to remember away from work. When you go to your art, it's just the art. The only thing I can ever think of is how the story is speaking to me. I never think about a reader other than myself when I'm at work.

Writing fiction is a beautiful, cleansing thing. I think I know something about the world when I start a book. I'm pretty quickly disabused of that notion in the middle of it, and by the time I finish a book, I realize that a lot of what I thought I knew was wrong—and that I know very little. After twenty books, I know a lot less than most people. I'm well on my way to knowing nothing at all, which is my goal.

An Interview with Percival Everett

Thea Brown / 2009

From *The L Magazine*, 3 February 2009. Reprinted with permission of *The L Magazine*.

Percival Everett is an award-winning author of nearly twenty books of fiction and poetry—including the acclaimed novels *Wounded* and *erasure*—as well as a painter, scholar, and teacher. His most recent book of poetry, *Abstraktion und Einfühlung*—a title borrowed from an essay by the early-twentieth-century art critic Wilhelm Worringer—was released earlier this year by Akashic. Everett recently took the time to email with *The L* to talk about his new collection.

TB: When and how did you first become acquainted with Wilhelm Worringer's theory of "abstract" art and "realist" art? Did it immediately strike you as something you wanted to investigate creatively?

PE: I was aware of Worringer long before I knew anything about his thinking about primitive art and, by extension, abstract art. I struggled through the work with my limited knowledge of German and my English/German dictionary. I didn't know when I was studying it that I would use it in any way.

TB: How did you decide to borrow the title of his essay for your collection?

PE: I love the title. Also, just like Worringer's work, it captures my thoughts about the nature of so-called non-representational art.

TB: How do you see your work in this collection in relation to Worringer's ideas? Were you aiming to demonstrate a process—a move from the realist to the abstract?

PE: I don't imagine this work in relation to Worringer. I appreciate the importance of his work in art history and criticism, but I cannot pretend to understand it so thoroughly as to exploit it. I am demonstrating a process, but it's perhaps more a fiction of my making.

TB: So, what level of comfort do you think an artist should or needs to have with another's work in order to engage with it creatively?
PE: One needs to understand well enough to play. I think one can neither worship nor despise the source, but there has to be a genuine engagement with the work. It may well be that my understanding is incorrect.

TB: As I understand it, Worringer's essay was primarily concerned with visual art. When you were working on your poems for this collection did you seek out (or happen to find) congruencies between the creative methods of your painting and your writing?
PE: I was very much attempting to employ my method of painting in writing these poems. I love non-representational art. I avoid the term abstract, because I find it misleading. I think non-representational paintings are realistic, perhaps more realistic than literal representations.

TB: How so?
PE: For me non-representational work is an extension of my vision rather than a replication of my perception.

TB: The distinction between realist and non-representational art seems as immediately applicable to poetry as to visual art. How do you think it might or does play out with fiction?
PE: In fiction it seems nearly impossible to be fully non-representational, whatever that "fully" means. I want very much to make a story or novel like one of my paintings.

TB: Meaning non-representational, or at least partially so?
PE: Yes.

TB: How did you choose the lines from the second sections of these poems to pull out and focus on for the third sections? Could you describe how you transformed those lines into their new incarnations?
PE: I wish I could explain my method. Actually, if I could explain it, I probably wouldn't share it.

TB: Fair enough! Your poems seem to point to a struggle, when dealing with art, to fully appreciate the work (i.e., glean all its implications, both literal and figurative) without losing meaning through over-analysis. Do you think there's a line that can be crossed with analysis in that sense?

PE: There is always a struggle, with every word, with every line, with every slash of paint. There is no line that cannot be blurred or crossed.

The Tipping Poitier

Drew Toal / 2009

Originally printed in *Time Out New York*, 28 May 2009. Reprinted with permission.

In the '60s, amid civil unrest and race riots in places such as Watts and Detroit, there was still one black man whom white Americans would almost trust to date their daughter—onscreen, at least. That man was Sidney Poitier, who played Dr. John Wade Prentice in the 1967 interracial-romance film *Guess Who's Coming to Dinner*. Author Percival Everett uses the actor as a jumping-off point in his biting and hilarious new novel *I Am Not Sidney Poitier*. Here, Everett explores the meaning of Poitier and the reasons that white America found him so unthreatening.

"I was interested in the icon of the palatable black man in the '60s or '70s," Everett, fifty-two, tells *TONY* from his home in Los Angeles, where he lives with his wife, novelist-memoirist Danzy Senna. He was drawn to Poitier because he is such a complicated figure—politically outspoken in public, and eminently "safe" onscreen ("Heaven forbid he should actually have sex in a movie," Everett deadpans). To research the book, the author spent many hours watching old Poitier films. "I knew them so well that I was just tired of them," he says of the experience. "It was then that I could own them."

You don't have to get far in *I Am Not Sidney Poitier* to realize that Everett has made the subject entirely his own. The book opens in 1968, as a woman, last name Poitier, names her newborn son Not Sidney. Though obviously eccentric, she has the foresight to invest every penny she has in Ted Turner's nascent media company. So when she dies, the teenage Not Sidney inherits an obscene amount of money. Turner, who over the years has become aware of the non-famous Poitier family, sees Not Sidney as something of a good-luck charm, despite the linguistic troubles his name causes ("What's your name?" "Not Sidney." "I know you're not Sidney, but what's your name?"). Turner promptly adopts the orphan and brings him to Atlanta.

At this point, Not Sidney—who already bears an uncanny physical resemblance to Sidney Poitier—embarks on an Odyssean journey that will see him molested by his high-school teacher Miss Hancock, visit with his light-skinned girlfriend's bigoted parents in D.C., and have a run-in with the redneck police department of Smuteye, Alabama, where he helps a group of nuns build their church (and finds himself embroiled in a local murder).

Everett has always displayed a formidable imagination (his novel *Glyph* concerns a hyperintelligent infant), and his absurdist sense of humor has garnered him a reputation as an "experimental" writer. It's easy to see why the author calls that a "bullshit label": Though his work defies literary norms, it's fun to read and comes laced with sturdy social commentary. In his novel *erasure*, a black author accused of writing "too white" ultimately finds financial success by writing a parody of ghetto fiction.

With its deeply layered hero—who is both like and not like the movie star he's named (or not named) after—*I Am Not Sidney Poitier* continues some of *erasure*'s themes: Both books are interested in race and the expectations that surround it. And like its predecessor, *I Am Not Sidney* tackles its subjects with satirical gusto. In one of the most evocative scenes in the book—a riff on the Poitier classic *Guess Who's Coming to Dinner*—Not Sidney is brought by his light-skinned girlfriend to her parents' house. There, our hero skillfully deals with his girlfriend's callow father, her horny sister, and extended bouts of squirm-inducing awkwardness.

This scene borders on farce, but Everett notes that it's not any more ludicrous than the film itself. "Why would this forty-year-old, really handsome, internationally acclaimed physician be interested in this twenty-year-old idiot, who just happens to be blond?" the author says about the film. In Everett's version, Not Sidney loses all interest in being acceptable, and the results are pure comic gold.

Even as he brings in issues of bigotry, sexual molestation, and murder, Everett effortlessly entertains. "If you can get someone's attention and confidence by having them laugh, you can pretty much do with them what you will," he says. And so he does. Unlike Poitier's screen image, Everett's book is a less polite beast, and refuses to be shy about speaking its mind.

The Bat Segundo Show #295
(Percival Everett)

Edward Champion / 2009

Transcript of interview recorded on 8 July 2009. Published by permission of Edward Champion (www.edrants.com).

EC: I'm here with Percival Everett, who is most recently the author of *I Am Not Sidney Poitier*. Percival, how are you doing?
PE: Fine, thank you for having me.

EC: I should point out that I've written an unpublished novel called "I Am Not Percival Everett," but let's talk about yours, which is probably better.
PE: You're just bragging. (Laughs.)

EC: No, I'm not. Actually, I should probably start off because you use so many opportunities in this book to make jokes about the character's name, and I wanted to ask you. What are your comedic roots? What did you read or listen to to be so obsessed? Because there are so many jokes in relation to both Not Sidney Poitier but also a number of internal metaphors and puns throughout this book that I absolutely loved. And I've always been curious—it's in all of your work—what you listen to and what you've written about to get this obsession with language and this obsession with puns. Like, for example, there's "My name is Jeremiah Cheeseboro and I'm a man of the cloth." I mean, very funny stuff. So how did this come about? What happened here?
PE: I love names. In fact, I have to tell you the best name that I now know—I don't know if I should tell you this, though, because this name does exist in the world. I don't know this person, but I had a friend who encountered this name. L-E-hyphen-A. Now how would you pronounce that?

EC: "Laya" or something.
PE: It's "Ladasha."

EC: Aha!
PE: It's genius. I absolutely love it, though I prefer the pronunciation "Lahy-phena." (Laughs.) But the name thing, I'm just fascinated by—what would you call it in philosophy—rigid designators. What makes a name a name? What's the name of a name? What we do when we name something. Identity.

EC: Literal misunderstandings then . . .
PE: Literal misunderstandings and desired misunderstandings.

EC: So you'd say half of your creative process is literally a literal misunderstanding? (Both laugh.)
PE: Most of my creative process is a literal misunderstanding. I just love the fact that not only can we mean stuff but that we can mean something that we don't intend.

EC: Well, in the case of this, since you are drawing from many real-life figures—Ted Turner, of course, Sidney Poitier . . .
PE: Is there really a Ted Turner?

EC: Well, I'm gonna get into this; that's part of the question. But also even the very funny riff on the Bill Cosby speech. And I'm curious. I should point out that I recently read Richard Powers's forthcoming novel *Generosity*, which deals with the notion of what a novel really is and what ideas and characters really are. And I'm very curious to put this question to you. To what degree do you need reality to start from? And to what degree do you feel the need to be faithful to reality? Or even faithful to real-life figures? Or can you accept a Percival Everett figure in this who also happens to have a book called *erasure*?
PE: First, I owe nothing to reality. But, of course, for any novel to work, in spite of my disregard, maybe even disdain, for facts, truth is important. If it's not true, you can't stay with it. You won't believe it. And there is no work. But truth has nothing to do with reality or facts.

EC: But you do have names to draw from not just in this book, but also in your previous books: Thomas Jefferson, Strom Thurmond. You're a guy who likes real names like this. And so, as such, I have to ask, is it just a constant influx of information from newspapers that is your creative muse? Where do you stop from reality and start with the inventive process? Or the misunderstandings we're talking about?

PE: Well, it depends on the work obviously. I read all the time, so it just depends on what comes to me. Some figures just present themselves as too alluring to ignore. I mean, how could I go through my life and not at some point address Strom Thurmond? (Laughs.)

EC: Yeah, sure. But it can't just be a simple impulse, because obviously . . .
PE: Why not? (Laughs.)

EC: Because I'm thinking when you set out to write a novel—and I'm not you obviously—but when you set out to find a concept or put your finger on something, is it a matter of instinctively knowing that that's something to riff on or something to expand further? Or do you have any plan like this?
PE: Sometimes I don't have a plan. Sometimes it's hit and miss, trial and error, feast or famine—all of those duals. (Laughs.) I don't know. For me, the way novels come is magic. And I only question it so much.

EC: Magic. Magic through pure work? You're a prolific guy.
PE: Yeah, I suppose. It won't get done unless I do it, so I try to do it. And I don't stress.

EC: You don't stress? Never stressed at all?
PE: Try not to be. There's no reason to get upset about anything, especially work. And then it happens. And the more it happens, the less stressed I become.

EC: I know that Robert Birnbaum interviewed you. And you said to him that you don't pay attention to the business of the publishing industry at all. That you just essentially write in an almost insolated vacuum. And I'm just curious if you feel that your art is possibly truer by keeping yourself insulated from any kind of obligation to sell or obligation to top another book or to improve upon another book. What is your relationship to your own work that would cause you to keep going if you feel no stress? Or does this no-stress scenario come from complete prolificity here and a complete work ethic?
PE: I make books. I don't understand business. I don't care about business. I

don't make a lot of money. But I make enough money that I'm happy. I make enough money that I can make the next book. And that's all that I want to do is make art. As long as I can do it . . .

EC: But in terms of readership, do you care about the reader at all?
PE: (Laughs.) No. (Laughs again.) I can't please everyone obviously. And I've written books about literary theory and deconstruction and Dionysus. I'm obviously not a guy with my thumb on the pulse of American popular culture. What am I supposed to do? I'm not . . . I don't write commercial successes. And if I could, you would see one on the shelf tomorrow. (Laughs.) But I have no interest in it.

EC: But you are entertaining in the prose, as we suggested earlier, with these names and with these literal misunderstandings and with the puns and the poetry—which is, I would argue, more comedic than dramatic. As such, there is at least some impulse to entertain. So where does that impulse come from? Is it just from the no stress, I'll just go ahead and . . .
PE: Well I like to play. And I find the world and the work amusing. And I would love to think that if any reader came to my work, if one ventured into the role of Dionysus that I've created, that it would in fact be funny for any reader in some way. In the same way that I have a novel, *The Water Cure*, that I'm told has funny places. But for me, it's just terribly depressing.

EC: So it seems to me that the amount of "funny" that a reader may attach to one of your books has no bearing to your own particular personal feelings. Wherefore then does the prism exist? Because if we understand a book to essentially be a prism between author and reader, what is the nature of your communication through that prism? Is it just the book, or . . .
PE: Well, the language is fantastic. I mean, if you find a note in the gutter it can mean something to you and it could have been nonsense to the person who wrote it. Once I let a book go, I have to let it go. I can't control what it does. I can't control what it means. I might have some intentions. But really, who gives a damn about what I meant? And again I can't affect it in any way. That's the beauty of doing this. That's why I do it. That's the exciting part of making a novel. It's that I have no idea what it's going to mean. I can entertain moments of vanity when I'm writing it saying, "This is not exactly what I mean." And, of course, I have to do that to create a whole work. But at the end of the process, I'm the mother bear kicking the cub out of the den and saying, "You have to go find your own food."

EC: Do you even want to know what it means?

PE: Oh, I love hearing what other people find in it. They often tell me more than I understand about what the work means. And I always take credit for it.

EC: But if people are imparting their own particular meaning, have you ever had a scenario in which you've heard someone's explanation—I'm sure— and said, "How could you have possibly come up with this? Because that's clearly not what I intended." Or have you essentially divorced yourself from the notion of authorial intention entirely?

PE: Well, I think I might well have. The words that you just supplied to me, but with a different inflection. Mine is, "WOW, how could you have come up with that?" And I really am thrilled that they did. I'm never dismayed by it, just always somewhat amazed by it. In a good way, even if it's really far afield and even if it makes me look like an ass. It's interesting.

EC: But this element of surprise that comes with reader response, so to speak, I'm curious how you keep yourself in a state of constant surprise. I'm also curious about these false starts that you alluded to earlier and how it ties in to this expectation within yourself or possibly the reader. Or maybe we can just keep it on you.

PE: Well, the book's not all that important. It's what the book does and what meaning gets made out of it. And that's what I'm interested in. I really have very little affection for a book once I'm done with it. I love the process. I think I know something when I start a work. And then by the end of it, I realize, well, I didn't know much at all. And after this many books, I know a lot less than anybody I know. At least my friends tell me. (Laughs.)

EC: Well, to what degree do you try to become better with each book? Or do you even care about becoming better? Is it just simply an act for you?

PE: Well, I do try to become better. I can't articulate what that comes to a lot. I try to become smarter about my play with language. And that doesn't mean more pyrotechnics. And often that means a novel like *Wounded*, where I found myself writing what I consider to be one of my more experimental novels, though everyone thinks it's really mimetic and a really realistic text. And to me it's about as strange as or stranger than anything I've written.

EC: This actually leads me to ask you also about, in this book in particular—

but it's in many of your other books—there's this tendency to have extremely outlandish, gargantuan figures. Such as everybody in Peckerwood County, who seem to come across as these extraordinarily one-dimensional characters. And yet at the same time, you do have, with the Cheeseboro scenario that I had mentioned, a lot of embedded metaphors, or rather more subdued metaphors, within the actual sentence itself. And I'm curious how you wrangle both of these forms of description and metaphor: the outlandish that's there in situation vs. the subtleties of the actual sentence. And sometimes the subtlety of the actual décor and the landscape and all that. Do you have any ground rules that you've set to establish how much something will be heightened vs. how subdued it might be on a basic sentence level?

PE: There are no rules. I don't believe in any rules when it comes to fiction. In fact, if I can make you believe it, then it's fair game. Probably when I'm working, if I can make myself believe it, then it's fair game. Because I don't know what you're going to believe. And it depends on the work. A novel like *Not Sidney*, where much of it is more a novel of ideas and the narrator is of a certain sort, can make bizarre perceptions or representations of the world and have the one-dimensional Peckerwood County. Whereas in other works, that simply wouldn't work. So the work talks to me. The most important part of the story is the story. And I can't impose my feelings or my desire to write a certain kind of thing that day on it.

EC: But in identifying *Not Sidney* as a novel of ideas, I would argue—and this is when we get into needless taxonomic arguments.

PE: (Laughs.)

EC: But I should point out that you are essentially saying, "Well, this is a novel of ideas, and maybe the story itself won't matter on some basic entertainment level . . ."

PE: Oh no, the story still matters.

EC: Okay. But I'm curious how committed you are to this idea of the novel of ideas. If it's entirely a construct, should we believe in it entirely? Or should we believe in the ideas?

PE: Well, if I've done it right, you should believe in it entirely. And superimposed upon this is the narrator's concept of this being a story of ideas. But you can't have—and this is not a rule—but for me I cannot have a novel where the story is secondary to anything. The world has to exist. So I have to make it, and I have to make it believable. How I do that can vary and come across in any different number of trajectories or strategies or whatever.

EC: But if the world exists, does it exist through the story or does it exist through a topography that you establish and advance a la Nabokov?
PE: From work to work that's going to vary.

EC: But in terms of the building of the house, surely there are some commonalities here in terms of coming up with a structure. Or devising where you're going to stem from. So I'm curious . . .
PE: Well, there are. But I believe these are constraints from my own experience, and there's a part of me that wants to find out if I don't have to dig a foundation to have a stable house. (Laughs.) You know, my graduate students come to me and ask me if I can teach them to write a novel. And my answer is very simple: No, I cannot. Because I don't know how to write a novel. I've written a lot of novels. By all evidence, I will write another novel. But every time I do it, I have no idea what I'm doing. And that's probably why I will do it again, because that's fun. (Laughs.)

EC: Working without a net.
PE: It's fun not knowing how this thing is going to go up.

EC: I'm curious if you delight in—if we're talking about the novel as a house, which possibly is too generalist an identification . . .
PE: Nah. It just depends where it goes. (Laughs.)

EC: Well, if we establish the house so that you can actually run the wrecking ball through the house . . .
PE: You bet.

EC: For you, artistic creation is a form of gleeful self-sabotage?
PE: It can be. Well, certainly if you consider disrupting all that you know about the world a kind of sabotage, yes. And I suppose in some ways that can be. If you're walking through life and you think you understand something, and you purposely take that away, then you feel sort of shaken up—your world view. And for some people that can be a sort of sabotage. For me, I consider that a necessary component of living.

EC: Well, the common figures and the common variables between our world and the world in your books ... I'm curious if in some sense this world that you're talking about, this gleeful anarchy that we're establishing here, whether this is your way of essentially creating an alternative to the world that we presently exist in, just for your own benefit and for the benefit of any reader who might latch upon and understand or come up with some entirely different understanding. Is this how your creative output serves or functions in any sense? Or is this something in which—again, we're getting into this notion of what the author here gets out of it and what the reader here gets out of it. But let's talk about what the author gets out of this.

PE: Well, first of all, I think that every one of my novels is a complete and accurate representation of the world around me. I don't believe they're abstract at all. I think they're concrete and absolutely real. So I don't find that they're at odds in any way with how I think the world is or how anyone else thinks the world is. The only constraints that are sometimes annoying, or maybe it's just one constraint, is the fact that the world I create has to exist between the covers of the book. And so when a reader comes to it, or even when I come to it again, I am immediately reminded of the artifice of the work and so taken away from the fact that it is in fact a reality that is around me.

EC: This makes me wonder how many copies of your own books you keep in the house. Because they may remind you of the fact that the world stops here. (Laughs.)

PE: No. They're around in various languages and uses. You know, things to level tables and whatever. (Laughs.) They don't remind me much of anything. Again, once I'm done with them, I don't have a lot of affection for them. I love all of my children, geniuses and idiots alike, which is a great line that comes from ... I think it's Walter Van Tilburg Clark who said that. I'd love to take credit for it. But it's really true. Maybe they're just reminders that I can do it again, having some books around.

EC: Going back to this notion of the novel as being world-building, a subject that doesn't get bandied about too much in literary fiction but more so in speculative fiction, particularly in recent years. It's actually become somewhat of a controversy. But this does lead me to wonder how much your own particular, subjective view, as represented through these characters, as represented through these perspectives, really is the world, the accurate world, the real world that you're insisting that these books are.

PE: Yes. (Laughs.)

EC: Can you expand upon that, sir? (Laughs.)

PE: Well, necessarily. That is necessarily true. It comes out of one consciousness—mine. I cannot be anyone else. Even were I to muster up the courage to have a multiple-personality disorder (laughs), the characters I would create, existing in the world, would come out of my subjective understanding of what those characters should be.

EC: Then how do you subvert that subjective understanding?

PE: You just accept that it's there. And again, for me, making fun of what I think and myself is often a way of creating distance between my own concerns and petty grievances with the world, or desires in it, with the world I'm trying to create.

EC: Let's go from anarchy to limitations. I'm curious if you impose any particular limitations on your writing or you work within a particular structure in order to poke through the wall in any sense. Or, going back to this earlier question of subverting your subjective view, I'm curious if limitations work in any way along these lines and likewise if how you give yourself permission to . . . I mean, if it's all anarchy, you need some kind of wall to bust your head against. So I'm curious what that process is like for you in terms of giving yourself permission. Is it just not having any stress? Your stuff is playful, but at the same time it can also be very punchy. And so I'm not entirely certain if I completely buy your no-stress viewpoint. I mean, there has to be some sort of edifice to smack your head against.

PE: Well, there are plenty of things that are sources of cultural, social, scientific, and philosophical angst for me. There's lots of stuff that interests me, lots of stuff that I'm unhappy with, lots of stuff that I want to explore, but as I say that, it's all stuff I want to do. So it's not stressful in that way. Also, I don't know if I would call my approach to the world anarchy. There's nothing sadder than an anarchist when all structure goes away. Because they have nothing to do. (Laughs.) And anarchy itself becomes a structure of resistance. So in a way it's self-contradictory. So I hesitate to adopt the anarchist model of the way I approach fiction. But I will approach, will take on the playground mentality about it. I'm tired of the swing. I'm gonna go do the slide now. (Laughs.) That's why they put it here.

EC: Got it. A big erector set exists at the ranch.

PE: Exactly. (Laughs.)

EC: I've actually been wanting to ask you about something for a while. It's in this book again. We have Not Sidney's obligation to build the church. We have of course Reverend Golightly, Jeffrey's Thanksgiving incantation "May your stuffing be tasty . . ."

PE: You're going to ask me about religion, aren't you?

EC: I am going to ask you about religion. How did you know? (Both laugh.) When you did interviews for *American Desert*, your novel about twenty-seven developmentally disabled Christs running around Area 51, you insisted that you were an apath, that you don't care if there's a God or not. But religiosity, yet again in this book. I'm curious as to what the . . .

PE: It's fun. (Laughs.) I don't know. I can't care. I can't be any more truthful than that about that question. However, in the world, this stuff is funny. (Laughs.) And I can't ignore it. And interesting often. I mean, the idea of someone speaking in tongues; to me, it's amazing. I don't find that particularly funny. But I am truly amazed by it. And I'm sure that it exists on various levels from the faking to the hypnotic. (Laughs.) So yeah, I'm interested in that . . . I mean, people are interesting.

EC: Is it possible that your attraction to religion in the form of putting religion into your narrative has much to do with the fact that this is an ideological system or even an intricate system that just simply is something that you have no desire to ken and you want to figure out why people are attracted mothlike to this flame, or what's the . . .

PE: Well, I wonder the same thing about psychics for horses. (Laughs.) People hire people to come and tell them what their horses are thinking. People will believe lots of things, and I'm fascinated by it.

EC: How much do you believe in something your character may believe as you're writing about the particular character? I'm curious. Because you have to be an actor in some sense. You have to get involved inside a character's head or inside a character's heart. It can sometimes be a tricky place. So do you feel that perhaps this notion of inhabiting allows you to learn about something like religion or something like these kinds of things that make people so interesting?

PE: Certainly I hope so. And I'd be disingenuous if I didn't say that I haven't had a character who is experiencing any kind of religious fervor. And that doesn't mean that I won't. But my own take on the world is often shaped by my raving atheist grandfather. (Laughs.) And so I accept that part of myself.

And I see that it shows up in the work. Just moving through the world, I don't care much. But I haven't been able to divorce my own disinterest in life from religion from most of my characters.

EC: I also wanted to ask you about laundry lists. There's a laundry list of terms: "a sitting duck, a dead duck, a chump, easy pickings, a babe in the woods." We sometimes get this Percival laundry list moment. And I'm curious if it extends not so much from language, but more from this notion of obsession or variables. Again, it goes back to the Thanksgiving incantation as well that we were talking about earlier. But there's often this series of words or phrases that will sometimes crop up within a particular moment. And I'm curious why that is exactly.

PE: I wish I could tell you. You know, I'm just an old cowboy. (Laughs.) I just write books. If I can find a strategy that works for me, I will employ it at that particular time. Why those particular words, for some reason, or those phrases? They appeal to me and they work, so . . .

EC: Well, to what degree do you resist language? Obviously you're a language guy. But at the same time, if you're dealing with a story, a story doesn't always match up to language tricks or even playful sentences.

PE: I don't believe in any kind of language tricks at all. The language is the language for the story, and anything that doesn't fit it will just be this huge— what is it? The gorilla in the room. (Laughs.) Unless I want to call attention to the language for some purpose, the language is subservient to the story.

EC: Even with one moment? There's a lovely sentence: "At the diner, I found Diana Frump shaking her apple rump under her white waitress dress to country music on the jukebox." Big internal rhyme there. So I must ask why that moment announces itself. It's a very nice sentence. It's a playful sentence. But you could have just had it serve the story. It calls attention to the sentence.

PE: Well, except that she's listening to music. And the rhyme is one that you might find in an R&B song on a jukebox.

EC: That's possible. However, I should also point out the "old man who is tossing pieces of bone onto the wrinkled surface of a spread out blanket." Well, wait a minute here. We've got some playfulness here with the old, with the wrinkled, and the bone. So he could have thrown something else besides bone, and I think it was just a . . .

PE: Except that people read bones. So I really wasn't trying to do anything terribly special with language. (Laughs.)

EC: Okay. But it is bone, wrinkled, and old man. So it's the symmetry there going on.
PE: Yeah, that worked out. And to some extent, you just have to let that stuff happen organically. Most times, if I think that you're doing that—well, if I think that I'm doing that, I just stop. It's true of all metaphor. In fact, I have a line that I have not used yet, but I use it for my students, and it is: "He sat there doing nothing, like a bad simile."

EC: This is interesting. To what extent can you be aware of, say, internal rhyme or internal metaphor cropping up? I mean these moments slipped out. And when I read them I was very aware of them, delightfully aware. So prose that calls attention to itself, even on a modest level, I don't think it's necessarily all bad.
PE: No, I don't think so either. However, that would not have worked had that been a third-person narration.

EC: That's true.
PE: You hopefully accept the rhythm and perception and movement through the world of this particular character, and you accept his voice. There are any number of ways I could have said these things that wouldn't have been his voice, that would have called attention to the language that would have been grating on you.

EC: So first-person perspective gives you the liberty then to pursue such moments?
PE: It does. But that doesn't mean that you're confined to first-person perspective to do that, again because there are no rules. If you give me a third-person narrator that in effect will become a first-person narrator who's simply telling the story in third person, because you'll be giving him or her agency, you can do it as well.

EC: Well, Percival, thanks very much. It's been a pleasure chatting with you.
PE: Thank you.

Where's Everett?

Susan Salter Reynolds / 2009

From *Los Angeles Times Book Review*, 12 July 2009, E5. Copyright © 2006, 2012. Los Angeles Times. Reprinted with Permission.

Percival Everett doesn't spend a lot of time considering his body of work. Instead, says the fifty-two-year-old author, whose new novel *I Am Not Sidney Poitier* came out last month, "I think about writing one book at a time. It's not that my books are non sequiturs—after all, you can't hide from yourself. It's just that I know something when I start and less when I finish."

This Zen-like approach might explain why, even after twenty-one books, Everett is not exactly a household name, even in Southern California, where he has lived and worked for many years. (He is a professor of English at USC.) Beginning with his first novel, *Suder*, in 1983, he has written about baseball, Vietnam, Greek myths, cowboys, Native Americans, revenge, genius, and hate crimes, among other subjects, all the while inserting himself, Zelig-like, into his own work.

He's not in it for the money, or even the fame. And that makes him pretty relaxed about it all. "There's nothing at stake," he says, sitting back among the cushions of a sofa in his high-ceilinged Los Angeles apartment. "I can't affect what readers think."

This sense of cool distance is the tone of *I Am Not Sidney Poitier*—a book about identity without the *Sturm und Drang* that usually accompanies books about identity. That makes it a thoroughly modern novel, in which the protagonist triumphs not by asserting his will over the world but by achieving a quiet comfort with his true nature, independent of race or class or religion or politics. It's a book about how much we don't know.

The narrator's name is Not Sidney, as in Not Sidney Poitier. His mother has named him that because their last name is Poitier and she wanted to avoid confusion. This is just the first of many ways in which the novel plays with the fixations of contemporary culture; a second comes when Not Sidney's mother invests all her money—around $30,000—"in a little-known company called the Turner Communications Group that would later become Turner Broadcasting System." At one point, Ted Turner pays her a visit because she owns so much stock in his company and because she represents "the kind of grass-roots, if not proletarian, person he wanted to imagine his media world touching." When Not Sidney is seven, in 1975, she dies in her sleep, leaving him to become "filthy, obscenely, uncomfortably rich." Turner invites Not Sidney to live in one of his houses.

Lest this seem like the stuff of a traditional Bildungsroman, Everett has something completely other than that in mind. "To Turner's credit," he writes early in the novel, "even he was not comfortable with the scenario of the rich do-gooding white man taking in the poor little black child. Television was polluted with that model, and it didn't take a genius to understand that something was wrong with it. My situation was somewhat different as I was in fact extremely wealthy as a result of my mother's business acumen."

Turner is a wise, avuncular presence, appearing now and then to offer oblique advice. One spring, he visits Not Sidney at college and offers the following: "Enjoy your break. And remember, be yourself. Unless you can think of someone better."

Not Sidney's other erstwhile mentor is one Percival Everett, professor and king of the koan. Everett's answers to Not Sidney's earnest questions are even more oblique than Turner's. "You want to know why people are so fucked up?" he asks Not Sidney, who is upset after a weekend with his girlfriend's snooty parents. "It's because they're people. People, my friend, are worse than anybody."

Is this Everett the writer, or Everett the character? Or is the line between them irrevocably blurred? It's easy to imagine Everett having some pointed fun with his readers, wanting to keep everyone on their toes. Among his students, he has a reputation for not suffering fools, while his editors know that if they talk about marketing his attention will fade fast. "I am paid," he is fond of saying when asked about teaching, "to write books and hang around smart young people."

The eerie thing is that even after spending a few hours with him, his physical presence remains elusive; it's hard to remember what he looks like. Your mind tries to recapture the details but it's like trying to catch the character in *The Soupy Sales Show*—the one who ran along the bottom of the screen. You think you saw him, but it's impossible to freeze the frame.

Everett teaches some fiction workshops, as well as classes in literary theory (Barthes, Derrida, and others) and a film course. *I Am Not Sidney Poitier* is punctuated by dream sequences modeled after the story lines of Sidney Poitier's films. "Poitier was the safe choice of white Americans interested in film," Everett explains. "An iconic, beautiful, sensuous dark man; politically progressive, someone who always kept a safe sexual distance from the camera and the story."

The dream sequences allow Everett to explore aspects of Poitier's experience that are not so safe—the sources of his distance and dignity. "There's a freedom of absurdity in dreams, enjoyed by drunks and babies," Everett says as he hugs his son Henry, two and a half, who has just returned from a walk with his mother, the novelist Danzy Senna. The couple also has a one-year-old named Miles.

Henry is given to wild dreams. Everett has learned to let him wail before trying to soothe him. He's interested, as both a father and a writer, in how we edit our dreams and our everyday experience to make sense of the world, in "how we make meaning." This is not plot, exactly, but something Everett calls "the inner thread of the story." Like Robert Coover, his friend and professor at Brown, where Everett got his A.M. in the early 1980s, he is interested in hyper-reality. "My books tend not to be chronological—sections don't follow each other logically. But I hope the overall impression is a continuous story." He laughs. "Unplotted. Fiction is an illusion, after all, a pretty cool trick. A lot of my work deals with people out in the world. My job is not to report real things but to make the fiction sound real. The beauty is that even when we know these tricks and recognize them, they work anyway."

Surely, writing about identity involves a certain sleight of hand. For Everett, though, it's more a matter of feeling his way into his novels. "I have a feeling about it," he says, "but I can't articulate what it looks like. I begin with a sense of weight. Then I find somebody, and I become that character. I inhabit that character."

When I bring up Not Sidney's innocence and truthfulness—which verge on naïveté—Everett almost betrays himself. "It's sad that we think because he's painfully honest, he's naïve," he says, ever-so-slightly protective of his character. "We take his modesty and conflate it with innocence."

As for how *I Am Not Sidney Poitier* does, "I hope the book sells, but I am constitutionally unable to participate," Everett says. Like many authors, he does not usually read reviews, although when he does, he prefers the bad ones because he learns more. For the most part, he finds reviews generally uninteresting and likens them to movie trailers.

"I make my money in France and Italy," Everett says. We talk about the earnest streak in American literature, a preference for clear morals and clear plot lines. Everett's books are anything but linear or predictable despite the fact that he studied mathematical logic and philosophy in college.

In much of his work, we get the not unpleasant sense of being mocked, of having our core beliefs taken apart by a mischievous author. But Everett is not in the business of judging.

"All thinking is good," he shrugs. "It sure beats an absence of thought."

The Water Cure: "In Any Novel, It Is the Reader Who Completes the Tale"

l'Humanité / 2009

From *l'Humanité* (Saint-Denis, France), 19 November 2009. Translated by Jennifer Kinney. Reprinted with permission of *l'Humanité*.

Water torture, or "waterboarding," has been widely used and considered by the Bush administration as a legal interrogation technique. In his latest novel, Percival Everett imagines a writer without a story who takes it upon himself to settle a personal vendetta against a man he believes, without proof, to have murdered his eleven-year-old daughter. The novel weaves together the story of the man, who becomes a torturer in aligning himself with his country's government, his outrageous beliefs about truth and language, and excerpts from romance novels he is writing, paralleled with enigmatic drawings. Invited by Les Belles Étrangères, the author, a leader in the contemporary American novel, speaks about this fascinating fiction that brings together all the possibilities of fiction writing.

Q: Your novel is titled *The Water Cure*, yet this scene occupies only part of the book . . .
PE: Even if torture is not present in an obvious way throughout the text, it is there in spirit, in every bit of the character's action. It is an expression of his discomfort but also the cure—in the same way that, during the Inquisition in the Middle Ages, torture was the cure for evil.

Q: One can also wonder if he is not the victim of a sort of psychosis . . .
PE: It is indeed a crowd behavior, a collective delusion, and the United States government uses the fact of having been victimized to justify extreme, illegal, and immoral behaviors. The character uses this as an excuse for his

criminal activities. And torture is shown to be a very precise technique that I describe.

Q: This person's behavior is frankly delusional . . .
PE: That's exactly the condition of the spirit of vengeance. The war against Iraq had nothing to do with terrorism, but sought to satisfy a totally irrational need for revenge. Someone had to pay.

Q: It is not just anybody doing this but a writer, someone who belongs to a group that claims to be rational and moral.
PE: This is what is terrifying in these group phenomena. Most Germans in 1936 and 1937 were good people, yet they ended up being seduced by Hitler. The terrorist in my novel is still at odds with his status as a writer. His name is Ishmael, the same as the narrator of *Moby-Dick*, and he writes romance novels under the name Estelle Gilliam. It's true this is a lie, but for market reasons many authors cannot afford to write according to their beliefs.

Q: Is that why the novel is strewn with fragments of philosophers' thoughts about the truth?
PE: Yes, it's related to his madness and the cleavage of his personality. But it is also his attempt to understand European culture. That's what allows him to remain indifferent to human life, its pettiness and its value.

Q: There are even reflections on language, including a list of "ten functions," which ends with "causing pain." This is unexpected.
PE: I'm glad we do not expect it, because pain is the last of the functions he attributes to it. That is what Ishmael thinks, and I fear he is right on this point.

Q: The book's structure is based on the principle of the fragment. This raises the question "How it is arranged?"
PE: My intention was to write a book in which there is no logical connection visible from one paragraph to another, so that the structure reflects the way in which we receive the world. We receive a set of stimuli, and given that perceptions are indistinct, each person chooses those that are necessary for the construction of the narrative that gives meaning to one's world.

Q: Is this not a way to avoid renouncing any of the possibilities that writing offers?

PE: I think that's true. Throughout the novel, the reader constructs the story as if looking at a photograph, choosing a particular angle or detail. It is impossible for the designer to introduce a hierarchy and to guide the reader. My plan was to destroy the fourth wall of the theatrical stage and immerse the spectator and the actor in the same moving stream of illusion.

Q: What is the status of the drawings found in the book?
PE: The children's drawings are the author's attempt to give meaning to his world by connecting him to his daughter's spirit after her death, imagining drawings she could have done. The drawings of the cat return to my interest in representation, and seek to answer the following question: How many elements are necessary to recognize an object, and how many can be taken away before the object is no longer recognizable?

Q: Is this a metaphor of the text itself?
PE: I think so.

Percival Everett:
Whites Want to Read "Black"

Tine Maria Winther /2010

Article by Tine Maria Winther, translated by Evelyn Meyer and Marte Hult, originally published in *Politiken & Politiken Weekly* (Copenhagen), 31 May 2010. Reprinted by permission of *Politiken & Politiken Weekly*.

Percival Everett is an award-winning author, American and black. In the U.S., the order of the words *American* and *black* is reversed, because a writer's being black is primarily what interests U.S. publishers and readers. Everett explains that being a black writer in America is synonymous with being limited to writing—or expected only to be able to write—about blacks at the bottom of society. He writes about this paradox in his acclaimed satirical novel *erasure*.

The protagonist is a black writer, Thelonious "Monk" Ellison, whose intellectual essays and experimental novels have produced a small readership. Around him, he can see other black writers succeed by "writing black," so Monk decides to publish a ghetto novel, *My Pafology*, using a pseudonym. The novel is written in ghetto slang, like this: "You gone wif to hit that K'rean muthafucka. I'm gone get my gun. Smooth nigger comin up in here pullin his piece and shit."

And, of course, the book ends up on the bestseller list, is nominated for prestigious literary prizes, and results in a Hollywood film contract.

"Whites want to read 'black,'" laughs Percival Everett, who in another of his novels has white people praise the *Pafology* part of *erasure* "for its authenticity."

It has been Everett's experience to be categorized as African American rather than simply as a writer. "In bookstores, my books are in the 'African American Literature' section, even my novel about Dionysus from Greek mythology and my Westerns. These books, moreover, are often adjacent to the 'Black Women Writers' section," says the author.

He is in Denmark to lecture to students at the Southern Danish University's Center for American Studies.

He shakes his head over large literary fairs such as the National Black Writers Conference which just took place for the tenth time in New York, although such events may have their justification. "If I were a white writer, I would not enjoy being invited to a white writers' fair," says Everett, who in several of his books does not reveal whether the protagonist is black or white.

The main characters in his breakthrough novel, *erasure*, and in his latest book, *I Am Not Sidney Poitier*, are, however, African American. The latter makes use of America's black darling of the 1960s, Sidney Poitier, to produce a political comedy of errors. (In this novel, the film rights for which, incidentally, have been sold to Hollywood, the protagonist's mother, whose surname was Poitier and who liked the name Sidney, named her son Not Sidney Poitier to avoid confusion. Of course, this effort failed.)

"Sidney Poitier was the safe choice for white-film America, a black icon for the previous generation. Sidney Poitier was the identifiable—no, he was *the* black actor—the only acceptable black man in 1960s' America. Although he was dark, he was tall and handsome, and although he could be sexy, he was not. He was safe," Everett observes, "and kept a safe sexual distance from both the story and the camera."

As private as he is in his writing, Percival Everett is a man who can see the comedy in things, and he laughs loudly as he retells the plot of *Guess Who's Coming to Dinner* with Spencer Tracy, in which the daughter of the house comes home with a black boyfriend in the person of Sidney Poitier. "This twenty-year-old daughter of a rich man has heretofore done nothing in/with her life, but the only way to make her decision to have a black boyfriend acceptable was to make him an ungodly handsome, intellectual superman, as if this would equalize things. It was inconceivable that he would just be a college student, for example. My character in the novel has a certain external likeness to Sidney Poitier, but he is in every way Not Sidney Poitier."

Comedy in Everett's novels is grounded in seriousness and love of intellectual knowledge. In *erasure*, he addresses issues such as the dumbing down of America, the fracturing of nuclear families, violence, racism, Nazism, and Alzheimer's. And always he plays with words, names, and fates. This is something he believes may have come from the South. William

Faulkner, for example, also plays with the names in his books. "As children in Georgia, we tirelessly put names together to make them funny: Rusty Steel, Blackburn . . . and of course a small pond named Ezra [a play on Ezra Pound]. It's as though I can't help myself."

As an adult, Everett, who now lives in Los Angeles, could never move back to the South. "When you get right down to it, the South is racist. The police there have a phrase they use over police radio—DWB, Driving While Black. It was and, I suppose, still is a quite common experience for young black men to be stopped by police, have their cars searched, and be asked to show their IDs. It happened to me in Florida, where I wasted a day sitting in prison because I was stubborn and wouldn't give my name," says Everett, who recalls that he had been stopped the same way in New Jersey. "They were searching for a 6'6" black bank robber, and they thought I might be that person. I'm not close to 6'6"."

Everett, who was a fundraiser for Barack Obama during the presidential campaign, does not believe that a black president in America will change much. "I was ecstatic when he was elected. Now I'm more subdued—perhaps disappointed. I don't believe that he's going to change much. People are people."

Percival Everett's books have not yet been translated into Danish, although he is popular in France, Italy, and Greece. But the Southern Danish University, acting on a "scoop," brought him here. As we say goodbye in front of his hotel on the Town Hall square, he points to a poster advertising *Precious* at the Dagmar cinema. It's an Oscar-winning film about a sixteen-year-old African American girl who for the second time becomes pregnant by her father and, after nine years of schooling, can neither read nor write. "I call it tolerant racism, when educated people go to see a film about poor blacks at the bottom of society. This even gains force by appearing to be authentic, and school groups go to see such films with their teachers. And in this way what it means to be black once again becomes cemented in viewers' minds. You don't see many movies with well-functioning blacks. . . . They might not be exotic enough."

Author Percival Everett
Talks Westerns, Serial Killers,
and His New Novel

inReads / 2011

From *inReads*, 28 November 2011. Reprinted by permission of *inReads*.

Percival Everett is about as prolific an author as you'll meet, with more than twenty books to his name and more in the works. His novels range widely in tone and topic but are all characterized by a probing intelligence and humor. His last novel, *I Am Not Sidney Poitier*, is the story of a boy named Not Sidney, who, in an unlikely twist, also happens to look exactly like the famous actor. In the book, Not Sidney's experiences are derived from famous Poitier films (for instance, Not Sidney has a hilarious *Guess Who's Coming to Dinner* moment) in an odyssey of race and identity. His latest book, *Assumption*, is more traditional fare (at least on the surface). The novel appears to have all of the trappings of a crime novel and follows Deputy Ogden Walker as he attempts to solve three different cases in Plata, New Mexico. But don't assume you know how this story is going to work itself out. We spoke to Everett about his new book, some old books, and the nature of banter.

inReads: So, there's something I've wondered about for awhile. Your author photo. What's the story with the bird perched on your shoulder?
PE: That was my crow, Jim. He was a pet for about two years. I raised him after he fell out of a nest.

inReads: Intelligent bird! Was it easy to train him to sit on your shoulder like that?
PE: He did that from the time he was a baby, but I kept wanting him to fly away and have a crow life. Finally, someone else walked toward him when I

was out of town, and he flew away and never came back, which was good. But a really monogamous bird.

inReads: *Assumption* is a crime novel but not your first foray into genre fiction. You've done a parody of the Western before. Was this a similar thing?

PE: For that book, I read a great number of pulp Westerns and watched fifty or sixty films so I could create a Western language that would sound like the West that wasn't. But this novel isn't really a parody. It is playing with the form, but I'm not having it on in any way.

inReads: I got through the last couple pages, and now I feel like I have to read the entire book again. So, um, thanks?

PE: It's not my intention to cause anyone extra work, but I am toying with the assumptions we have when we enter into that kind of story. You assume that your protagonist is a certain way, and you take some things for granted that maybe in real life you wouldn't. And you also have some assumptions about the writer and the space that you're entering.

inReads: Ogden is a likeable character.

PE: Yes. Well, one of the things that intrigues me is when people interview the neighbor of the serial killer and they say, "Well he was always such a nice guy." You know. "He was a great neighbor!"

inReads: It's always the nice ones you have to keep an eye on.

PE: Yeah, you never hear, "That guy was a bastard."

inReads: You'd want to keep a low profile, while you're doing your serial killing.

PE: If you're really a serial killer now, you make it appear as if you actually are one, so no one would suspect you.

inReads: Well, you've clearly given this thing a lot of thought. It's scaring me a bit, so I'm changing the subject. How does the process of writing a book like *Assumption* differ from writing something personal like *erasure*?

PE: In a way I'm distanced from the work necessarily because I'm employing that formula, but the challenge for me was how I could make my experience with that book my own and not simply the construction of a story that fit the model. So that's what I was trying to do. And I think I'm the wrong person to ask if that was successful. But that was my aim.

inReads: There is a lot of good banter between Ogden and his fellow deputy Warren Fragua. Banter is a deceptively difficult thing to do right, as it has to be pitch-perfect and sound realistic. What's your secret?

PE: Well, you just put your finger on what it is. It's realistic-sounding. Dialogue is never "real" dialogue. It's never what people actually say in the world. It creates the illusion that you're there and hearing it. If you actually memorized some of that dialogue and went out into the world and performed it without people knowing what you were doing, they'd think you were nuts. Likewise if I just recorded real banter and transcribed it, it would read as terrible dialogue in fiction. Part of my job is to make it sound real.

inReads: The banter in pulps is how I'd like to sound, although I guess you're right that people would think you're insane if you started talking to them like that.

PE: Well we could try.

inReads: I'm not the person to pull that off.

PE: Me neither. I'd be thinking too long for the next thing I'd say.

inReads: I think of good rejoinders ten minutes after the moment.

PE: I've only had one perfectly timed rejoinder. I used to work ranches out in Idaho and eastern Oregon and I was delivering some cows to this guy, but I had to find his house in the town of Baker, Oregon. And I don't know if you've been out there, but there are not very many black people out there. I stopped this woman on the street and asked her where to find this address, and she said, "It's three blacks that way." And it's the only time I've ever had the perfect thing to say. I said, "It can't be nearly that far."

inReads: Yes!

PE: That's worth a novel right there.

inReads: Indeed. Speaking of new novels, I understand that you have one in the works called *Percival Everett*. Is it about you or the bizarro version of you from *I Am Not Sidney Poitier*? Or neither?

PE: Neither. It's a novel and it comes out of Frege's Puzzle, the problem that you have reconciling sense and reference. And so it's really about that, about two things that can have the same name and not be the same thing. That's not very helpful, is it?

inReads: No, but I'm still going to read the book. I'm sure it will all become clear.

PE: Well thanks for the vote of confidence. (Laughs.)

inReads: You don't strike me as the type of man who uses an e-reader. Am I wrong in that assumption?

PE: I don't particularly like them, because I like books. But what I have found is that when traveling with the stupid iPad—although I don't know if it's worth the money, but I didn't pay for it—I get to carry a five-hundred-page volume of Shelby Foote's narrative of the Civil War with me, where I just hate to pack it. So yeah, for some things it's great, but it doesn't replace books, because it can't sit on the shelf and call to me. It's probably great for genre fiction, something I'm not going to read again once I'm done.

inReads: Shelby knew his Civil War.

PE: I do like Shelby Foote's Civil War history. I read it maybe ten years ago, and then I did the thing that I do. I saw it sitting on the shelf and thought, "God this is good, I'm going to read them all again." Three volumes of this thing, and it takes forever not because it's so long, but because after every paragraph I think, "That was great!" and go back and read it again.

inReads: Shelby really hogged the camera in Ken Burns's documentary . . .

PE: Well, he would have to.

Key Resources

Other Significant Everett Interviews

Bucci, Tonino. "Percival Everett." *Liberazione* (Rome) 27 May 2009: 13. [Focused on *Wounded*, racism, and being free to write what one wishes (in Italian)]

Franti, David, and Elena Torre. "Intervista a Percival Everett." *Mangialibri* July 2009. Web. http://www.mangialibri.com/node/4640. [Focused on *Wounded* and contemporary American politics, but also touches on the effect of Everett's having read the Greek and Roman classics since his youth (in Italian)]

Lorini, Teo. "Interview: Percival Everett." *Pulp Libri* (Italy) 83 (January/February 2010): 22–26. [Especially good on *American Desert* (in Italian)]

Pierantozzi, Alcide. "Percival Everett." *Rolling Stone* (Italy) February 2010: 36. [Focused on *American Desert* and *Wounded* (in Italian)]

Fanjul, Sergio C. "'Las cosas entretenidas no suelen generar pensamieto.'" *El País* 20 Aug. 2011. Web. http://elpais.com/diario/2011/08/20/babelia/1313799136_850215 .html. [Heavily focused on *erasure* (in Spanish)]

Piña, Begoña. "Percival Everett." *Qué Leer* 26 February 2012. Web. http://www.que -leer.com/14216/percival-everett.html. [Almost exclusively focused on *erasure* (in Spanish)]

Important Nonfictional Statements by Everett

"Signing to the Blind." *Callaloo* 14.1 (Winter 1991): 9–11.

"The Revolution Will Not Be Televised." *Hungry Mind Review* 45 (Spring 1998): 16.

"Why I'm from Texas." *Callaloo* 24.1 (Winter 2001): 62–63.

"Raising Horses, Writing Novels." *Speakeasy* (Minneapolis) 1.4 (March/April 2003): 14–15.

"Red States?" *What We Do Now.* Ed. Dennis Loy Johnson and Valerie Merians. Hoboken, NJ: Melville House, 2004. 21–25.

"'Getting Lost in the Fictive Distance': Addressing a Villa Gillet Session." *Reading Percival Everett: European Perspectives.* Eds. Claude Julien and Anne-Laure Tissut. Tours: Presses universitaires François Rabelais, 2007. 209–12.

"Freedom's Just Another Word for Nothing Left to Lose." *Vida: Women in the Arts*

7 November 2010. Web. http://www.vidaweb.org/freedom%E2%80%99s-just-an other-word-for-nothing-left-to-lose.

Significant Biocritical Essays on Everett

Bates, Joseph. "The Writing Life: Percival Everett, Characteristically Uncharacteristic." *2008 Novel & Short Story Writer's Market.* Eds. Lauren Mosko and Michael Schweer. Cincinnati: Writer's Digest Books, 2007. 5–9. [Includes interspersed comments by Everett]

Flota, Brian. "Percival Everett." *Twenty-First-Century American Writers,* 2nd Ser. Dictionary of Literary Biography 350. Eds. Wanda H. Giles and James R. Giles. Detroit, MI: Gale, 2009. 86–97.

Guzzio, Tracie Church. "Percival Everett (1956–)." *American Writers: A Collection of Literary Biographies. Supplement XVIII (Charles Frederick Briggs to Robert Wrigley).* Ed. Jay Parini. Farmington Hills, MI: Gale, 2008. 53–67.

Masiki, Trent. "Irony and Ecstasy: A Profile of Percival Everett." *Poets & Writers Magazine* 32 (May/June 2004): 32–39. [Includes interspersed comments by Everett]

Collections of Scholarly Essays on Everett's Work

Callaloo 28.2 (2005): 291-381. [Special Everett section]

Canadian Review of American Studies 43.1 (2013). [Special Everett issue]

Julien, Claude, and Anne-Laure Tissut, eds. *Reading Percival Everett: European Perspectives.* Tours: Presses universitaires François Rabelais, 2007.

Maniez, Claire, and Anne-Laure Tissut, eds. *Percival Everett: Transatlantic Readings.* Éditions Le Manuscrit, 2007.

Mitchell, Keith B., and Robin G. Vander, eds. *Perspectives on Percival Everett.* Jackson: UP of Mississippi, 2013.

Most Significant Uncollected Essays on Everett's Work

Baker, Houston A., Jr. "'If you see Robert Penn Warren, ask him: Who *does* speak for the Negro?': Reflections on Monk, Black Writing, and Percival Everett's *erasure*." *I Don't Hate the South: Reflections on Faulkner, Family, and the South.* New York: Oxford UP, 2007. 121–50.

Bauer, Sylvie. "'Nouns, Names, Verbs' in *The Water Cure* by Percival Everett, or, 'Can a Scream be Articulate?'" *Revue française d'études américaines* No. 128 (2011): 99–108.

Berben-Masi, Jacqueline. "'Inverser la plaisanterie afin de secouer le joug'; ou, comment vicier un stéréotype." *Revue LISA/LISA e-journal* 7.1 (2009): 89–100. Web. http://lisa.revues.org/792. [Discusses "The Appropriation of Cultures" (in French)]

———. "Percival Everett's *Glyph*: Prisons of the Body Physical, Political, and Academic." *In the Grip of the Law: Trials, Prisons and the Space Between*. Eds. Monika Fludernik and Greta Olson. Frankfurt am Main: Peter Lang, 2004. 223–39.

Birat, Kathie. "Percival Everett and the Epistolary Novel." *Lettres noires: L'insistance de la lettre dans la culture afro-américaine*. Profils américains No. 23. Ed. Claudine Raynaud. Montpelllier: PULM, 2012. 123–43. [Discusses *A History of the African-American People*]

Coombes, Sam. "La parodie et l'ironie au service d'une critique des stratégies politiques identitaires dans *erasure* de Percival Everett." *Bulletin de la Société de Stylistique Anglaise* 29 (2007): 127–39. [In French]

Demirtürk, E. Lâle. "Rescripted Performances of Blackness as 'Parodies of Whiteness': Discursive Frames of Recognition in Percival Everett's *I Am Not Sidney Poitier*." *The Contemporary African American Novel: Multiple Cities, Multiple Subjectivities, and Discursive Practices of Whiteness in Everyday Urban Encounters*. Madison, NJ: Fairleigh Dickinson UP, 2012. 85-109.

Feith, Michel. "Blueprint for Studies in the African American (Neo)Baroque: John Edgar Wideman, Percival Everett." *Transatlantica* 1 (2009). Web. http://transatlantica.revues.org/4266. [Discusses *Frenzy*, *American Desert*, and *erasure*]

———. "Ellison avec Barthes: Occultation et désoccultation du 'canon ethnique' dans *erasure* de Percival Everett." *Revue française d'études américaines* No. 110 (2006): 61–77. [In French]

Gibson, Scott Thomas. "Invisibility and the Commodification of Blackness in Ralph Ellison's *Invisible Man* and Percival Everett's *erasure*." *Canadian Review of Comparative Literature* 37.4 (2010): 354–70.

Gunning, Dave. "Concentric and Centripetal Narratives of Race: Caryl Phillips's *Dancing in the Dark* and Percival Everett's *erasure*." *Caryl Phillips: Writing in the Key of Life*. Cross/Cultures 146. Eds. Bénédicte Ledent and Daria Tunca. Amsterdam: Rodopi, 2012. 359–74.

Johnson, Michael K. "Looking at the Big Picture: Percival Everett's Western Fiction." *Western American Literature* 42.1 (2007): 26–53.

Lambert, Raphaël. "Negotiating Black Identity: Percival Everett's *erasure*." *Journal of the American Literature Society of Japan* 7 (March 2008): 32–50.

Moynihan, Sinéad. "Living Parchments, Human Documents: Passing, Racial Identity and the Literary Marketplace." *Passing into the Present: Contemporary American*

Fiction of Racial and Gender Passing. Manchester: Manchester UP, 2010. 21–50. [Discusses *erasure*]

Ramsey, William M. "Knowing Their Place: Three Black Writers and the Postmodern South." *Southern Literary Journal* 31.2 (Summer 2005): 119–39. [Discusses *Suder* and several stories]

Ruffin, Kimberly N. "Bones and Water: Telling on Myth." *Black on Earth: African American Ecoliterary Traditions.* Athens: U of Georgia P, 2010. 111–35. [Discusses *God's Country, Watershed,* and *Grand Canyon, Inc.*]

Sánchez-Arce, Ana Mariá. "'Authenticism,' or the Authority of Authenticity." *Mosaic* 40.3 (2007): 139–55. [Discusses *erasure*]

Schur, Richard. "Stomping the Blues No More?: Hip Hop Aesthetics and Contemporary African American Literature." *New Essays on the African American Novel: From Hurston and Ellison to Morrison and Whitehead.* Eds. Lovalerie King and Linda F. Selzer. New York: Palgrave Macmillan, 2008. 201–20. [Discusses *erasure*]

Stewart, Anthony. "Giving the People What They Want: The African American Exception as Racial Cliché in Percival Everett's *erasure.*" *American Exceptionalisms: From Winthrop to Winfrey.* Eds. Sylvia Söderlind and James Taylor Carson. Albany: State U of New York P, 2011. 167–89.

Tissut, Anne Laure. "'Still Beautiful but Inadequate': Des vicissitudes de l'autorité dans *erasure*, de Percival Everett." *L'autorité en question.* Eds. Yves-Charles Grandjeat and Christian Lerat. Pessac: Maison des sciences de l'homme d'Aquitaine, 2005. 151–64. [In French]

——. "This Is an Elephant: How to Do Things with Fiction." *Études Anglaises* 63.2 (2010): 150–60. [Discusses *The Water Cure*]

Yost, Brian. "The Changing Same: The Evolution of Racial Self-Definition and Commercialization." *Callaloo* 31.4 (2008): 1314–34. [Discusses *erasure*]

Everett Bibliography

Weixlmann, Joe. "Percival Everett: A Primary and Secondary Bibliography." *African American Review* E-Project 2012. Web. http://aar.slu.edu/everett.html. [Regularly updated, comprehensive bibliography of works by and about Everett]

Index